GOD STILL SPEAKS: LISTEN!

Biblical Abbreviations

OLD TESTAMENT

Genesis	Gn	Nehemiah	Ne	Baruch	Ba
Exodus	Ex	Tobit	Tb	Ezekiel	Ezk
Leviticus	Lv	Judith	Jdt	Daniel	Dn
Numbers	Nb	Esther	Est	Hosea	Ho
Deuteronomy	Dt	1 Maccabees	1 M	Joel	Jl
Joshua	Jos	2 Maccabees	2 M	Amos	Am
Judges	Jg	Job	Jb	Obadiah	Ob
Ruth	Rt	Psalms	Ps	Jonah	Jon
1 Samuel	1 S	Proverbs	Pr	Micah	Mi
2 Samuel	2 S	Ecclesiastes	Ec	Nahum	Na
1 Kings	1 K	Song of Songs	Sg	Habakkuk	Hab
2 Kings	2 K	Wisdom	Ws	Zephaniah	Zp
1 Chronicles	1 Ch	Sirach	Si	Haggai	Hg
2 Chronicles	2 Ch	Isaiah	Is	Malachi	Ml
Ezra	Ezr	Jeremiah	Jr	Zechariah	Zc
		Lamentations	Lm		

NEW TESTAMENT

Matthew	Mt	Ephesians	Eph	Hebrews	Heb
Mark	Mk	Philippians	Ph	James	Jm
Luke	Lk	Colossians	Col	1 Peter	1 P
John	Jn	1 Thessalonians	1 Th	2 Peter	2 P
Acts	Ac	2 Thessalonians	2 Th	1 John	1 Jn
Romans	Rm	1 Timothy	1 Tm	2 John	2 Jn
1 Corinthians	1 Cor	2 Timothy	2 Tm	3 John	3 Jn
2 Corinthians	2 Cor	Titus	Tt	Jude	Jude
Galatians	Gal	Philemon	Phm	Revelation	Rv

GOD STILL SPEAKS: LISTEN!

Homily Reflections for Sundays and Holy Days:

Cycle A

HAROLD A. BUETOW, PhD JD

ALBA·HOUSE   NEW·YORK

SOCIETY OF ST. PAUL, 2187 VICTORY BLVD., STATEN ISLAND, NEW YORK 10314

Library of Congress Cataloging-in-Publication Data

Buetow, Harold A.
    Homily reflections for Sundays and Holy Days / Harold A. Buetow.
        p.   cm.
    Includes bibliographical references.
    Contents: Cycle A. God still speaks — listen!
    ISBN 0-8189-0727-4
    1. Church year sermons. 2. Catholic Church — Sermons. 3. Sermons,
American.
    BX1756.B826H66   1995
    252'.6 — dc20   95-20679
                                                     CIP

Produced and designed in the United States of America by the
Fathers and Brothers of the Society of St. Paul,
2187 Victory Boulevard, Staten Island, New York 10314,
as part of their communications apostolate.

ISBN: 0-8189-0727-4

Printing Information:

Current Printing - first digit   1   2   3   4   5   6   7   8   9   10

Year of Current Printing - first year shown

1995	1996	1997	1998	1999	2000

TABLE OF CONTENTS

PREFACE TO ALL THREE VOLUMES

Need and Importance of Homilies

Among the many reasons for the need of the homily, one of the greatest is the secularization of our culture. Under the Third Republic in France, *morale laïque* (secular morality) made great inroads in divorcing morality from religion. Emile Durkheim (1857-1917), an influential founder of modern sociology, completed its tendencies: the total disengagement of ethics from religious dogma and the founding of morality in society alone. In the United States, secular morality has relevance to a society which is torn between conservative "born-again" religion and liberal "secular humanism" and which is experiencing a decline in public and private morality. Good homilies are one way to provide an opportunity, brief though it be, for handing on Christian values.

Yet the homily is one of the most frequently criticized areas of complaint from church-goers. Many church-goers parish-hop in search of good preaching. Many others have become non-church-going because what has been coming from the pulpit has no meaning for them and, at a time when messages from outside the Church constitute a serious challenge to Christian values, no help with some unavoidable new issues. The time when many people were willing to overlook poor preaching is long past.

Although today's pulpit is a lonely place, the homily is important. The word of God must come alive for our times. It was God's word which created everything: it unfolded God's plan of salvation, God spoke through Jesus, Jesus was the Word made flesh, Jesus proclaimed the Good News, and God's word convenes the assembly of believers and creates their unity. The proclamation of the word is the introduction to Christian congregation. The homilist is to engage in the Word of God more than in words about God. The better the proclamation and the living out of the word, the more authentic the Church.

An effective homily evangelizes the one who delivers it and those who hear it. It creates an atmosphere of love in a parish — but for that the homily needs to be relevant in theme, clear in presentation, and above all a message of God from heart to heart. Vatican Council II's "Constitution on the Sacred Liturgy"[1] emphasized the importance of preaching; ever since, in liturgical publications, the restoration of the homily to the Eucharist has continued.

What Is a Homily?

Nature

"Homily" comes from the Greek *homilia*, which implies a more personal and conversational form of address than what might today be connected with communicating with a crowd. The word most frequently used in the New Testament for preaching is *keryssein*, "to proclaim," a word which takes for granted that preachers are heralds who announce that which they are commissioned to announce, not by their own authority, but by the authority of the one who sends them. In fact, however, the New Testament does not actually use a specific technical word to describe the kind of preaching we mean by a "homily." That came to the fore in the early Church, when the homily was the bishop's or pastor's talk to his people, on a personal and familiar level, about a scriptural text of the liturgy.

The United States bishops define the homily as "a scriptural interpretation of human existence which enables a community to recognize God's active presence, to respond to that presence in faith through liturgical word and gesture, and beyond the liturgical assembly, through a life lived in conformity with the Gospel."[2] It takes place during the celebration of the Eucharist, a point of encounter between the local Christian community and God's word; in such a framework, the homily is a time when this encounter can be especially intense and personal. Whereas Vatican II pointed out that the homily is part of the liturgy, the *General Instruction of the Roman Missal* goes even further, noting that the homily is an *integral part* of the Mass, and a *necessary source* of spiritual nourishment for Christian living.[3]

The homily is directed to faith. As St. Paul asked, "How can they believe unless they have heard of him? And how can they hear unless there is someone to preach?"[4] Our faith is a way of seeing or interpreting the world: it accepts and affirms the world as a creation of a loving God who sent His son to rescue it.

For its theme the homily is, of course, guided by the Lectionary. In its selection of scriptural texts, the Lectionary in turn is guided by two principles. One is the thematic principle, by which readings are chosen to correspond to the theme of a feast or season. Whereas Advent, Lent, and Easter provide the best harmonization among the readings for each Mass, many Sundays of the year have no unified theme. And that's where the second principle comes in: the "semi-continuous" principle, whereby readings are taken in order from a book of the Bible which is being read over a period of time.

The Introduction to the Lectionary (which homilists can read with profit) provides some concepts behind the readings. It illustrates the basic unity of both Testaments and of the history of salvation, with Christ as the center. The Lectionary's central principle is that of Vatican II: that Scripture should be the soul of theology. In its three-year cycle, the Lectionary makes an effort to let Scripture speak for itself. The Gospel is central, and it allows each evangelist to present his own theology. In many cases, the readings from the Jewish Scriptures have been chosen for their relationship to the Gospel passages.

Homilists proclaim the deeds of God through His prophets, kings, psalmists, poets, evangelists, and saints in order to enable us all, homilist as well as congregation, to see our incorporation in God's saving process. We reflect upon the many passages about Israel in exile so that we can recognize our own pilgrim journey (with its successes and its failures) and provide encouragement in failure and a challenge to fidelity. We proclaim the mysteries of our faith and the principles for Christian living, and show that the mystery continues to be active among us, especially in the liturgy.

The homily is not a talk given *on the occasion* of a liturgical celebration; it is *part* of the liturgy itself. This obviously contains implications for the way in which the homily is composed and delivered. The homily should flow naturally out of the readings and into the entire liturgical action. Its style should be personal: a mean between being too chatty and casual on the one hand and too cold and detached on the other. In accord with its eucharistic function to enable people to lift up their hearts in praise and thanks to the Lord for his presence in their lives, its language should be specific, graphic, and imaginative. Above all it must be genuine and true. It ought to be the lived involvement of the homilist, reflected upon in prayer, and then shared humbly with God's people.

Many years ago, I read two books in the same period of time. One, by a navy chaplain, dealt with his participation in action during World War II. The other, an autobiographical account of a man's conversion, didn't have much action other than that of divine grace. Yet the former was dull, the latter exciting, compelling, and attractive. In free time I reached for the latter. Why? Because the first was full of clichès, redolent of textbook style, and relatively uninteresting. The latter was by a journalist who knew his trade well, used picturesque words, and communicated life and suspense in simple, meaningful sentences. Do our homilies grip hearts in that way? Shouldn't they?

They will indubitably do so when we homilists, with integrity and honesty, recognize the active presence of God in our own lives. That's true no matter how shattered and broken we may feel our lives to be at a given time. It is, in fact, perhaps precisely at such a time that we have most to share with a broken world. We should always remember that our celebration of the Eucharist, including the homily which is an integral part of it, is done in memory of Jesus Christ who, knowing that he had done and said enough to cause his death to be near, *on the very night before he died* turned to God and praised and thanked Him out of his very depths.

The implication of all that is, of course, that the homily be *substantive*. People have come to expect substance of every public speaker. A supposedly true story is told of an elderly lady of determined mien who took a seat in the front pew. When the homilist began, she opened a little wooden box and extracted an elaborate hearing device, which she arranged, screwed together, and adjusted to her ear. Two or three minutes into his homily, she removed the receiver, unscrewed the mechanism, and packed its component parts snugly away again in the box. She gave the homilist something to think about as he struggled to finish talking.

Purpose

The *overall purpose* of homilies is salvation — salvation of the homilist and of the listeners. It is to lead listeners to respond in faith and love, to be converted, to follow the Lord Jesus who is our only way to the Father. As the United States bishops put it:

> Although we have received this good news, believed in it, and sealed our belief in the sacrament of baptism, we need to rediscover the truth of it again and again in our lives. Our faith grows weak, we are deceived by appearances, overwhelmed by suffering, plagued by doubt, anguished by the dreadful silence of God. . . . We come [to break bread in the Eucharist] expecting to hear a Word from the Lord that will again help us to see the meaning of our lives.[5]

Another purpose is to form apostles. It is the last of three stages. The first of these is *kerygma*, meaning proclamation, the first teaching of the basic truths of the faith. The second is *didascalia* or *didache*, which is further instruction along doctrinal lines. And the last is *homilia* — originally, as we said, a fatherly talk from a presiding bishop or priest to his people explaining the Scriptures in a simple way.

So our primary purpose is "to lead the assembly to lift up their hearts, not fill up their minds."[6] We "dwell with the word not for information but for transformation."[7] Homilies spring primarily "from contemplation, a lump in the throat, a bush in flames, a touch of the poet."[8] In giving them, there are great books to help, such as *The Catechism of the Catholic Church*.[9] Despite some criticisms, among its many advantages are that

> it presents faith, morality and worship in organic unity; it focuses centrally on God and on the missions of Christ and the Holy Spirit; it acknowledges the primacy of love in the entire Christian life; it respects the integrity of personal conscience and the need of formation in a community of faith and prayer; it attends to the value of liturgical worship for catechesis itself, and it incorporates Catholic social teaching and adverts to the structural aspects of morality. Building in an ecumenical dimension, it also acknowledges the values of Judaism and, in a general way, of other religions.[10]

But God's word in homilies is to be *alive*, not just read or heard in a static non-involved way. Stella Adler, teacher of actors like Marlon Brando, Warren Beatty, and Robert De Niro, counseled: "You cannot teach acting. You can only stimulate what's already there." Often blunt, as a young actor mumbled through a monologue she shouted, "Everything is Hoboken to you!"

Along with the prayers and the readings of the liturgical seasons, homilies retell the epic of salvation history for a different purpose than would a lesson in history, literature, or philosophy — or even the exegesis of a Scripture class. The homily aims rather to draw on the texts of the Bible, presented so as to move people to reconciliation with God and with one another.

Each individual homily should have an *immediate purpose* too, arising out of the homily's one main theme. This theme, if treated adequately, accurately, and logically, eliminating all irrelevancies, will certainly achieve its goal. But, as Aristotle said, no wind is favorable to a ship that does not have a destination.

Preaching that Is Christian

Our preaching is in the name of Jesus Christ, and is a sharing in his work. Homilists are sometimes accused of wanting only to tickle the ears of their congregation — to water down Christ's message in favor of "pop" psychology, sociology, or personal exaltation. This may or may not be true, but there is also a danger in preachers' not paying sufficient attention to acceptable ways of presenting Christ's message so that they can be helpful to people where they are.

Homilists are also accused of not being faithful to preaching the cross — that they don't make this "obstacle to some," as St. Paul called it, sufficiently central to modern Christian preaching. We *must* preach the mystery both of Christ crucified in love and the daily cross carried in love. But to harp on the bad points of individuals or societies is to miss the true Christian message of Good News. Jesus Christ did not choose the cross; He was no sadist. He chose his Father's will in love. We must choose Jesus Christ, follow him, and accept the cross that is inherent in the daily struggle of Christian living.

A Theology of the Homily

When Jesus appeared to the two disciples at Emmaus after his resurrection (Lk 24:13-35), a key idea was "life." That word is still used in a major way in advertising. Scripture contained the idea of life then, and the homily now. The preached word looks back to Scripture and forward to the Eucharist.

The preached word supposes exegesis of the Scriptural Word, the Word "then." There is no foundation for exhortation today without the literal meaning of the text. The preached word is also a new moment, the "today" moment. The past is to touch the present. Jesus at Nazareth (Lk 4:16-22) brought the past into the present, for which the crowds marveled; homilies are to do the same.

Thus preaching is to make us present to ourselves. Martin Buber said that to the degree that we are present to ourselves, and only to that degree, can we be saved. Self-knowledge reveals our negativity (that is, that we are loveless [unloved, unloving]), which is something we avoid and repress. Jesus' pity for the crowds to which he preached (Mt 9:36-37) was directed at things deep beneath the surface in human nature: namely, guilt, love-lessness, death. Homilists will speak with authority similar to Jesus' if they really touch something deep in human nature: depth speaking to depth.

And preaching, by giving us self-knowledge, prepares us for the Eucharist. Only people who are *aware* that their anxiety comes from lovelessness, and of their need for the power to love, and *eager to receive* it, and *expect* it, will *ask* sincerely and receive the gift of the Spirit.

The Liturgy of the Word gives us Jesus' mind and dispositions (Ph 2:5; Jn 13:34). The aim of liturgical preaching is to lead us to Jesus' faith surrender which will be re-presented. This is similar to what Jesus did with the disciples at Emmaus: by Scripture, he homilized them to "recognize him in the breaking of bread."

The homily flows out of Scripture into the liturgical action which follows. Without preaching the Sacrament is silent. The homily says what Jesus is doing in the Sacrament: inviting us into his story. Without preaching, the Sacraments move toward magic and are divorced from life. Flooded with the meaning which comes from Jesus' story represented to us, we are ready to "lift up our hearts" and "give the Father thanks and praise." We have no right to say "lift up your hearts; let us give thanks to the Lord our God," unless our liturgical preaching has given people a reason for doing so.

A Noble Tradition

When Joan was 14 and her sister Barbara 7, their parents died. The two girls were taken from their home to live with people who were strangers to them. Every night when the girls were alone, Barbara, the younger sister, would ask, "Tell me about mama," or "Tell me about daddy." Then Joan would recount all she could remember about their parents. When they grew up, Joan realized what they were trying to do. In a new and frightening world the two girls were trying to hold on to their identity in order to meet the problems of a new environment. After a year, Joan and Barbara were separated. Today Barbara has no memory of her parents and very little of her first seven years. There was no one to help her keep the memory alive. The homily is an opportunity to keep Christ's memory alive.

Christian preaching is a human work, but also divine: the work of a human instrument who speaks words, but words that come from the depths within, where the life-giving Spirit dwells. It has a noble tradition, beginning with the blunt, practical, and Scripture-based John the Baptist, "proclaiming a baptism of repentance which led to the forgiveness of sins."[11] In the beginning of his ministry, Jesus continued John's mission, but in his own way: "After John's arrest, Jesus appeared in Galilee proclaiming the good news of God: 'This is the time of fulfillment. The reign of God is at hand! Reform your lives and believe in the Gospel.'"[12]

Jesus' method does not need further elaboration here. It was simple in style, filled with images for ordinary folk, used short stories called parables for reflection, and gave attention to the Sacred Scriptures. It was nourished by prayer and backed up by his life — a model for all of us. It was honed by rejection and disappointments — with his fellow citizens of Nazareth, with his disciples, with the leaders, and with the holy city of Jerusalem over which he wept. He showed his awareness of the fate of the preacher in statements like "Unless the grain of wheat falls to the earth and dies, it remains just a grain of wheat. But if it dies, it produces much fruit."[13]

The Apostles, in the measure of their ability, followed in his footsteps. They were dedicated to prayer and preaching.[14] The Acts of the Apostles provide us with the first Christian homilies after Jesus' ministry. St. Peter preached on the first Pentecost, after the lame man's cure at the Temple gate, and to the Sanhedrin,[15] and provided the origins of what was probably a baptismal homily.[16]

The final chapters of Acts — more than half — center on the preaching of St. Paul.[17] He preached with power in the synagogues of Antioch, until his life was threatened; in Jerusalem, until the Church sent him away for his own safety; in the synagogues at Cyprus; in Antioch of Pisidia; at Iconium, Lystra, Philippi, Thessalonica, Athens, Corinth, and Ephesus; before Governor Festus, King Agrippa, and Bernice; and, lastly, at Rome.

The other Apostles were no less dedicated: Stephen, for example, before the Sanhedrin; Philip to the Ethiopian official; and James to the Christian council at Jerusalem. They showed the truth of the maxim that the good is diffusive of itself; in the present context, that means that we can't be wholly Christian and keep the Good News to ourselves.

The early Church showed the same enthusiasm as the Apostles. Ignatius of Antioch, on his way to martyrdom in Rome in about the year 110, wrote beautiful and touching letters to the churches. The *Didache* in about 150 A.D. spoke of instructions for catechumens. At around the same time, Justin Martyr, a lay teacher at Rome, described the Sunday Eucharist (not much different from our own). Hippolytus, a third-century church writer and martyr, spoke of *agape*, the practice of the highest love, mentioning that on some mornings there took place prayer and instruction on the word. Tertullian, outstanding third-century theologian, noted that the preaching in North Africa strengthened and encouraged the people.

Through the ages, great names carried on the tradition: Athanasius, Gregory Nazianzen, Basil the Great, John Chrysostom, Jerome, Cyril of Jerusalem, Ambrose of Milan, Augustine of Hippo, Leo the Great, Caesarius of Arles, Gregory the Great, Bede, and Charles Borromeo, to cite a few. Church Councils have encouraged the tradition.

Various religious orders dedicated themselves in one way or another to preaching: Franciscans, Dominicans, Carmelites, Augustinians, and Jesuits among them. The Protestant Reformation and subsequent tradition focused heavily upon the importance of preaching. The advent of the radio in the 1920's and of television in the 1950's provided new opportunities for an expansion of the tradition to larger audiences than theretofore dreamed possible. Vatican Council II (1962-65) was most notable, its "Constitution on the Liturgy" being in the forefront.

The Hearers: the Assembly

Homilists ought to be intensely concerned about understanding their audience. That audience is a special and unique assembly, the Church, the visible sacrament of the saving unity to which God calls all people, the instrument for the redemption of all. It is comprised of the light of the world and the salt of the earth, and needs to be treated with respect and, indeed, reverence.

Admittedly, the identity of the assembly is difficult to assess with precision. There is great diversity: men and women, old and young, successes and failures, the joyful and the bereaved, fervent and half-hearted, strong and weak, bright and ignorant, schooled and unschooled, rich and poor, wise and foolish. Each member has his or her specific need, so the conflicting expectations make for a dynamic and volatile entity. But there is also unity — all God's people are baptized into the one body of Christ; they share a common faith, a specific way of interpreting the world around them.

The homilist can be sure that the assembly thirsts to be understood, to have burdens lifted, to be given hope, to know they matter. Jesus always spoke with compassion ("suffering *with*"), and so the multitude heard and followed. The homilist ought in Jesus' name to try to get to know them well enough to provide words to meet their need for God. But *knowing* them without *loving* them will bear little fruit. The homily needs to touch the *heart* so as to release hidden springs of faith, hope, and love, and thus evoke a personal response that will lead to commitment.

The Homilist

Mission

It's good to remember that the homilist is *sent* to give God's message. The Father sent the Lord Jesus as the Word to be our light. He in turn sent his Apostles to teach all nations to believe in him and obey his commands. The Church continued this same *mission* or sending of preachers in Christ's name. In order to carry out the ministry of preaching to God's people in the name of Christ and his Church, preachers have to be sent officially — that is, given a mandate. Like St. Paul, he has to be called and sent to proclaim the message. When such persons speak the word of God in the name of His Church, it is God Himself who uses the preacher's humanity to speak to His people.

Preaching, therefore, is done only by those who are called by God, and whose call is recognized by the Church when it sends them to preach in its name. It is Christ who is the supreme preacher. Homilists must necessarily try to live close to Christ so as to be able to transmit entrusted truth; they are mediators of Christ's message of salvation to his people.

Homilists also represent the community, by giving voice to its concerns and possible solutions, and by enabling it to gain some understanding of the reverses afflicting it. This means that homilists should recognize their pastoral role: they should know and be able to identify with the people to whom they are speaking, with a sensitive and concerned awareness of the struggles, doubts, sorrows, and joys of the members of the local assembly.

History has shown what can happen when homilists grow away from their people. At the end of the seventeenth century, for example, paradoxically after France had completed the process of founding seminaries for the training of future priests, the better-trained clergy unfortunately started to grow away from the common people whom they were supposed to lead, without drawing them closer to the Good News. This resulted in France's anticlericalism of the eighteenth century and the more straightforward detachment and indifference of the nineteenth. In happy contrast was St.

John Vianney, the Curè of Ars, whose simplicity and genuineness was quickly recognized and appreciated by the people. They thronged so continuously to his little town of Ars that the French railroads had to put on extra trains.

The homilist truly represents the Lord by offering the community God's word of healing and pardon, and by providing compassionate love. It is a primary duty of the minister to proclaim the Gospel of God to all.[18] The other duties of the minister are considered properly presbyterial to the degree that they support the proclamation of the Gospel, and "a key moment in the proclamation of the Gospel is preaching."[19] Here as elsewhere the model is Jesus, who was especially poignant as lector and homilist in the synagogue at Nazareth.[20]

Qualities

No one by virtue of ordination to the active ministry has the qualities required for a good homilist. Others may be able to do it better. In Samoa on one occasion, when a missionary doctor was given an honor by a native king and arose to accept, he was jerked back into his seat by a native doctor, who whispered, "Here in Samoa we don't believe that a man who is a good physician is necessarily a good speaker. We have arranged a speaker for you. You can be sure he will say what you were intending to, and will do it even better." The native doctor was right. The surrogate speaker drew enormous applause for his acceptance speech. The ordained clergyman, however, must still try. And he should agree to some extent with the taciturn small-town Vermonter who said, "We have an understanding here 'bouts that no one's to speak unless he's sure he can improve on silence."

It has been said that the perfect homilist is 28 years old — and has 30 years of preaching experience. The homilist shares with every speaker the observation of Aristotle that "the man who is to be in command [of effecting persuasion] must. . . be able (1) to reason logically, (2) to understand human character and goodness in their various forms, and (3) to understand the emotions."[21] Aristotle adds that "persuasion is achieved by the speaker's personal character. . . We believe good men more fully and more readily than others."[22]

In the Judeo-Christian tradition, that notion is reflected first in Isaiah. To purify him as one who was to speak for God, a seraphim held a burning ember to his lips. In the Roman liturgy, the celebrant at Mass still makes symbolic reference to this incident just before he reads the Gospel. Over and above all that, the homilist imitates Christ: the greatest homily is the preachers' own living of the word they proclaim.[23] With Paul, who came to understand that the cross is God's wisdom,[24] the homilist shares that wisdom. The homilist will realize further the truth of St. Augustine's words: "Our pilgrimage on earth cannot be exempt from trial. We progress by means of trial. No one knows himself except through trial, or receives a crown except after victory, or strives except against an enemy or temptations."[25]

Good homilists are bold in preaching the word. They are, after all, a gift of God's Spirit in answer to the community's prayer.[26] They have *constancy* and *courage*.[27] They are persons of *prayer*,[28] and their prayer-life must not be simply alongside of their homiletic life, or over and above it, but the very warp and woof of it. Good homilists pray for those who hear the word, both those who accept it and those who exercise the freedom given them by God to reject it. That isn't easy. It's interesting that the *Catechism of the Catholic Church* entitles its entire Article 2 in its section on Christian Prayer "The Battle of Prayer."[29] Paul in his prayer for the Ephesians gives an idea of the prayer of the good homilist for his people:

> I pray that [the Father] will bestow on you gifts in keeping with the riches of his glory. May he strengthen you inwardly through the working of his Spirit. May Christ dwell in your hearts through faith, and may charity be the root and foundation of your life. Thus you will be able to grasp fully, with all the holy ones, the breadth and length and height and depth of Christ's love, and experience this love which surpasses all knowledge, so that you may attain to the fullness of God himself.[30]

In addition to those supernatural considerations, the homilist ought to have qualities of nature. He should, for example, remember that he is fundamentally a communicator, competing with other communicators who are polished professionals. No matter how sincere the homilist's intentions, if his communication is to be effective it is essential that he possess certain qualities. One is a passion for the beauty of language. In this respect, he ought to be many cuts above the ordinary, like the two girls overheard discussing the art of conversation. One said, "Take 'I'll say' and 'I'll tell the world' away from some people, and you cut their conversation practically to zero." Her companion rejoined, "I hope to tell you! Ain't it the truth!"

The homilist's passion for the beauty of language should be more like that of writers who use their facility for language to their advantage. Mark Twain advised: "Use the right word, not its second cousin. The difference between the almost right word and the right word is. . . the difference between the lightning bug and lightning."

The homilist should be akin to the blind man who, one sunny day near a park, was tapping for attention with his cane and carrying on his chest a sign: "Help the blind." No one paid much attention to him. A little farther on another blind beggar was doing better. Practically every passer-by put a coin in his cup, some even turning back to make their contribution. His sign said, "It is May — and I am blind!"

Commercial enterprises, whose children are more calculating than the children of light (Lk 16:8), study language intensely to further their own goals. A waiter is told not to ask if you'll have an egg in your malted milk, but to hold up an egg in each hand and ask whether you'd like one egg or two. Clerks in filling stations, hotels, and department and chain stores are instructed never to give a customer the choice between something and nothing and not to ask questions easily answered in the negative.

None of this is to say, however, that the homilist shouldn't use big words on occasion — not for pedantry, but to show that God's word can be more profound and elevated than many people think, and more learned than any physician's prescription sheet or lawyer's technical verbiage. Some people value brains and venerate what they find mysterious; this applies to religions, too. There's nothing wrong, for example, with speaking occasionally of "*epiklesis*" or "*anamnesis*," provided that the homilist makes clear his meaning.

How to Give a Homily

Preparation

Remote

Good homilists study not only Scripture and Theology, but also literary and speaking technique; the world's greatest literature, painting, sculpture, and musical achievements; popular art forms like movies, which can point to truths if used sensitively; and the cultural, social, political, and economic forces at work in our world. Their people, no matter how poor or uneducated, are accustomed to good presentations on TV, in movies, and in public speeches. The studies of homilists are preparatory to their hearers' receiving the grace of God, which builds upon nature and, but for miracles, doesn't contradict it.

A simple test for homilists (and others) to discover their range of interest is to take up the newspaper, especially the Sunday edition, and see how much interests them in many sections: foreign news, national news, athletics, the theater, music, books, and so forth. If areas of interest are many, the reader is very much alive. Not only does this mean richness of life and a continually enlarging curiosity, but it's the best form of insurance against senility.

Sherwood Anderson, the writer, relished life and found it a great adventure, despite some of his frustrations. He wrote in a letter to a friend, "Even at its worst, I sometimes wish I could have a thousand years of life." Others have tried to look upon life as drama, to have as much fun as if they were sitting in their own private theater. Thus they are able to enjoy even the faults of friends, or men and women who theretofore got their goat. Charles Dickens was probably not annoyed when he found Uriah Heep in real life, and Voltaire, Goethe, and Shakespeare probably had nothing but enjoyment in knowing the prototypes of the bounders and hypocrites they created for their and our enjoyment.

With particular reference to the heartpiece of homilies, the Scriptures, the homilist's studies need not be at the highest exegetical level. Scholars devote entire lives to that. Since homilists are proclaiming the faith of the Church, not merely their own, some good basic tools, in addition to the Bible, are a Bible dictionary, concordance, Gospel parallels, and commentaries. Homilists' caring pastoral nature will override their fear that, in this age of alienation from Christian concepts, their message may not be understood.

At the same time, homilists should not suppose that their congregation is on a very exalted level of scriptural knowledge. At the end of a radio broadcast of stories from the Bible, an announcer said: "Will Cain kill Abel? Tune in at the same time tomorrow and find out." That kind of phenomenon shouldn't dishearten a person of God.

Good preaching flows from contact with and concern for the lives of the people. In this connection, good homilists will also prepare themselves remotely for their homilies by listening with understanding to the deep rhythm of the heart of their people. This empathy will result in a message that is encouraging and relevant to the people's lives as well as a challenge to homilists to live the Gospel they preach. Thus authenticity marks homilists' lives, their message, and their relationships with their people.

Proximate

Preparing a *particular homily* for a *specific occasion* involves components of any creative process — data gathering, gestation, insight, and expression — all in the time frame of a week at most. Homilists will do well to begin early in the week, prayerfully reading and re-reading the liturgical texts. They aim to make these texts *fresh* so that their own spirit be graced and renewed. The homilist reads them aloud, in different versions, from the Bible for context as well as from the liturgy, with pen in hand to jot down ideas.

There comes a point, however, when commentaries, concordances, Gospel harmonies, and the like may result in being academic rather than intimate and pertinent: preaching *about* God's word rather than letting God's word speak within hearts. An academic homily can make hearers passive, non-involved, and even somnolent. We need the courage to risk letting go in order to allow the Holy Spirit Himself to work within us, giving that moment of insight, that incomparable "aha!" experience when God's Spirit moves over our darkness bringing light.

The homilist then needs further study and reflection. This facilitates getting away from slavishly following the thoughts of others and trusting rather the gift of God's Spirit. It enables homilists to use their *imagination* — a special gift of God — to make suitable application for themselves and for their people. Picturesque symbols can speak eloquently, attract, and persuade. Perennial truth can be presented by analogies and metaphors pertinent to time, place, and occasion. Through it all, the homilist remains theologically sound but pastorally in tune with the real lives of the people.

At least two days before the actual preaching, drafting on paper may begin. This will allow time for the easily overlooked revising and editing. Now it is more possible to arrange the material so as to arouse attention and invite a deeper faith response. The homilist makes sure of the central theme, stated clearly at the outset and repeated when emphasis and clarity require it. The theme is an integral part of the liturgy of the Church, celebrated in the Church by the Church, and thus has a charism that surpasses a talk at a liturgical convention.

This whole procedure can be made much easier by using a word processor. (All parishes, whenever financially possible, need modern equipment which helps in the service of the Lord; practice of the homily on videotape is also good.) A homily preparation group can powerfully involve members of the congregation, the parish staff, and even ministers of other faiths. The scriptural passages can be read and explored, the good

news shared, applications made. Such group involvement provides the
richness of new insights and the touchstone of feedback before the actual
homily is delivered. If the preparation has been careful and prayerful
there's little to fear.

It helps to have a clear outline in mind. The outline can be written and
briefly referred to not as a crutch but a landmark. The homily's order of
readings is usually 3-1-2: that is, the Gospel first, then the first reading
(usually a passage from the Jewish Scriptures, ordinarily connected with
the Gospel), and lastly the moral exhortation of the second reading (usually
an Epistle, and usually from St. Paul).

The outline might consist of only a few words with subcategories. If
one were to outline the Second Sunday of Advent in Cycle A, for example,
aside from the Introduction and Conclusion (which the homilist should
have almost memorized), the key words would be "John the Baptist" and
"Jesus." Under John the Baptist, one would include desert, message, diet,
crowds, religious leaders, and Jesus. Under "Jesus" would come fire, Spirit,
and fulfillment (which would include the first and second readings).

If the material tumbles from your mouth out of the order of your
outline, don't worry! Trust your gift of the Spirit who knows you and your
people and provides for their needs. One preacher who had written his
homily carefully found himself at the church without his manuscript. "As
I've forgotten my notes," he began his homily, "I will rely on the Lord for
guidance. Tonight I'll come better prepared."

As we said, commit the specific ideas of your introduction and your
conclusion to memory. Familiarity with your introduction will overcome
initial nervousness and make for a confident beginning. Knowing your
conclusion as specifically and as graphically as possible will have at least
two beneficial results: (1) You will leave your audience with a clear,
concise thought, and (2) if perchance you get stuck in mid-stream you can
always reach land by a strong conclusion.

In the Pulpit

In their growth and improvement, people are helped by the witness
of others. The homilist's congregation often knows all the truths to be
presented, but they need to see someone giving witness. Thus their faith
is strengthened by experiencing it as vibrant in the behavior of the homilist.
They can then return to their faith-less world with new conviction,
renewed motivation to try again, reassured by witnessing in another person
that faith really matters in and to their lives.

Two beautiful words hopefully describe the person in the pulpit. They are enthusiasm and vivacity. The word enthusiasm comes from the Greek *en*, "in," plus *theos*, "God." Unfortunately, its etymology is often forgotten. Enthusiasm comes from within, from the inner depths where God dwells. The outer manifestation of the interior working of the Spirit will be apparent to an audience by the presentation, involvement, and commitment of homilists, so that what they're saying is clearly "*in* God," but also *with* God, and most of all *for* God. It's been said that the worst bankrupt is the person who's lost his enthusiasm.

The second word, vivacity, comes from the Latin *vivere*, "to live," and can therefore also mean liveliness or aliveness. Homilists will inevitably communicate their degree of this quality to their audience. A story is told of a man who, sitting in a pew, heaved a sigh and died in church during the sermon. An usher called an ambulance. The medics arrived, and carried away the dead parishioner while the pastor droned on. One of the medics was overheard saying to the usher: "You know, we picked up six people before we got to the right one."

The homilist's aliveness should communicate itself in his voice as well as his gestures and bearing. We speak, of course, of enthusiasm and vivacity that are interior realities and not superficial substitutes. Well-prepared homilies will be effective to the degree that Christ, who is Life, is allowed to show that life through the homily, thus calling forth life in the hearers. People desire and need to be revived and renewed. In short, they need the communication of life through a homilist who is truly alive — in Christ.

Should homilists read their homily in the pulpit from a written text? Many reasons are given for doing so. Among them are that homilists are competing with television and can only in this way provide the words they have so carefully crafted on paper, that only by reading can they properly vary sentence length and structure, that this is the best method to lead the congregation through a series of connected and developed points, that it fosters trust in the homilist by the congregation, that it puts the congregation at ease and better able to listen, that it leads the congregation to believe that the homilist has something important to say, that it proves that the homilist is prepared, that it gives the congregation a sense of its own dignity and worth, that it puts the homilist at ease, that it prevents repetition, that it permits the homilist to present more quality material in a shorter time, that it is a written record of what was actually said.

Yet there is a difference between *reading* a homily and *delivering* it. Reading it can get in the way of the enthusiasm, vivacity, dynamism, vigor, zest, robustness, and passion that people have a right to expect from a homilist. Reading can also prevent the surges of inspiration that can come even in the pulpit. Therefore, wherever possible, we recommend that the homilist prepare well, perhaps use whatever minimum notes may be necessary, and humbly leave the rest to God. Should the homilist find it necessary for whatever reason to read the homily in the pulpit, he might be well advised to investigate the use of a Teleprompter or similar device. In no case should the homilist read from the pulpit "canned" material of others.

None of these requirements of homilists is hampered by their being brief. One great preacher, while receiving compliments on his sermon, thanked each parishioner for the kind remarks, then suddenly realized what one of them had actually said: "Pastor, your sermon this morning was like water to a drowning man."

Brevity does not detract from — indeed it enhances — consideration of the congregation, substantive study, prayerful reflection, remote and proximate preparation, skill in communicating, enthusiasm, and vivaciousness. Students of creative writing were told that a good short story contained four elements. They were religion, royalty, sex, and mystery: religion because people are interested in eternal verities, royalty in the sense that readers would be more interested in people high on the socioeconomic scale, sex because that's always with us, and mystery because the writer has to hold the reader's interest. The students were then assigned the task of writing in class a brief story that contained those elements. Most of the fledgling writers needed the entire class period to finish. But one young man was done quickly. His entry: "My God, the queen is pregnant! Who did it?"

How to Use these Books

The use of published homily "helps" can be a hindrance. Homilists who use them to replace the prayer, study, and work required are hurting themselves and their congregations. If, however, these homily materials are used according to the suggestions in the "Introduction" below, they can provide valuable possibilities for the development of a homily, especially in indicating some ways in which the biblical word can be seen as God's present word to His people.

Toward those ends, these homilies:
— contain materials that can be outlined personally — for example, for dynamic delivery or improvisation;
— include examples drawn from life as well as provide lessons which apply to life;
— embody much of the overall Christian message as presented by the liturgy;
— aim to be practical as well as speculative;
— encompass enough material to be, without harm, lengthened as well as shortened for particular occasions;
— try to be perennial as well as timely;
— when used meditatively, add further thoughts to the experience, prayer, and readings of the user;
— use short stories, metaphors, and similes which aptly encapsulate wisdom and truth; and
— were, in most instances, written in connection with the liturgical occasion commemorated, and preached on the occasion.

The work therefore has many potential uses and users in addition to homilists:
— At home by individuals, families, and groups. The homilies evoke reflection and encourage prayer, especially prayer joined to the whole Church.
— In prayer groups, as one of a wide variety of prayer forms.
— In Bible study groups. This series provides one more help in what all Christians are called upon to do: compose their own life of Christ; see if one has wandered from the ideal; discover the truly Christian life; and have a basis for action and judgment.
— For catechists, for whom these pages provide material for one desirable component of classes: the week's liturgy.
— With catechumenate programs, for whom these materials can help orient lives toward the Mystical Body.
— For lectors, deacons, commentators, priests, and other ministers, these homilies can help in preparing for proper inflection, emphasis, and other modes of interpretation of God's word.
— For church bulletins, when excerpted.
— By all Christian denominations, especially those who have Sunday Scripture readings similar to the Roman Catholic.

Content

Old traditions outlined theological presentations into variant components to which they gave such titles as "Creed, Code, Cult," "Dogma, Morals, and Worship," "Belief, Commandments, and Sacraments," and "Faith, Practice, and Grace." The *Catechism of the Catholic Church*, adhering to the "four pillars" of catechesis that have been traditional since the Middle Ages, divides its content into *The Profession of Faith* (that is, the Creed), *The Celebration of the Christian Mystery* (Liturgy and the Sacraments), *Life in Christ* (Commandments), and *Christian Prayer*. Choosing topics and titles as dictated by the Liturgy does not, of course, permit an orderly presentation, and there is inevitable overlapping for emphasis.

To the question, "Is this three-year cycle of homilies comprehensive?," the answer is in the affirmative with two reservations. First, we presume that the listeners are already familiar with the basics, at least, of sound doctrine. Secondly, we realize that the Church at times chose the readings for reasons other than the themes we see; while we believe our choices are legitimate and beneficial, we admit to other good possibilities.

God is a central theme. In addition to the fact that all homilies are shot through with God, many are specifically on God: His relevance, His care, His detailed provision for us. Last year, somewhere on the leaves of a forgotten sugar-cane plant, a bit of sunlight ended its eight-minute dash to earth. Somehow, the plant turned that sunlight into sugar. Somehow that sugar got into your morning tea. You sipped last year's sunshine at breakfast. Now it starts to feed your tired muscles. As you walk and work, the muscled sunlight becomes motion power. Then at night, were you to bicycle and provide power for the headlamp, it becomes light again. That's God at work!

Jesus is, of course, another main theme, and many homilies specifically deal with him. Mary is another theme that permeates these homilies, as does the Church.

Another theme that is important in our day is the identity of human personhood and a consequent realization of our dignity. Solutions to many current problems depend on that. As Galileo said, "The sun, with all those planets revolving around it and dependent on it, can still ripen a bunch of grapes as if it had nothing else in the universe to do." We have, therefore, many presentations especially on the dignity and uniqueness of all human beings, especially the powerless and underprivileged. Some problems, like sin and suffering, are with us perennially, and many references try to understand sin and to give meaning to suffering.

In our time, when a very effective media shove Christian values to the background and incessantly tout secular values, it's extremely urgent to preach our values. The most forceful of them is love. In addition to its being interwoven in all homilies, it receives special treatment in many specific ones. Consequent upon love are other values that receive special treatment: forgiveness, service, purity, humility, obedience, peacemaking. Faith, too, is interwoven throughout and receives special treatment in individual homilies.

In a time when money-grubbing is encouraged by our whole milieu, when the measure of one's worth is judged by one's possessions, and when the worth of one's work is measured by its salary, we must remind ourselves of the importance of another value: detachment. Some of these homilies therefore deal specifically with our choices about money. And extremely important among Christian values is wisdom. This is especially relevant to a society that treasures statistics, information, and data processing over worthwhile knowledge, insight, and understanding.

One who looks for life as it really is, and not as some people say or think it is, is wise with the wisdom of God. So these volumes address such other Christian values as the quality of life, whether our beatitudes coincide with Jesus', Christian priorities, active risk over passive acceptance, the ideal family, the root meaning of life, the imitation of Christ, feasting and fasting, role models, life values that reflect faith, the family as creator, genuine religion, Christ's teachings as an ongoing stimulus to human growth and potential, the meaning of salvation, the meaning of being "human," and holiness true and false.

Other areas receiving attention are witnessing and evangelization: being present to others, being prophetic, the nature of the Good News, witnessing to Jesus, and apostleship. Last but by no means least, although our world has solved many technological problems, eradicated much pain, lengthened life, discovered cures for many diseases, and invented many comforts, it is still vexed by one event it hasn't been able to solve: death. So these homilies take advantage of the frequent opportunities provided by the Church's liturgy to talk about death, vigilance, and preparedness.

The purpose of the entire content is, of course, the healthy growth of a strong interior life. That, too, receives much generic as well as specific treatment.

Method

Some time ago, in Lille, France, I met the principal of a High School that had just been built. He was obviously proud of the building. I asked who designed it.

"The educational authorities in Paris," he boasted.

"Do they design all school buildings throughout the country?" I asked.

"Yes," he said.

"Do they put in the same number of windows and radiators in the cold, damp weather here near the Belgian border as in the warm, sunny cote d'azur in the south?" I continued.

"Yes," he answered, now a bit uncomfortable. He had evidently never questioned the wisdom of the centralized "educational authorities in Paris."

No human work, including this one, fits all times and places. We hope that homilists will be able to put these homilies to good use, but they are going to have to help with their own experience, vision, and imagination.

As for *experience*, it's wise to remember that its use is fraught with ambivalence. On the positive side, personal experience can often present material in ways that are memorable, due to aliveness in presentation, picturesqueness of words, and the speaker's involvement. Using experience can simplify complex notions. It can also result in *encounter*, an important experience between homilist and congregation.

On the negative side, one's personal experience is inadequate. It's a drop in the bucket of the human record, compared with such exposure as history or anthropology. Those who consider experience the only teacher or the final test for the validity of any idea are in great measure pragmatists, empiricists, and positivists, whose philosophies often exclude any "givens," objective truth, speculative values, supernatural realities, and emphasis on intellectualism. They also usually exclude "mystical experience," which is genuinely verified paranormal spiritual experience. Empiricism by definition excludes the possibility of anything being in the mind other than sensations and perceptions. Plato, in speaking of one who would be a leader, said that "knowledge should be his guide, not personal experience."

The sacred cow of American culture has become the self. Especially in literature and philosophy, subjectivity has gained a new ascendancy. Throughout our culture, the old notions of "truth" and "knowledge" are in danger of being replaced by the new ones of "opinion," and "perception." Polls are conducted on everything from the state of the nation to the state of one's marriage. Never mind that respondents sometimes offer opinions on matters they know nothing about. (In one famous poll, just to give an example, students cheerfully dispensed opinions on three completely fictional nationalities — the Pireneans, the Danireans, and the Wallonians.) Young writers are constantly told, "Write what you know." There's nothing wrong with that rule as a starting point, but it seems to get quickly magnified into an unspoken maxim: "The only valid experience is personal experience."

For one to use personal experience in a homily, there are several cautions and guidelines. Experience as a solitary encounter, with little or no reflection, should not be considered worthwhile. The homilist (and everyone else) should not consider as experience whatever *happens* to you, but what you *do* with what happens to you. Those who relate experiences must themselves contribute something by way of inference, interpretation, or construction: experience must, at least in part, be the work of the mind. If one's life is so busy doing and experiencing with no time for reflection, one can't grow in suffering or prayer or anything else. Wisdom, for example, doesn't come from suffering, but from suffering reflected on and assimilated. If there is no time for reflection, life becomes not a connected whole but a pile of beads without a string.

One priest introduced his homily — apropos of nothing — by saying that he'd been at a fast-food emporium with golden arches, and asked the audience to identify where he'd been. They, of course, got it right. He went on to say that, when he went in, the sign outside said "85 billion sold." When he came out fifteen minutes later, he was disappointed to see that the sign didn't read "85 billion and one." Aside from the inane waste of time, it had absolutely no reference to the point of the homily. The encounter was a misuse of experience.

T.S. Eliot said when he wrote of the tragedy of some people's lives, "We've had the experience, but we've missed the meaning." That could be a true epitaph for many people. The homilist's aim, on the other hand, should be to go beyond discovering truth that can be *experienced*, to a discovery of truth that *defies* sensory perception.

An important question about experience is the problem of vicariousness. If learning is not always by direct individual experience of the world, and most agree that it is not, by what means can we learn about the world from the experience of others? The picture of the lone human being faced with the task, unassisted, of constructing his world, is not shared by many.

Learning a particular context is not like learning to wiggle your ears. It is steeped in prior contexts that are relevant to it. People who travel the world are repeatedly astonished by ideas, developments, trends, and movements that were virtually ignored by their experience at home. Even the well-read cannot be assured that their vicarious experience is presenting them with an adequate picture of reality.

As for *vision* — the second way of putting these homilies to good use — the origin of the Hershey bar is a helpful illustration. Milton Snavely Hershey (1858-1945) went through seven schools before dropping out at age 15 well behind his classmates. He lost an apprenticeship in a print shop after clumsily handling type. He failed at business in Philadelphia, Chicago, and New York. With only the clothes on his back, he returned to Lancaster, PA. That's where his vision came in. While roaming out West between business failures, he'd seen in Denver a recipe for caramels different from his own, one that called for milk. At an exposition in Chicago, he'd seen a German chocolate-making machine. In New York and Philadelphia, he'd seen the demand for candy on street corners. From childhood, he'd known of the dairy farms in Pennsylvania. He made associations, and set out to make a chocolate bar — long considered a luxury for only the rich — in quantity and affordable to the common man. So he borrowed $700 and turned that loan into a million-dollar caramel company. When he died in 1945 at age 88, he left behind a multimillion-dollar corporation.

With regard to *imagination*, the third way of putting these homilies to good use, it's too often true that, as Jesus said, the children of this world are more prudent in dealing with their own generation than are the children of light. When, for example, a publisher was overstocked with a novel that wasn't selling, he resorted to a Tom Sawyer technique: he printed an ad that read: "Millionaire, young, good-looking, wishes to meet, with a view to marriage, a girl like the heroine of M_____'s novel." Within 24 hours the novel was sold out. Not admirable ethics, but "A" for imagination — the kind that homilists should have.

Users of these homilies are expected to adapt them to their own time and place. With regard to time, studies have revealed the obvious: older persons and younger persons do not speak the same language, and homilies, like other means of communication, can profitably use the catchphrases, slogans, and idioms of a particular audience. With regard to place, studies conclude, equally obviously, that people in one country appreciate different styles from those in another, rural from urban, academic from agricultural, and the like. Though the essential message will not change, the packaging must.

This means that homilists must be prepared to break down the thousand-dollar bills of the Good News into the nickels and dimes of where people live. We therefore urge that ministers of the word of God bring God's precious truths to life through illustrations from the daily experiences of their particular congregation, use their imagination to be as specific, picturesque, and apt as possible, and utter Gospel truths with the conviction of their own hearts.

The homilies here are probably longer than desired for most pulpit presentations. This is not to suggest long homilies. To the contrary, we agree with the old pastor who advised his new associate, "We have no rule on how long you can talk, but we're of the firm opinion that no souls are saved after the first fifteen minutes." Perhaps a comedian put it better when he said, "The secret of a good homily is a good beginning and a good ending. And having them as close together as possible."

Rather, the homilies in these books are presented with the conviction that it's advisable not to have to grope for ideas, and better to have to condense rather than expand. Our thought is that there's enough here to give a respectable homily even if one forgets parts of the written material. A homilist might prefer to take one idea from a homily presented here and develop it. Or the homilist may wish to take a meaty scriptural sentence (for example, "Put out into deep water" [Lk 5:4; Fifth Sunday in Ordinary Time, Cycle C]) or even a momentous word (for example, the oft-occurring "repentance") and run with it. Thus these books may be used for many years, with a different emphasis each time.

Conclusion

One preacher told his congregation, "My job is to speak to you. Your job is to listen. If you finish before I do, please raise your hand." In the congregation, you will see people who are holier than you, more intelligent, more creative, and more talented. But they're not in the pulpit: you are, and if you have God on your side (that is, in your heart), whom can you fear?[31] Their jobs as doctor, lawyer, or Indian Chief called for intellectual training in their respective fields. Applicable to all preachers is Anatole France's story about the young postulant in a monastery dedicated to Our Lady, whose only skill was juggling. Driven by the desire to serve, in the dead of night, walking furtively lest he be seen and mocked by his brethren, he made his ardent way to the altar with his sackful of wooden balls, and did his act for Our Lady.

You have a special calling to goodness and renewal through your preaching: there's much less of that around than of intellectual ability and training, and in today's world it's at least as important. What you do is utter God's hidden wisdom.[32]

Footnotes

[1] In *The Documents of Vatican II*, ed. by Walter Abbott and Joseph Gallagher (New York: Guild Press, etc., 1966), pp. 137-177.

[2] The Bishops' Committee on Priestly Life and Ministry, *Fulfilled in Your Hearing: The Homily in the Sunday Assembly* (Washington, DC: United States Catholic Conference, 1982), p. 29.

[3] *General Instruction of the Roman Missal*, No. 41.

[4] Rm 10:14.

[5] *Fulfilled in Your Hearing*, p. 19.

[6] Robert P. Waznak, "The Catechism and The Sunday Homily," *America*, Vol. 171, No. 12 (October 22, 1994), p. 20.

[7] Ibid.

[8] Ibid.

[9] The *Catechism of the Catholic Church* (Vatican City: Libreria Editrice Vaticana, 1994).

[10] Avery Dulles, "Books on the New Catechism," *America*, Vol. 171, No. 12 (October 22, 1994), p. 22 (citing Berard L. Marthaler, ed., *Introducing the Catechism of the Catholic Church: Traditional Themes and Contemporary Issues* (Mahwah, NJ: Paulist Press, 1994).

[11] Mk 1:4.

[12] Mk 1:14f.

[13] Jn 12:24.

[14] Ac 6:4; 4:24-31.

[15] Ac 2:14-41; 3:12-26; 4:8-12, 19f.; 5:19, 29-32.

[16] 1 P 1:3 - 4:11.

[17] Ac 12:25 to end.

[18] Vatican Council II, "Decree on the Ministry and Life of Priests," No. 4, in Austin Flannery, ed., *Vatican Council II: The Conciliar and Post Conciliar Documents* (2 vols., Northport, NY: Costello Publishing Co., 1975), Vol. 1, p. 868.

[19] The Bishops' Committee on Priestly Life and Ministry, *Fulfilled in Your Hearing*, op. cit., p. 1.

[20] Lk 4:14-22a.

[21] Aristotle, *Rhetoric*, 1.2.1356a20-25.

[22] Ibid. 1.2.1356a1-13.

[23] See 1 Cor 11:1; Mt. 5:16; 7:21-25.

[24] Ac 9:16; 14:22; 1 Cor 1:21-25; 2:1-16.

[25] St. Augustine, *Commentary on the Psalms* (Ps 60, 2-3; CCL 39, 766), as in *The Liturgy of the Hours*, Second Reading of the Office of Readings for the First Sunday of Lent.

[26] Ac 4:24-31; see also Lk 11:13.

[27] 2 Tm 4:1-5; see also the rest of the pastoral epistles to Titus and Timothy.

[28] Eph 1:15-20; 3:14-21.

[29] The *Catechism of the Catholic Church*, op. cit., nos. 2725-2745.

[30] Eph 3:14-20.

[31] See Lk 12:4f.

[32] 1 Cor 2:7.

INTRODUCTION TO CYCLE A
GOD STILL SPEAKS: LISTEN!

The Introduction to Liturgical Cycle B, entitled *All Things Made New*, deals with the newness of human life in Christianity as illustrated by all the volumes, but especially in Cycle B. The Introduction to Cycle C, entitled *Ode to Joy*, points out the three cycles' overall emphasis on that fundamental quality of Christianity. In this Introduction to Cycle A, *God Still Speaks: Listen!*, we deal with another important area: the fact that God continues to speak to us, that one of His ways is through homilies, that we ought to listen, and that listening has its rewards as well as its price.

Some people today seem to feel that God speaking to people happened only long ago — with the prophets, with Jesus, with the Apostles, and, if relatively recently, with some saints. Now, these people say, it's all over, and God no longer speaks to people. Part of the reason for that belief is the way people imagine God's coming in the past. Some Church art contributes to their belief that God's voice is a shout, or at least an unmistakable audible voice, its hearers piously holding a hand at their breast and looking sanctimoniously upward toward the supposed source of the voice.

God

Much of what we believe about God still speaking to people depends on our idea of God. Jesus taught us about God in word and action, much of it relevant here. The very beginning of the Lord's Prayer, where he taught us to call God our "Father," transports us at once into a new era of insight into the mercy and gentleness of God. Any father delights in providing for his children; our loving heavenly Father delights even more.

Such a heavenly Father would not leave us bereft. The ascension of his son Jesus into heaven does not commemorate a departure, but celebrates the living and lasting presence of him who at his birth was called

"Emmanuel" — "God with us" — and whose last words in St. Matthew's Gospel tell us that he is with us always (28:20). And the Holy Spirit was sent to guide us to all truth (Jn 16:12) and to give us power to be God's witnesses to the ends of the earth (Ac 1:8).

Still Speaks

Where Do We Find His Voice?

Moses found God on a mountain-top, and his face shone from the glory of that meeting. God spoke to Job out of a storm (Jb 38:1). Elijah found God not in a thundering earthquake, or in crushing rock, where he expected, but in a still small voice. Where will we find Him?

The prime way in which God speaks and we have the opportunity to listen is through what we call *grace*. Grace is God's creative, transforming gift of love — in other words, God Himself freely seeking to give Himself to us. It's favor and generosity; it's by our being generous in turn that we make real in our lives what St. Paul wishes for everybody: "The grace of the Lord Jesus Christ, and the love of God, and the fellowship of the Holy Spirit" (2 Cor 13:13). We sometimes extend that greeting to each other at the beginning of Mass.

Paul calls it the grace "of Jesus" because, of all human beings, Jesus is the one in whom God finds an adequate response, and in him infinite love is embraced, embodied, and lived out. When Paul wishes us "the love of God," he means the same reality under a different aspect: not Jesus who makes love known, but Jesus who is love's unseen source. God's "grace," "love," and "fellowship" will be with us only insofar as we are "graceful," "loving," and "sharing." Only those arms that are empty of self can stretch out to receive the gift of grace — the poor rich young man, for example, could not accept Jesus' invitation to become a disciple because he had so many possessions (Mk 10:28).

Humility, sometimes prompted by having few possessions, is the only way we can be open to God's grace; anyone who has dealt with proud people knows how closed and aloof they are and how difficult to reach. Humility doesn't mean an undue abasement that makes one demeaned, degraded, or embarrassed. Nor is it a passive surrender in the face of suffering. Nor does it consist in a pride that apes humility: people being proud that they are not proud. Rather, humility is an active and faith-filled openness to God's voice in our lives. Many people like the promise but not the price.

Under proper conditions of searching for God's voice, our soul can grow in grace as does a corn stalk. Within eight weeks of its own ideal circumstances, the corn stalk establishes a root system which, if laid end to end, would extend for seven miles. In ideal weather the plant often grows as much as four inches a day, giving rise to the legend that "you can hear the corn grow."

One of Jesus' parables in this volume (Mk 4:26-34, Eleventh Sunday in Ordinary Time) compares our soul's growth to nature's growth. Nature's growth is often imperceptible; we can see it only by using a time-lapse camera or by returning at intervals. So, too, is our soul's life. Nature's growth is constant: It takes place night and day, day and night, whether people are awake or asleep. In contrast, our soul's growth is spasmodic; one day we may take a giant step forward, the next day a baby step backward. Nature's growth is inevitable, our soul's growth anything but.

One sure way to the grace of finding God's voice is *prayer*. Jesus himself heard the Father's voice by going often to a mountain alone to pray (Mt 14:23). His prayers were often in the face of difficulties, not unlike the prayer of the two disciples on the way to Emmaus after his resurrection. In their disappointed prayer, Jesus accepted them exactly where they were. He understood their anger, frustration, and pent-up feelings. They revealed the false expectations they had of the Messiah. He knew that the two must vent all this before they would be ready to listen to him. That is what Jesus was waiting for with them, and that's what he waits for with us (Lk 24:17).

That's what prayer is about. Jesus is with us in the midst of our problems; he knows about them, but we need to get in touch with them and express them to him. Then, when we're rid of a lot of choking obstacles, Jesus can begin to speak to us. We can see that with the two disciples. Very soon Jesus had their full attention as he assured them that they had been unable to see the saving hand of God in his sufferings and death, as shown in all the Scriptures beginning from Moses to his day (Lk 24:27).

The *Sacred Scriptures* are another good way to hear God's voice. The Scriptures themselves tell us this. The Second Letter to Timothy, for example, speaks of Scripture being good for revealing God's wisdom, for salvation, for teaching, for training in holiness, and for helping to correct ourselves (3:14 - 4:2). And the letter is speaking of the First Testament, for the New Testament had not yet been written. How much more does this advice apply now that we have the New Testament as well!

A superb way of receiving grace, and thus hearing God's word, is through the *seven Sacraments*. Indeed, Jesus instituted them precisely for this purpose. They initiate us to himself through Baptism, bring us back to God and His people through the sacrament of Reconciliation, strengthen us for adulthood through Confirmation, minister to growth into the fullness of life through the sacrament of Marriage, help with ministry through Holy Orders, and prepare us in sickness by Holy Anointing. The sacrament *par excellence* is the Eucharist, our bread of life; our active participation in the Mass and receiving Holy Communion can bring God's voice to us with His "Good News."

To hear God's voice, we must not forget the members of Christ's Body, *his Church*: "Where two or three are gathered together in my name, there am I in the midst of them." This Church, at times as vacillating as Peter, stubborn as Thomas, and irascible as Paul, but always as faithful as Mary Magdalene, the mother of Jesus, and the Beloved Disciple, continues to proclaim God's saving truth generation after generation. Our Church, still learning, communal, praying, and overall happy, is the voice of God!

Still another way in which we have the opportunity to hear God's voice is *in the everyday circumstances of our lives* and *in ourselves*. We do not look for God only "up in heaven." The Alternative Opening Prayer for Trinity Sunday in Cycle B says that one of the areas where we may expect to meet God is in the depths of our being. God told St. Catherine of Siena, "I call the soul 'heaven' because I make heaven wherever I dwell by grace."

If in all these circumstances we want to hear God's voice, we must watch for Jesus. To watch for Jesus means, as Cardinal Newman said (*Parochial and Plain Sermons*), to be awake, alive, quick-sighted, zealously honoring him; to look out for him in all that happens; to be detached from what is present, and to live in what is unseen; to live in the thought of Christ as he came once, and as he will come again; to desire his Second Coming, from our affectionate and grateful remembrance of his First.

Homilies as God's Voice

It's most pertinent that the voice of God is present also in *homilies*. We have said much about homilies and homilists in our Preface, and will therefore address here only a few words to their being the voice of God. Homilies help in the essential meaning of the Sabbath: as a celebration of life, a time to pause from our daily work, a time of blessing, a fiesta of all the moments of our lives and of our community. The homily helps encourage the kind of listening that is the starting point of authentic celebration. The homily helps avoid our Sabbath becoming empty, repetitive, and stifling.

Homilists share preeminently in the duty of all God's people to be prophets, to speak for God. Like the prophet, the homilist is to address the heart, with the deeply-felt words with which a lover woos his beloved. Homilists are to follow Isaiah's beautiful injunction to "speak tenderly" (Is 40:2).

The role of prophet, though, is not always an honored one. People don't like to hear the truth when it requires them to change who they are or how they live. The whistle-blower in industry often gets fired, the reforming politician doesn't necessarily get elected, and the preacher is often avoided. Sometimes, even today, the prophet gets killed — at least metaphorically.

But does speaking for God to others require us to express everything that is on our minds? Are prophets expected to be "reality talkers" — people who always tell the complete and unvarnished truth, no matter what the consequences? Do you say to your host, "Wow, this food tastes awful"? Isaiah, like every good preacher, had no illusions about human nature — its occasional blindness, foolishness, and stupidity. But despite being a reality therapist who told it as it was, he had a message of hope: after all, there's a basic goodness in everything in our world; God is alive and well, and no matter what the difficulties of any time or place the facts of God's plan for the world are in the final analysis friendly (See the Fifteenth Sunday in Ordinary Time in this Cycle A).

What do we look for in those homilists who, like prophets, purport to be speaking for God? Certainly preaching should never be an ego trip; egotism is the only disease that makes everyone sick but the person who has it. Nor is mere willingness necessarily one of the qualities. Disordered desires and resistance to God existed together in the great prophet Jeremiah, as they do with most of us. But at the same time the urge to speak in behalf of God was irresistible for him, becoming, as Jeremiah put it, "like fire burning in my heart." Jeremiah, in love with life, had to proclaim a message of doom and death; a devout worshipper, he had to foretell the destruction of the Temple at Jerusalem; a loyal Jew, he had to announce the fall of his nation if his people didn't stop sinning.

Homilists' uneasy task, regardless of how well or ill others receive the message, is to keep their own integrity by speaking out — positively as well as negatively. Their homilies, to more closely approximate God's voice, should include encouraging peoples' gifts, helping them discover the unique talents with which the Lord has blessed them, and putting all at the service of the whole body of Christ that is the Church. Altogether, their speaking in God's behalf signifies meaningful presence to others.

Broken down into the nickels and dimes of everyday living, among good homilies, many necessary qualities are compassion, patience, gentleness, humility, sincerity, reverence, delicacy, tact, true listening, going beyond mere justice and showing mercy, serenity in crises, authenticity, honesty, and insightfulness. Homilies must show prudence in superabundant measure — for example, realizing with St. Paul that if you want to overcome others' faults you first praise their virtues (1 Th 1:1-5).

Analogous to prudence, but not the same, is another supereminent virtue for homilies that speak with God's voice: wisdom. St. James gives some descriptive adjectives for the wise people who are endowed from above, which contrast with people who are only street smart. He says (3:17) that people imbued with God's wisdom are *pure* enough to approach God; *peaceable*, maintaining a right relationship between person and person and between people and God; *gentle*, knowing how to forgive even when strict justice may give the right to condemn; *compliant*, being sensitive to other people, allowing themselves to be persuaded, and knowing when to yield; *full of mercy and good fruits*, giving sympathy to people who are in trouble even though they brought their trouble on themselves; *constant*, not hesitating to make decisions; and *sincere*, having no trace whatever of hypocrisy.

Another virtue which homilies which speak for God must show in superabundance is *moral courage* that comes from *love*. This means not only to stand up against evil, but to give to God what is God's. The true measure of our worth is not the likeness and inscription on our coins, but on our person. As Caesar cast the denarius in his image, God has cast us in His. As Caesar sends out as wage and calls back in tax, God sends out the bearers of His likeness and calls back, demanding of us the sum of our lives.

In truth, it's sometimes difficult to discern God's voice. One night as the boy Samuel had the watch in the Temple, just before dawn he fell asleep. When the Lord called to Samuel (1 S 3:4), Samuel in his drowsiness had no way of recognizing the voice as that of the Lord (v. 7). When he finally recognized the voice, he eagerly answered in the words given him by Eli: "Speak, Lord, for your servant is listening" (vv. 9f.). Samuel's attitude, like the attitude of all who are close to God, was that of the Psalm: "Here am I, Lord; I come to do your will."

Listen!

True listening doesn't mean simply maintaining a polite silence while we're rehearsing in our mind what we want to say or do next. It means trying to see the matter at hand the way the speaker sees it. This means not merely sympathy, which is feeling for the other, but empathy, which is going out to the other. True listening requires entering actively and imaginatively into the other's situation and trying to understand a frame of reference different from our own.

There are many unworthy reasons why people listen in general: to a spouse to keep peace, to children out of frustration, to an employer because there's no other way out. There are "listenings" of criticism, of resentment, of superiority, of indifference.

The only true way we should listen to God and other people, however, is through sensitivity. This takes a certain largeness. When at age 12 Jesus was instructing in the Temple, he was not, as often pictured, a precocious boy dominating his seniors, but an eager student: He was "listening to them and asking them questions" (Lk 2:46).

As the prophet's task to speak is not easy, neither is the task of listening to the prophetic word. What is Good News for people of open heart, listening ear, and upturned eye is bad news for those who sense only empty words. Such people go on their way sad and unconverted. Jesus still speaks, but they don't hear his voice. He enters their lives and they let him go, unrecognized. "Today, if you hear His voice, harden not your heart" (Ps 96 [95]:8).

Frequently we do not hear God's call because we don't listen well. We can't always distinguish God's call from the noises around us. Those who believe in a life of prayer and alertness to discern God revealing His plans in His own good time are rewarded. The devout Simeon was one of these. He was the quiet man, the person who listens. As a result of listening to the Holy Spirit, he came into the Temple (Lk 2:27) and held the baby Jesus in his arms.

God's hospitable word is broad and generous, open to all. The glorious letter to the Colossians reveals the special and unique insight that

God's "Good News" is an invitation for all people of good will every-where. Not everyone can be a thinker, or a creative artist, or a charismatic leader, or a good lover. But everyone's gifts are sufficient to enable listening to God and growing into Jesus.

Mary, the sister of Martha, "sat beside the Lord at his feet listening to him speak" (Lk 10:39). Jesus, rejecting the Talmudic view that it was "better to burn the Torah than to teach it to women," welcomed her. And, challenging the then-current notion that a woman was unable to learn, he taught her. Martha, showing a familiarity which suggests that she had known Jesus for a long time, said to him, "Lord, do you not care that my sister has left me by myself to do the serving?" (v. 40).

Jesus spoke to Martha those often-misunderstood words that apply to all of us: "There is need of only one thing" (v. 42). What is this one thing? Many have thought that Jesus was contrasting Martha with Mary, that Martha had missed out completely on "the better part," that there is a conflict between listening and doing, that there are two opposing states of life — the contemplative and the active — and somehow the contempla-tive life is better. No, the one thing that Jesus wants is that we listen to his word, that we open ourselves to him. We have to look at Martha and Mary together. Far from there being a conflict between listening and doing, the one must accompany the other.

An important requirement for hearing is to get rid of preconceived ideas. In Jesus' life, even the day after the people had received a miraculous meal and Jesus was teaching about the bread of life, they wanted God to come to them on their terms (Jn 6). Despite the fact that God was speaking to them in ways that they should have understood, they wanted God's signs to be accommodated to them. But God is in His own image, not in ours, and Jesus was showing Him as He is. If we listen, we can learn.

The Results of Listening

Anyone who listens to Jesus can be initiated more deeply into his life. Peter, the man of action, glimpsed in his meeting with God on Matthew's Mountain of Transfiguration (17:1) the first steps of contem-plation. He experienced, without really understanding, the wonder of God, and he longed to stay there. This is the magic of God in our lives; whenever His almighty power and presence touch us in ways beyond our human experience, we're struck with awe and wonder. Peter succumbed; words failed him, and he could only babble. The babbling made little sense except to God, who understood because He reads hearts. He saw hidden within Peter's foolish babbling the germ of his real desire: "I want to stay with you."

Perhaps we're like Peter. He was generous to a fault, blew hot and cold, was ambiguous and inconsistent, sometimes insightful and sometimes obtuse, sometimes brave and at other times weak. Like him, we are, for reasons we cannot fathom, God's choice to have faith. Like him, we should allow Jesus to speak to our heart and then "put out into deep water" (Lk 5:4).

Having listened to God's voice and truly heard, we obey — we "let go, and let God." What symphony conductor Herbert Von Karajan said about conducting applies to life: "Technique you can learn. But what comes out of it is what you give as a human being." To listen to Jesus' message is to give oneself to constantly renewing one's cooperation with God's grace; those who only take and never give find it hard to justify their existence.

Listening to the voice of God will result in a life chock full of meaning. That, of course, goes beyond skimming the surface, and realizes that most of what is really essential is invisible to the eye. This may involve a turning around of one's whole value system — away from self and toward intense service in behalf of God and others. God offers us eternal life. Eternal life is not simply ordinary human life "without end," but the fullness of human existence.

Those who have listened and want to put what they heard into action inevitably face some degree of difficulty. For one thing, they are bound to be the conscience of the world. They must speak up whenever morality is offensive, and they're caught in the perpetual clash between Jesus and the world. For another, to adhere to Christ's values sometimes means the hardship of going against one's own selfish desires.

Supereminently as a result of listening, we will recognize our call to holiness, the definition of true greatness, the meaning of faith and trust, the loneliness of leadership, and joy and suffering in perspective. These are some of the results that are mentioned in the homily for the Second Sunday of Lent in this Cycle A from which this volume is named: *God Still Speaks: Listen!*

The first reading of the Mass for that day (Gn 12:1-4) begins a family photo-album of our forefathers in faith: Abraham, Moses, and David. The name of the seventy-five-year-old Abram would be changed to Abraham because of his faithfulness. God appeared to him in his home town of Haran in Mesopotamia to tell him to travel to Canaan to fulfill the destiny that God had in mind for him there. Although the possessions of this nomad were not many, it's not difficult to imagine his hardships in having to leave his home, his family, and all the things that made up his world to face the perils and uncertainty of the unknown. But Abram loved God and lived his life searching for God's voice and, being a good man, when he heard it he took the risk of letting go of all that was secure and familiar in order to journey by faith into the completely unknown.

A couple of thousand years later, Jesus likewise listened and obeyed. It had become obvious that he was going to suffer and die at the hands of the leaders of the people, whom he had challenged and defied. Now, as he was preparing for the ultimate letting go, he listened to his heavenly Father in prayer to learn whether he was right in setting his face to Jerusalem for further confrontation with worldly power.

The second reading from that same Mass (2 Tm 1:8-10) reminds us that God has not stopped speaking to people. As Abram was called by God, and as Jesus listened to his heavenly Father, people of all time are called to listen and become holy. But God's Good News can entail hardship. The timid and fearful St. Timothy was here being asked to preach the Good News despite the fact that St. Paul, who was writing him, was in jail for doing just that.

The liturgy of the Sixth Sunday of Easter in this Cycle A, *Be an Apologist and a Protestant for Jesus*, tells us that our listening is not to result in mere understanding or fine words: we're to act upon what we hear. Jesus said, "Everyone who listens to these words of mine and acts on them will be like a wise man" (Mt 7:24, as in the Ninth Sunday in Ordinary Time in this Cycle A). Many people — all of us at one time or other — confess God with our lips and deny Him with our lives. It is seldom hard to recite our Creed, but it is often hard to live the Christian life.

A Gospel personification of those who hesitate is Nicodemus. John the Evangelist, in comparing those who believe in Jesus as coming into the light and those who don't believe as remaining in darkness, might be said to be speaking of Nicodemus as only coming *near* the light. A symbol of those who respond promptly, on the other hand, is St. Matthew. In view of his having loved money enough to defy Jewish sensitivities by becoming a tax collector, his getting up and following Jesus is surprising. When Matthew weighed in the balance his material losses over and against his potential spiritual gains, though, he decisively opted for Jesus. Grace had been freely and generously given him and Matthew freely and generously responded. Then to celebrate he threw a farewell dinner party for his friends: "many tax collectors and those known as sinners" (Mt 9:10) — Damon Runyon characters and jailbirds rolled into one.

An Exemplar of Listening

When a woman from a crowd called out in praise of Jesus, "Blessed is the womb that carried you and the breasts at which you nursed," his answer was, "Rather, blessed are those who hear the word of God and keep it" (Lk 11:27f.). That declaration of the supereminence of spiritual relationship to God included Mary, the outstanding model for disciples of Jesus who want to listen to his Good News.

Mary is a special example of the efficacy of God's grace when combined with a person's cooperation. She shows the paradox of Christianity that's revealed in all the saints: a tremulous joy at her great privilege and, at the same time, a sword which pierces her heart.

We need her for our spiritual lives. An anonymously-written poem tells about a magician entertaining at an orphanage. The little children's eyes became twice their normal size as they watched him pull things out of his big black hat. The last verse of the poem describes one of the little boys questioning the magician, and is applicable to our need for Mary:

> "But can you," asked a small boy edging nigh
> And trying hard his sobbing now to smother,
> "But can you get out anything you try?"
> "Sure, Sonny, one's as easy as the other."
> Then smiling through a mist upon each eye
> He begged, "Please, Mister, get me out a mother!"

FEAST OF THE IMMACULATE CONCEPTION

Gn 3:9-15, 20   Eph 1:3-6, 11f.   Lk 1:26-38

The Courage to Love and to Risk

The Fullness of the Fruits of Redemption;
Commitment in the Adventure of Faith

Contrary to the plaster-cast piety that often imprisons Mary the mother of Jesus, she's a person to whom our contemporary people, men and women, can relate. As part of our prelude to Christmas, we pay honor to her who was to be the first dwelling-place of the Word Incarnate.

At the time of God's announcement to Mary, she was betrothed (v. 27), roughly the equivalent of our "engagement," entailing a commitment but no sexual privileges. At that time and place, betrothal occurred at the age of about twelve-and-a-half years and the couple usually married about a year later.

Mary is the personification of the fullness of the fruits of her Son's redemption. The difference between her and us isn't that she possessed great gifts and we not, but that she possessed them *in an incomparable way*. That's why we commemorate on this Feast of the Immaculate Conception that at the moment of her conception Mary was preserved from the defilement of original sin. But of herself she had nothing, as she testifies in her *Magnificat*.

God didn't intend anything substantial for Jesus' mother without intending the same for us. As today's portion of the letter to the Ephesians reminds us, God loves us too, has redeemed us, makes us the temple in which He dwells, fills us with His light and life, and sends us as a light into darkness — all as happened with Mary. So there is no call for envy here.

Because St. Luke tells us that it was an angel who came to speak to Mary, imagination conjures up wonderful images. The truth is that we don't know much about the messenger: Luke was relating salvation history, in which the important thing is not the medium but the message. In the Jewish scriptures, the term "angel" often means simply the presence of God.

Note: This homily is mostly on Luke; Cycle B is mostly on Genesis;
     Cycle C mostly on Ephesians.

1

Six months before this God's message had told the priest Zechariah, within the gold-plated walls of the temple at Jerusalem about the birth of John the Baptist. Now with a far more august message the angel was coming to a humble maiden in a common home in insignificant Nazareth (v. 26), a town never mentioned in the First Testament, or the Talmud, or by the Jewish historian Josephus; the town was despised in Jesus' time (Jn 1:46) and inhabited by jealous, material-minded people (Lk 4:23-30). And the message was delivered by Gabriel, no less — the angel who calls to mind the revelations he made to Daniel.

The contrast between the messages and between their recipients, Mary and Zechariah, were considerable. Though the angel had come to Zechariah without first addressing any greeting, now — because of the importance of the event — the angel greeted Mary in highly complimentary terms (v. 28). Mary, more than any other human being in the Bible, was the recipient of the most impressive salutations (Lk 1:28, 30, 35, 42-45; 2:34). The present message began by hailing her as a favored one — that is, full of grace, a phrase associated with joy and wisdom. "The Lord is with you," added the angel, indicating Mary's special prerogative. Mary is the moon, God is the sun. Mary is the peripheral instrument, Christ the center.

Whereas Zechariah had been fearful at seeing the angel, Mary was merely greatly troubled — not by the sight of the angel, but at what was said (v. 29). It was amazement at the high-sounding titles, but not fear. And she pondered — implying intense, prolonged reflection in a spirit of faith. The angel, understanding her perplexity, told her not to fear (v. 30), and in a kind reassurance called her by name.

Then (v. 31) came the essence of the message: She will conceive in her womb and bear a son. Did Mary understand by these words that her son would be divine, the second person of the Blessed Trinity? Probably not. Mary, as a Semite, wasn't accustomed to thinking in philosophical terms, like "person" and "nature," which would come only hundreds of years later. And there are indications that before Pentecost Mary didn't fully understand her son's divine mission (Lk 2:48-50). Mary pondered, ever anew, Jesus' words and works; through the light of the Spirit at Pentecost, she would plumb more deeply the mysteries in which she was involved.

Her wonder and awe at possibilities not consciously grasped prompted her direct question about how all this could possibly be. Several months were yet to elapse before her final marriage ceremony to Joseph. Mary was well aware that being an unmarried mother wasn't only regarded by pious Jews as a scandal; any woman who was unfaithful to her husband, or even to her promised partner, could be brought outside the town walls and stoned to death. Unlike Zechariah's difficulty about whether his wife could conceive and give birth, which was physical because of her advanced age, Mary's was moral.

Respect for virginity had no parallel in pagan cults, and perhaps far too many young women today consider virginity as a form of immaturity that has to be discarded, like losing baby teeth, or as a failure of courage. Experience has displaced innocence as a virtue — which leaves us wondering why, with all the new options available, young people don't seem to be notably happier than they were generations ago. Is it possible that when women discarded the idea of virginity they also discarded a source of happiness and feminine strength without understanding what they were throwing away?

Nowadays, women are exposed to the idea of "use it or lose it": to make themselves sexually available or stand accused of abnormality or the most vicious form of teasing. A woman who chooses not to fall into bed with a man finds herself branded with the scarlet letter A, which now stands for Abstinence. So many years after the sexual revolution, it seems that women have accomplished only a change from one form of repression to another. Perhaps what women learned while virginity was still in fashion was that the hymen was a reminder that their bodies ought to be used to help promote their inner growth..

Yet virginity refers not merely to physiological or external fact, but even more to a quality, an inner attitude. A virgin in this sense isn't only a person (man or woman) who abstains from sexual intercourse, but one who matures to wholeness as a complete person and is liberated — not subject to any other human being — so as to be free to serve God. More than abstinence, true virginity is a wholeness of human-ness, a quality of mind and spirit more than body. For some, what passes for virginity paves the way to a useful bachelor- or spinsterhood. For others, like Mary, true virginity liberates for the mission of giving one's all out of love and commitment, at the expense of self.

Why, then, would Mary become betrothed? For several reasons. There was, for example, the tyranny of established custom — "either marriage or the grave," said her contemporaries. In that tradition, the Jews took seriously God's very first command to humankind after the creation of Adam and Eve: that they be fertile and multiply (Gn 1:28). They wanted to propagate the Chosen People and the true faith. A childless man had his name struck out of family registers. And men wanted to have sons to pray for them at their graveside, especially the Mourner's Kaddish.

Most importantly, Mary's betrothal wasn't to just anybody, but to Joseph. He could have been of the same mind as she in reconciling the vow of virginity with an intention of marrying. Marriage, in this sense, would have been a protection to her vow. The angel's answer, that the Holy Spirit would come upon her (v. 35), indicated a sign of God's favor.

As a pledge, God's messenger told Mary about the approaching maternity of the aged and sterile Elizabeth (v. 36). That sign increased Mary's joy and gave her the opportunity to visit her cousin Elizabeth. The reminder that nothing is impossible for God (v. 37) revealed a new depth of meaning to Mary's virginity: Answering the usual questions about the incompatibility of virginity with giving birth, it posits complete trust and obedience before God. Mary's words of surrender are beautiful, revealing the true liberated spirit: She's the handmaid of the Lord (v. 38). Mary didn't ask that God's will be *changed*, but that it be *done*. That's the essence of holiness.

We who now read the story of Mary already know that everything was going to be all right. But at this point Mary didn't know that. We may fail to marvel at the incredible courage and indomitable spirit of this young woman who, not knowing what the outcome might be, said "yes" to her God.

That "yes" to God risked everything Mary had a right to hold dear: her family, her friends, her security, her respectability. She was aware that her "yes" meant much pain, but also much trust. Her "yes" was no less of a risk than we must take every day, when:

> To laugh is to risk appearing a fool.
> To weep is to risk appearing sentimental.
> To reach out for another is to risk involvement.
> To expose feelings is to risk rejection.
> To place your dreams before the crowd is to risk ridicule.
> To love is to risk not being loved in return.
> To go forward in the face of overwhelming odds is to risk failure.

But risks must be taken. If you risk nothing, then you risk everything. People who risk nothing do nothing, have nothing, are nothing. Such people may avoid suffering and sorrow, but they can't feel, grow, or love. Chained by their certitudes, they've forfeited their freedom. Only a person who takes risks is free.

Mary was the first Christian to commit herself to Christ in the adventure of faith; it's fitting that God fill her with grace, the fruits of her Son's redemption— because this simple girl had the courage to love her God and to risk everything by trusting Him.

FIRST SUNDAY OF ADVENT
Is 2:1-5   Rm 13:11-14   Mt 24:37-44

Rise from a Night Far Spent to the Day Drawing Near
Vigilance; Christmas, the End of our Lives, and the
End of the World; Jesus' Comings; True Security

Some think that retirement age was set at 65 because job performance is poor after that. But there's no such relationship. When German Chancellor Otto von Bismarck set up the first social security plan in the 1880's, his main purpose was to halt the spread of socialism by giving workers benefits. He chose 65 as the age to begin pension payments because few Germans then lived much past 65! Other nations later used the age set by Germany.

The truth is that older folk can remain youthful by cultivating a sense of humor and staying active. God can accomplish His purposes through those who many people think are washed up and worn out. If we think that God can use only the vigorous and the young, we limit His vast power.

In the Bible, God often entrusted leadership to oldtimers at key turning points in history. Abraham was old when he began the Israelite nation, Moses was old when he led it, and Solomon was active in his senior years. As for women in the Bible, Sarah was so old that, at the prospect of the birth of Isaac, she laughed out loud. Naomi was a senior who trusted God in tough times. Anna was elderly when she had to bravely face grief. Elizabeth, the mother of John the Baptist, was old when she gave birth. Zechariah, Elizabeth's husband, was an old man, but he continued to work as a priest.

In more modern times, at age 88 Michelangelo was designing churches and Frank Lloyd Wright designed a civic center. At 90, Peter Roget was updating his thesaurus and Justice Oliver Wendell Holmes was still writing Supreme Court decisions. Leo Tolstoy learned to ride a bike at 67, and Albert Schweitzer was operating his hospital in Africa at 89. Benjamin Franklin helped write the United States Constitution at 81. At age 80, Goethe completed *Faust*; at 98, Titian was still painting masterpieces. At 100 Grandma Moses was still painting pictures. Leopold Stokowski signed a six-year recording contract at 94. Pianist Arthur Rubinstein was still performing at 90. George Bernard Shaw was writing plays at 91.

The wives of some of these men probably didn't want them to retire because, like wives today, when men retire the wives get half as much money and twice as much husband. Today, people marry for better or for worse, but not for lunch. And perspectives change with age. At age 20, we worry about what others think of us. At 50, we don't care what others think of us. At 70, we discover that people haven't been thinking of us. And at 80, we learn that people are glad to forget us.

There's nothing wrong with looking for security to see ourselves through sickness, financial emergency, and old age. Some people, however, seek it unwisely — in get-rich-quick schemes, for example. That's why "boiler rooms" flourish — dingy cubicles where confidence men make telephone pitches from prepared scripts to entice the unsophisticated into all kinds of get-rich schemes like oil, real estate, precious metals, and banking.

The Apostles frequently looked for security. They often asked Jesus about his coming at the end of the world. Today, the First Sunday of Advent, we consider some aspects of Jesus' coming. As Advent moves along, the Church shuttles from the theme of awaiting Christ's glorious coming at the end of time to preparing spiritually for Christmas, the commemoration of his birth.

The special Gospel during the coming liturgical year (Cycle A), of which today is the first day, is St. Matthew. In today's passage, Jesus is replying to the Apostles' insecurity. Without their understanding what he was talking about, he referred to his Second Coming. Throughout Advent, our liturgy will refer frequently to that word "coming." The very word "Advent" means "coming." Jesus' comings are in *history*, *mystery*, and *majesty*.

Historically, though Advent is a time of waiting for Jesus' coming it's not a time of make-believe. We don't pretend that Jesus hasn't already been born of Mary, preached a public life, died, and rose. In *mystery*, we recognize Jesus' presence among us in his Spirit, his Word, his Sacraments, and one another. We also await his final coming among us at our death and in *majesty* in the last days of creation. No matter which coming we refer to — Christmas, or any time during the days of our lives, or at our death, or at the end of the world — Jesus' message is that, rather than knowing the exact details of time, it's more important that we be always vigilant and prepared.

To get that message across, Jesus presents three little stories. His first is that of Noah (vv. 37-40). Jesus' Second Coming will be comparable to what happened in Noah's time (v. 37), for three reasons: (1) both events come suddenly, (2) only a relatively few people are prepared, and (3) most people are preoccupied with worldly concerns. Note that what the unprepared people of Noah's time *did* was acceptable. It was what they *failed to do* for which they were blameworthy: That is, they didn't take God into consideration. Noah himself, on the other hand, never became so immersed in time as to forget eternity; he prepared himself in calm weather and was ready for the flood when it came. There's plenty of food for thought there, especially when we're alone in our perception of God's will and ridiculed for it.

Jesus' second story is the parable of the workers (vv. 40-41). The men are doing field work, the women making flour. All are busy working, which is commendable, but in each case one of the two persons is too busy, again not taking God's words to heart.

Jesus' third story uses a strange metaphor for God (v. 43). We would be ready for his calling the heavenly Father "bread" or "light" — he had already done that — but now he compares God to a thief. This may not be as strange as it first appears. In a sense Satan has control over the world. The only way to wrest control from him is to tie him securely and rob him. Later New Testament writers continued the theme of God as thief. So we must constantly watch. We can't be like the Scarlett O'Hara's of the world, whose motto in the face of unpleasantness in *Gone With The Wind* is, "I'll think of that tomorrow."

An old fable tells of three young devils in training as to what best to tell people on earth for the greatest effectiveness. One said, "I'll tell

them there's no God." The others voted that down for the reason that too
many people already believe. A second said, "I'll tell them there's no
hell." That, too, was voted down because of long-standing traditions.
The third said, "I'll tell them there's no hurry." The fable says that that's
the teaching the devil has used with great success ever since.

In the final analysis, true security can come if we, remembering
that no one gets out of this world alive, are at the same time mindful that
it's *God* for whom we wait, after all, so our watching should be of joy-
producing expectation. Although no one lives very far from the end of
the world, our faith gives hope for the future.

That's where Isaiah, who provides today's first reading, comes in.
Isaiah — and all the prophets — were much more concerned with
shaping the future than *foretelling* it. They were courageous witnesses
to God, even in the face of imprisonment and death. Isaiah, because he
looked forward with joy to the coming of Jesus, has a prominent place
in the liturgies of Advent and Christmas.

Part of Isaiah's vision was that the future Messianic kingdom
would be a time of justice and peace, and a time when all nations would
come together. Isaiah's "days to come" (v. 2), originally an unspecified
time, later came to mean the final age of history, the days of the Messiah.
Isaiah's idea that the mountain of the Lord's house would be established, to which all nations would stream, was a very ancient one. His
vision of beating swords into plowshares (v. 4) is a vision of Messianic
peace. The vision, along with that of Micah (4:1-3), is paraphrased in
an inscription on a wall across from the United Nations headquarters in
New York. But complementing these sentiments are the words of Joel
(4:10) to beat your plowshares into swords. Decisions on how to act
properly — even those based on Sacred Scripture — require careful
reading and prudent judgment.

So it's still necessary to put forth the same reminders that Jesus
did. That's what St. Paul does in today's second reading. It comes from
his major theological work, his letter to the largely Jewish-Christian
church at Rome, and is a reminder to live in such a way that we will be
ready for Christ's coming — during our lives, and at the hour of our
death, and at the end of the world. This section will be ever-famous for
having had a part in the conversion of St. Augustine. Miserable in his
addiction to sin and despondent over his failure at goodness, Augustine
snatched up the Scriptures and fell upon this passage, which completely
changed his life.

Paul specifically mentions (v. 13) six sins that are typical of life without Christ: *carousing*, in which the pagans had engaged with friends after victory in athletic games; *drunkenness*, which was disgraceful even to the pagans because it took away the glory of reason which distinguishes the human being from the rest of the world; *sexual excess*, which places no value on fidelity; *lust*, ugly because it means being lost even to shame; *quarreling*, born of unbridled competition that results in the negation of Christian love; and *jealousy*, which begrudges preeminence to anybody other than ourselves. These works of darkness are essentially no different from today, when we speak of "safe sex" (and there's no such thing), marital "lapses" (as we so delicately describe our infidelities), abuse of controlled substances, and other self-destructive behavior. There are no new sins.

People who commit such sins don't usually commit them at high noon at the city's main intersection; like athlete's foot, they hide in out-of-the-way places under the cover of darkness. Our present time of preparation is another chance to throw off the works of darkness (v. 12). We can't afford to remain in the unprotected condition of spiritually asleep people who are scantily dressed, when the time in which we're living calls for alertness, action, and armor — the armor of God, which Paul tells us elsewhere is faith, hope, charity, fidelity, and uprightness.

As we begin our preparation for the historical coming of Christ at Christmas, his mysterious comings during our lives and at the time of our death, and his majestic coming at the end of the world, let's sort out our priorities. In our band of vision, which is more than occasionally narrow, ordinary life may seem dull, with only occasional moments of light. Today's readings teach us a different message: that the seeming ordinariness of life crackles, like a radio receiving a communication from some other planet, with cosmic forces, restless life, development, and hope.

As we await the coming of Jesus in the new and eternal Jerusalem, let's have the same joy that today's Responsorial Psalm says the pilgrims had as they approached Jerusalem and caught first sight of the city. Let's be responsive to God's presence in our family, our parish, our community, our world, and in nature. If we do that, Jesus' comings will take care of themselves.

SECOND SUNDAY OF ADVENT
Is 11:1-10   Rm 15:4-9   Mt 3:1-12

Change of Heart: A Fundamental Option
The Axe at the Foundations of the World; Preparing the
Day of the Lord; Hope; The Final Age of the World; Conversion

Although the stores are probably way ahead of us, we're moving along in our preparations for Christmas. Today's liturgy speaks of personal change of heart, or conversion. In today's Gospel, St. Matthew presents St. John the Baptist as the one who introduces Jesus to the world. The Church chooses him as a personification of many themes of Advent.

John appeared, almost out of nowhere, in a hilly place of arid soil, deep gulches, and rocky precipices in Judea northwest of the Dead Sea (v. 1). His message was a good one for our Advent preparation for Christmas: Reform your lives! (v. 2). Quoting Isaiah (40:3-5), Matthew referred to John as a herald in the desert (v. 3). A herald was a crier preceding a king when the king was about to make a journey, to forewarn the inhabitants of his arrival so that the local populace could repair their roads. The roads were for the most part dirt paths — so bad that most people seldom left home. Any roads that were surfaced in any way were made for the king, repaired only as the king needed them, and designated as "the king's highway."

John's task, though, was straightening out human hearts. John always imparted truth as he saw it — to Herod, to all the people and, here, to the religious leaders: secular (Sadducees) and clerical (Pharisees). He was a voice to summon people to justice and right — a signpost to God. And the Jews respected him. While his mission was like that of Isaiah, his clothing (v. 4), like much else about him, reminded people of Elijah. In fact, Jesus would speak of John as Elijah (Mt 17:12). Elijah's ministry was identified with fire: He appeared like fire, was able to call fire down upon earth, and went to heaven in a chariot with fiery horses. Fire is a good symbol. It provides illumination and warmth, and at the same time purification, and it signifies one committed to the Lord's words. Tongues of fire would descend from heaven on the first Pentecost.

The grasshoppers John ate provided his body with needed protein, and his honey from wild bees or the sweet sap of certain shrubs or trees provided sugar. Those who are squeamish about that kind of food should consider some current diets. Dragonfly larvae, for example — plump, juicy, high-protein, low-fat — are considered a delicacy in places like Bali, where they're fried in coconut oil and served with vegetables, and in Thailand, where they're roasted and eaten plain. Dog meat is a treat in China, and horse meat is sold in many parts of Europe. And far less clean-living animals, such as lobsters and oysters, are consumed by the millions in the United States.

In John's time, many thought the Messiah would make his appearance in the desert. Perhaps that's one reason why huge crowds of people (v. 5) left the relative comfort of the cities to enter the desert with its unbearably hot days and cold nights to hear the voice of this skinny man with the piercing eyes, leather-like skin, hard legs, calloused feet, emaciated and stern face, and unkempt beard and hair. Though no one knows who told John what to say or do, he had a majesty of bearing and an authority that commanded respect and obedience.

John's message (vv. 7-12) demonstrated his forthright self. It contained both a warning and a promise, both apt for Advent. When he saw the Pharisees and Sadducees stepping forward (v. 7), he was agitated at their hypocrisy. The Pharisees and Sadducees were united on little other than their hostility to challenges to their authority and power — represented now by John, later by Jesus.

John's calling them a brood of vipers is the same invective that Jesus would use later against the same class of people. The picturesque comparison is meaningful. The viper is a snake whose presence is unsuspected, but which hurts and can kill. People in that category could aptly be considered worthy offspring of the devil, the ancient serpent. Such people deceive others and kill souls with the poison of false morality.

If in this desert of short, dried-up grass and bushes stunted for want of rain a fire broke out or a reaper came, the animals that had used the brush as shelter would scurry for their lives: snakes, scorpions, field mice, rats. That the Pharisees and Sadducees flee from the coming wrath meant that they were like that — animals running for their lives. Their smugness, like smugness everywhere, precluded their feeling any need for repentance. John wanted evidence of repentance in action (v. 8), not just self-assured words of reliance on Abraham as their physical forebear (v. 9). It's *spiritual* descent from Abraham, achieved by grace, that counts in God's eyes. It will be the Christian community who will turn out to be the true children of Abraham.

After all, an axe is striking at the very foundations of the world (v. 10)! As with people of most times, however, including our own, people manage to retreat from the important issues to think about trivia. In 1453 in Byzantium, which was then besieged by the armies of Mohammed II and about to fall, some of the questions which excited the passion of public opinion were: Are angels male or female? Were the Virgin Mary's eyes blue or brown? When a fly falls into a basin of holy water, does it pollute the water? We aren't so different from the Byzantines.

Between John and Jesus, the one who's coming after him (v. 11), there are striking similarities. People called John a preacher; Jesus would also proclaim God's word. A common location was the desert, where John worked and where Jesus was tempted. The audience of both was large crowds. The opponents of both were the Pharisees and Sadducees, important groups of the Jewish nation. The central message of both was reform, repentance, and the coming of the Kingdom. Both baptized. The fate of both was to be rejected by the leaders, suffer persecution under them, and be killed at their hands. Both were buried by their own followers.

But John was only a *voice*, whereas Jesus is the *Word*; John was a herald, Jesus the One Who establishes the reality. John cut a more eccentric figure than Jesus. John didn't seem to have much faith in humanity; Jesus says we can bring about the Kingdom of God here and now. John somberly but justifiably made people feel guilty; Jesus inspires us with hope. Jesus' baptism is unique, greater by far than the baptism of John. John says that Jesus will baptize with the Holy Spirit and fire.

We've already spoken of fire. The Spirit — Hebrew *ruach* — can mean many things. It means breath, for example, and breath is life; it's what God exhaled into Adam at his creation, and thereafter *ruach* is that which invigorates people when God's Spirit enters them. It also means wind — less gentle than breath, full of power; so God's Spirit in a person transforms weakness into power, enabling us to face and overcome difficulties. *Ruach* is also connected with the works of creation: God's Spirit upon the face of the waters in the very beginning (Gn 1:2), for example, creating the cosmos out of chaos, another work of transformation.

This is the same Spirit to whom Isaiah refers in today's first reading (v. 2). God had made a promise to King David through the prophet Nathan that David's kingdom would last forever (2 S 7:8-16).

But the kings descended from David were worthless, weak, and usually corrupt. By Isaiah's time (eighth century B.C.), with an invasion by Assyria threatening them, many doubted Nathan's words: Judah was hardly likely to survive an attack. Others, like Isaiah, believed that God's promise would be kept: One day there would be another king as great as David, a man after God's own heart.

For Christians, that prophecy is fulfilled in Jesus — whom we call Christ, "the anointed one." It's of him that Isaiah says that the spirit (*ruach*) of the Lord shall rest upon him (v. 2). This new king will be committed to God's own moral standards. Isaiah then mentions what mystical theology has come to know as the Gifts of the Holy Spirit — all of them practical, all orientated towards action, and all down to earth. The passage concludes (vv. 6-9) with images drawn from the Garden of Eden as a dramatic symbol of the universal peace and justice of messianic times. That justice — referred to also in the Responsorial Psalm — means not simply a king whose judgments won't be corrupt or based on appearances or decided by kickbacks, as with the Davidic kings, but by uprightness which comes from the goodness of God.

Today's portion of St. Paul's letter to the Romans takes up Isaiah's metaphor of justice and peace, very telling to the people of Rome, accustomed as they were to the clanging of arms as they watched their legions marching off to conquer the corners of the world. Like all people everywhere, they also knew the discouragement of disagreements with those who were closest to them. Their community was divided by questions of day-to-day practice.

Paul's letter, filled with hope, encouragement, and expectation, intertwines the cosmic vision of Isaiah and the everyday life of the Christian in the process of seeking peace and reconciliation. Go to Scripture, says Paul, because it was written that we might have hope (v. 4). Paul knows that only God can bring about a communion of love between people who are in many ways diverse. His advice is a good Advent program of reconciliation: Accept one another as Christ accepted us.

We Christians don't give in to despair or pessimism, because we believe in God and in him whom God sent. We enjoy life, because we enjoy God. But every generation needs its own shoot springing up from its own tradition, its own breath (*ruach*) of fresh air blowing across the land, its own people who aren't co-opted by the prosperity of the moment. It includes the central biblical vision that our conversion from sin toward God takes place in our innermost self — in the place where we say "I," as in "I believe" or "I have sinned." As part of our program of preparing for Christmas, let's see what we find in this inner core of our being, ask for the grace to see how we're in need of conversion, and request the strength to repent and convert. And let's make our program of conversion a matter not of misery and dreariness, but a matter of joy, of getting rid of things that make us unfree.

THIRD SUNDAY OF ADVENT
Is 35:1-6, 10   Jm 5:7-10   Mt 11:2-11

Discovery of Identities: One's Own, Jesus', and Others'
The Signs of God's Presence; The True Image of God;
Courage and Patience; We Need the Lord to Come and Save Us

The Merchant of Venice is a comedy by Shakespeare in which a vengeful Jewish moneylender, Shylock, demands a pound of flesh from a non-Jewish debtor who is in default of payment. The play is dominated by Shylock. The stage history of the drama shows variations on three Shylocks: the comic ogre in a red wig that almost certainly ruled early performances; the demonic, vengeful figure, part First Testament character, part wild beast; and the wronged, saintly, tragic figure, the only gentleman in the play. This mythical figure is one of the most coveted roles for Shakespearean actors, because it is full of possibilities for an actor to give an identity to the character.

The discovery of identity is one of our greatest jobs in life. That begins with our own. If we get to know who we are, we're not tense and agitated, troubled with suspicions, a constant irritant to ourselves and to others. We're visibly happy, peaceful, and easier to live with. Then we're able to go out of ourselves and discover the identity of others. That brings understanding among members of families, among friends, among acquaintances, and eventually among nations.

Christians can't properly or completely discover identity, their own or others', until and unless they discover the identity of Jesus. He is that central to our worldview. Whether Jesus was God, or man, or both; whether his teachings were wholly true or enable us to pick and choose among them; whether his values bear the weight of God's own authority —all have a bearing on how we experience the distance between who we really are and who we've been called to be.

Today's two-part Gospel is about discovering the identity of Jesus as well as John the Baptist. In jail for bluntly condemning Herod for his defiant adultery with his brother's wife, from his prison cell John anxiously sent his disciples to searchingly inquire of Jesus whether he was "He-Who-Is-To-Come" — the Messiah, the long-expected savior of the Jewish people — or whether they had to wait for someone else.

Some scholars interpret John's question as being for the benefit of his followers. Some of these followers had been shocked by the contrast between John and Jesus, and at times they were envious of Jesus and his followers. Others say that John was asking this information for his own benefit. Good people like John often find it difficult to accept the differences between their expectations and the way God comes into their lives.

Imagine John's mindset. The prison where this man of the open spaces was now confined was possibly Machaerus, a frontier fortress on a high plateau east of the Dead Sea. We can be sure that Herod's treatment of John was as cruel as he could devise, especially since his motive was to frighten John into silence. The soldiers in charge would be the meanest goons who could administer effective brainwashing. If John were asking the question about whether Jesus was the Messiah for his own sake, what agonizing hours of doubt he must have had!

In the solitude of his hard prison cell, he pondered, and he wondered, and he reflected, and he considered, and he ruminated — about everything, but especially about those beliefs he shared with his fellow Jews about the Messiah. If Jesus was the Messiah, why didn't he start acting like it? Where was the battle in which the army of the Messiah was supposed to vanquish the forces of evil, of which army John wanted to be a part on the side of goodness?

In any case, what nobility of character John had! He who had intended his reputation to decrease while Jesus' reputation increased was showing himself willing to let go of even the consoling companionship of his few followers in an alien world. (Some of John's later followers were so loyal to him that they never did come to follow Jesus; they ended up separate from their Jewish roots and remained anti-Christian.)

John's question posed a problem for Jesus. If he answered "yes," he would be creating trouble for himself. The Pharisees would have loved to have that kind of evidence — which they would interpret as blasphemy. And the people, including John's disciples, had false ideas of "The-One-Who-Is-To-Come," looking upon him as a political liberator who would lead the Jews from under the heel of Rome into superabundant prosperity.

But if Jesus answered "No," he would be lying.

So he resorted to the section of the prophet Isaiah in today's first reading, knowing that the intelligent among the people would realize that he was answering "Yes, I am the Messiah," but in an astute way that would give the leaders a hard time if they tried to pin him down in court. "Go back and report to John what you hear and see," he said. "The blind can see again, cripples walk, lepers are cured, the deaf hear, dead people are raised to life, and" — most important of all in a time that had no high regard for ordinary people — he added that "the poor have the Good News of salvation preached to them."

Isaiah had foretold these special events as a proof of the Messiah, and everyone recognized Isaiah in Jesus' words. Isaiah, about seven hundred years before, had delivered God's high-sounding promises at a time when the Jewish people were having their own identity crisis. Jerusalem, their sacred city, had been destroyed, their leaders were in captivity in Babylon, and only peasants remained in the Holy Land to till the hard soil. And yet God through Isaiah raised their eyes to the image of a wilderness blooming, a vision of a miracle of life, a surge of new vitality into tired hearts, all seeming to go against common-sense reality. The Jews took Isaiah's words so literally that they've always expected instant perfection at the Messiah's coming, and they still today can't acknowledge that the Messiah has already come.

Jesus, too, was going against the reality of his time. He exploded the term "Messiah." Considering the popular mentality of the time, he concluded his answer by asserting another beatitude: Blessed is the one who takes no offense at me (v. 6). He would be a stumbling block to all whose preconceived notions of his identity blinded them to the truth of who he *really* was.

In the second part of today's Gospel, Matthew shows that after establishing his own identity, Jesus went on to establish the full identity of John as a prophet — that is, one of those people who spoke on God's behalf in shaping the moral character of Judaism. Despite John's emaciated look, rags, and imprisonment, Jesus gave him great praise. But, lest Jesus give the impression of currying favor with John or his disciples, he waited until John's disciples were out of earshot before giving it. Knowing full well that everybody recognized that John's blunt, courageous character was anything but weak, Jesus asked the people if they thought John comparable to the vacillation of a reed swaying in the wind, or to those who dress luxuriously. His questions were a neat reference to Herod.

Despite that testimony to John's greatness, though, Jesus said that the least born into the kingdom of God is greater than John. Why? Because John, great though he was, understood only half of the identity of God as shown through Jesus. John preached a God of divine retribution; Jesus preached a God of divine love. John lived before the cross, so he could never know the full extent of God's love; God has given the least of us His gift of knowing His love through the cross.

In our pursuit of our personal identity with which we can be happy, we must follow the advice in today's portion of the letter of James: Be patient — with a particular kind of patience. It's a patience that doesn't lose hope, no matter how hard the situation; a patience that's strong and at the same time gentle. It's a patience that's not supine and passive, but active. It's a patience that manifests a quiet, everyday sort of strength — less admired than its dashing cousin Bravery. Bravery crosses raging floodwaters to rescue a family of twelve; patience shares its house with them while their own is rebuilt. Don't lose heart, just as the farmer in the water-scarce Holy Land has to wait patiently for rain to bring about the yield of the soil. Meanwhile, we cry out with today's Responsorial Psalm, "Lord, come and save us!"

The important thing is whether we're trying. You can tell the difference in people who, knowing themselves, are trying with God's help to realize more fully their potential, and those who, neither knowing themselves nor God, can't find their way in peace. Those who haven't fully arrived must, like the farmer in James's letter, be patient and wait. But they can't *only* wait. A farmer who did that would wind up with no harvest, and probably no farm! God will do His part; we must do ours. Our part can't be in silence or inaction; we must be moved to heal, to care, and to reconcile — all with joy and hope, so that people may see God's love through us.

When we've discovered our identity, we're able to rid ourselves of all that keeps us confined: our lack of trust, our fears, our bitterness.

When we've cleared the desert of our lives of all that clutter, we can burst into flower.

So there's an urgency in our Advent cry of longing: "Lord, come and save us." We mean it now especially in connection with Christmas — most particularly today when our vestments and Advent wreath's candle are a different color to show our rejoicing — but we know too that there is his other, final coming. Are we comfortable enough with knowing our identity — warts and all — that we can say "Come" to Jesus now and mean it?

FOURTH SUNDAY OF ADVENT
Is 7:10-14   Rm 1:1-7   Mt 1:18-24

Let the Lord Enter
Trust in Weapons, or in the Son of God?; God With Us; Depth
and Breadth of Vision; Promise and Fulfillment; Surprises and Gifts

Some of us are celebrating this wondrous season in the happy family situations we see on television sitcoms or around the Christmas crib, others in the loneliness and isolation depicted by some newspaper headlines. The latter can be very close to the situation of the Holy Family, who didn't have a very cozy time at this season.

To help guide us on how not to be lonely even though we may be alone, we have at our option two contrasting ways to live our lives. *The first way is personified by St. Joseph* in today's Gospel, the second by King Ahaz in Isaiah. Joseph represents a life in which the individual trusts in God even when God throws in a few surprises. As G.K. Chesterton wrote, whoever tries to fit God into their minds ends up with a cracked skull. This way of life, despite the astonishments, leads to joy and fulfillment due to the freeing of the spirit through commitment, responsibility, and trust in God. In contrast, Ahaz represents a life built on trusting things of the world — leading to an unfulfilled existence where emptiness abounds.

St. Matthew begins with the betrothal of Joseph and Mary (v. 18), before the two had come together as man and wife. Mary was with child.

Joseph knew he wasn't responsible for Mary's pregnancy; this presented him with a lonely dilemma which differs from depictions of some holy cards and sticky-sweet carols. On the one side, he was a righteous man, one who observed the Mosaic Law. That Law entitled him, at the very least, to repudiate his marriage agreement by signing a declaration to that effect in the presence of witnesses, but without stating his reasons in public. The Law also gave him the right to renounce Mary publicly, and the punishment for her transgression would be death.

But if Joseph did nothing, there could be other bad consequences. For one thing, it wouldn't be honorable for him to assume the paternity of a child whom he knew wasn't his, especially in view of the Mosaic Law's requirements of justice. And should he fail to denounce Mary, his failure, if the true paternity came to light, might be taken as evidence of a disgraceful connivance on his part in her sin.

Neither in this domestic crisis nor in any other events of life did Joseph, a just man, want to do anything unkind. He would quietly divorce Mary and disappear from a mystery beyond his comprehension. When his sincerity reached its limit, there came further mystery: a message from God came to him in a dream telling him not to be afraid to take Mary his wife into his home.

Have you ever wondered why, whenever the people in the Scriptures are confronted directly by the divine presence, someone has to come along and say, "Don't be afraid"? This is because acting out in commitment to love is a fearful thing, and it demands of us the greatest trust in God — which is the only true courage. Many people today avoid it.

The message said that it was through the Holy Spirit that this child had been conceived (v. 20). In Jewish thought the Spirit had several functions: to bring God's truth to people, to perform God's work of creation, and — even more — to do God's work of re-creation.

The message went on to direct Joseph to assume the responsibility of naming the child. He was to call him Jesus because he was to save his people from their sins (v. 21). Others would call him "Emmanuel" — "God-with-us" (which means that the Lord is with His people) — because that's the way people would perceive him. This included Matthew, the writer of the Gospel, who considered this appellation so important that the very last sentence of his Gospel has Jesus say "I am with you always" (28:20). To Joseph, although the overall message wasn't very clear, one thing was certain: God was making it abundantly plain that Mary's child was special.

The second way of life is personified by Ahaz, King of the Jews' Southern Kingdom, Judah, a descendant of David who was as weak and corrupt as his forebears. Twenty years old when he began his sixteen-year rule, he had immolated his infant son by fire to the pagan god Moloch (2 K 16:3). Now, around 735 B.C., Assyria's armies were going to invade Judah at any moment. On another front, the Northern Kingdom (Israel) and Syria, though ordinarily enemies of each other, had joined in a powerful coalition to attack, and were already on Judah's soil.

Which side was Ahaz, who was beside himself with fear, to take? Awaiting his decision, his people trembled. He could let Israel and Syria have their way, or turn to Assyria for help — in either case ending Judah's independence. Or he could listen to Isaiah, who was calling for reliance upon God.

Isaiah announced that if Ahaz put his trust in Assyria, their army would roar through Jerusalem as though the mighty river Euphrates in flood were to sweep over its banks and roar through the country up to the people's neck (Is 8:5-8). Isaiah's advice was concerned with the preservation of Judah in distress, but even more especially with the fulfillment of God's earlier promise to David of the coming of Emmanuel as the ideal king.

Ahaz answered Isaiah's advice with hypocritical piety by saying that he would not put the Lord to the test (v. 12), thus invoking the same prohibition from Deuteronomy (6:16) that Jesus would quote during his temptation in the desert. We needn't deplore Ahaz's lack of responsibility as though we don't know it in our time. In the United States, there are cases to show how similar to Ahaz we've become: A man steals a car from a parking lot and is killed while driving it, and his family subsequently sues the parking-lot owner for failing to take steps to prevent such thefts; a bicyclist compares disrespect toward bicyclists to cross burning, swastika painting, gay bashing, and other hate crimes.

The plaintive refrain has become, "I'm a victim"; "I'm not responsible"; "It's not my fault." This victim status is now claimed not only by members of minority groups, but increasingly by the middle class, by millionaire artists, students at Ivy League colleges, and other "adult" children.

It seems to have become a generalized cultural impulse to deny personal responsibility and to resort to the grievances of the insatiable self. It stems in part from Americans' unwillingness to acknowledge the limitations and disappointments inherent in the human condition. Americans have enshrined the infinite expectation — for psychological gratification, self-actualization, self-realization, and happiness — not as a goal to be won but as an entitlement.

To Ahaz, God Himself provided a sign (v. 13). To us, that sign, when taken literally, is mysterious. There was a woman (v. 14), known to both Isaiah and Ahaz but not to us, of marriageable age, who was either pregnant or would soon be, who would give birth to a child who would help the Davidic line. Historically, that child may have been Ahaz's son Hezekiah, one of only two good kings of Judah after David, who might truly be called "God Is With Us," for in his birth Judah would see a renewal of the promise God made to David. But Ahaz, like many after him, considered it easier to put faith in chariots and horses than in God (Ps 20:8). It was the wrong decision and, as a result, Judah suffered the prophesied fate.

Jewish tradition never considered Isaiah's sign of a virgin with child (v. 14) as being Mary. In truth, Isaiah didn't predict the virginal conception of Jesus unless vaguely and indirectly in the statement of faith: God alone saves. Isaiah's use of the term "Emmanuel" lends credence to the opinion that Isaiah's perspective was deeper and broader than even he knew. In the nature of prophecy, Isaiah needn't have known all the meanings of his own words.

Matthew's Gospel sees the fulfillment of Isaiah's prophecy beyond Isaiah's scope. The "Emmanuel" to whom he refers is Jesus. Jesus is God's new revelation of Himself. In Jesus, God is with us, sharing all the hopes and fears that we have in our imperfection. No matter how much or how little of Matthew's story is factual, his message is to show that Jesus is the fulfillment of the hopes of Judaism. The word "Emmanuel" isn't only a statement, but a promise: God comes to us still.

It was Joseph who was the prophecy's hope. In contrast to King Ahaz, Joseph had confidence in the confusing sign of the child mysteriously conceived in Mary the virgin. Despite the problems involved, he accepted his responsibility, because he saw it as the will of God. So, thanks to him, it would be possible for the child to be born to the royal line of David. Thanks to his faith, the child would receive the name made known to him: Jesus — that is, Savior.

St. Paul, who wrote today's passage of his letter to the Romans from Corinth at the end of his third missionary journey, was three things: a slave, an apostle, and one set apart (v. 1). As a slave, this Roman citizen, with all its rights and privileges, proud of his education as a rabbi and his financial independence as a craftsman, nevertheless called himself a slave to God's will — as Joseph was. As an apostle, he was one who was sent to preach God's word, in continuation of Older Covenant figures (v. 2) like Isaiah. As one set apart, Paul was consecrated for God's work as Jesus was. We too are God's servants, apostles, and people set apart for a special role in God's work. No one's life is without purpose.

Paul emphasized the two over-riding aspects of Jesus we should think about in this season: Jesus' humanity and his divinity. Jesus was not a legendary half-man half-god, but *truly* fully man as well as fully God. In Jesus' humanity, he descended from David (v. 3) and was the Jesus of Nazareth who was beset by weakness, subject to the laws of nature, and liable to death. As an early Church Father said: "He became what we are, to make us what he is."

Jesus is also uniquely Son of God. He lives in the spirit of holiness not only in possessing the divine nature but, more than that, in his glorified state he is the dynamic source of holiness who vivifies the whole human race. His being the life-giving spirit who is able to communicate God's life comes by virtue of his resurrection from the dead. Without that, Jesus might have been numbered among the great and heroic figures of this world, but *e pluribus unum* — one among many. His resurrection makes him unmatched. Of all this divine largess, we're the beneficiaries. We're called to belong to Jesus Christ (v. 6). We, like the Romans to whom Paul wrote, are beloved of God (v. 7) and called to be holy.

That means finding our wellsprings. Different people do that in different ways. The Australian aborigine or the Native American find their sense of Self in their land; to take them away from that is to disconnect them from Self and results in tragedies like alcoholism and suicide. Jews find their major roots in their Temple and Synagogue. We Christians find our sense of belonging and meaning in great measure in our Church and home. Let's remember that in these few days that remain for coming home for Christmas.

Let our way of life not be that of Ahaz, who trusted in the power of this world and found frustration and hollowness, but the way of

Joseph who, though surprised at God's way of doing things, trusted in God, welcomed Jesus, and thus found joy and peace.

CHRISTMAS

Is 62:1-5   Ac 13:16f, 22-25   Mt 1:1-25

Look to God and Respond to His Message
Look Up, not Down; The Goodness of the Lord; Harden Not
Your Heart; Jesus, Our Only Hope; the Fulfillment of Hope

Most of the animals of the world look downward, toward the earth. The human being, the animal best fitted to look upward, too often allows himself to be earthbound like the other animals. We witness murders, abortions, children starving, and individuals pursuing self to the exclusion of others. And in recent years more and more people are saying that they dread Christmas, that it has become a time of strain, anxiety, and stress. That's sad.

But sometimes people become wise and look upward. Then our spirits rise as we see hills and mountains and, in the night sky, the stars. There are far more stars in the universe than grains of sand on the average beach: by latest estimates, about 1,000 times as many. As our instruments improve, that estimate will go up. In the lower left-hand corner of the great square of Pegasus, we see the spiral galaxy of Andromeda. It's as large as our Milky Way. It's one of a hundred million galaxies. It's 750,000 light years away. It consists of a hundred billion suns, each one larger than our own.

When on a star-lit night we contemplate the vastness of the universe, we might think of our smallness and insignificance. But we should rather think of our grandeur. The spirit of the human being is much greater than all these universes, because the human being can contemplate and comprehend all of these, whereas all these worlds put together cannot comprehend a single human being.

Note: This homily is on the Vigil Mass. For the Night Mass, see Cycle B;
    for the Mass at Dawn and the Mass During the Day, Cycle C.

All these worlds are composed of simple molecules such as the hydrogen molecule, which consists of only a nucleus and an electron, whereas the human body consists of much more complex molecules and, in addition, possesses the gift of life — a life whose complexity transcends by far that of the molecular world.

Although the radius of the universe measures one hundred thousand million light-years, it has definite limits, and even the most inferior of human beings is greater than the entire material universe; human beings have a greatness of a different order, which surpasses any mere quantitative greatness: We possess consciousness and the capability of being aflame with love.

And all these worlds are silent. But we, human beings, are the voice and the consciousness of these worlds. And so, in the wonder and the vastness of it all, we think of God. And, inspired to find out more about Him, we go to the Scriptures.

Even there, the issues sometimes become complex. Take today's Gospel. St. Matthew begins his story of God coming to earth with a list of the human ancestors of Jesus. The Jews were very much interested in genealogies, because they thought of one's ancestors as revealing what sort of person one is. In addition, any mixture of foreign blood caused a Jew to lose his right to be numbered among the people of God.

In Matthew's genealogy of Jesus, a most unusual feature is that women are named in it. With the Jews of his time, women, although held in higher regard than with many contemporary tribes, had no legal rights and were for the most part at the disposal of men. In his regular morning prayer, the Jewish male thanked God that He hadn't made him "a Gentile, a slave, or a woman."

Even more amazing in this genealogy are the four women who are named. Rahab was a Canaanite prostitute; with courage and intelligence, she saved two of her Israelite clients and her entire family. As the king of Jericho sought to arrest the two clients who were in her house, she helped them to flee (Jos 2:1-7), thus sparing her whole clan in the conquest of Jericho. Ruth was a pagan of the Moabite tribe (Rt 1:4), an alien and hated people. After the death of her Jewish husband, she renounced her own people to make her husband's people and land her own. Prompted by her mother-in-law, Naomi, she "tricked" a wealthy relative of the family, Boas, into marrying her. Thus his and Ruth's child saved the line of Naomi from extinction and assured both women of provision and security in their old age.

Tamar was a deliberate seducer and an adulteress. The widow of Judah's first-born son, not wanting to die childless, dressed up as a prostitute and slept with her father-in-law, Judah, became pregnant, and bore twins (Gn 38). Then she cleverly secured the legal recognition of the children; in this way she exploited her in-laws to help her dead husband to have offspring who would bear his name. The wife of Uriah whom David had seduced (2 Sm 11 & 12) was Bathsheba. The story of David's adultery with her is well-known. David could marry her only by ensuring that Uriah was killed in battle, which he did. The first child of this adulterous liaison died, but the son of their marriage, Solomon, became a glorious king of Israel.

Why did Matthew single these women out in his genealogy? If he wanted to give Jesus the most distinguished and respected ancestry, why didn't he choose such highly regarded foremothers in Israel as Sarah, Hagar, Rebecca, Rachel, or Leah? Perhaps Matthew wanted to announce a theme that runs through his entire Gospel: the message of Jesus is also for the pagans.

Perhaps more likely, Matthew was making the point that in salvation history not everything is neat and tidy; God could afford to renounce the luxury of a "squeaky clean" ancestry. All these women are "mothers of life" because they fought for the continuity of the generations and were ready to stake their lives and reputations for that end. The genealogy tells us about the human Jesus. He is son of Abraham, to whom God first revealed Himself, and son of David, most of whose successors were weak sinners. In addition to Jesus' being descended from Abraham and David, courageous women and bold undertakings played a part in salvation history.

Aside from sentimentalists and romantics, Christmas has been for most of its history very realistic. Indeed, its roots are intermingled with ancient winter festivals and saturnalias celebrated by pagans, and many of the trappings that we now associate with the holiday —evergreens, for example, and mistletoe — are also pagan in their origins. Today's Christmas is a bridge between the world as it is and the world as it should be. It's a vision of family gatherings, warm homes, presents, Christmas trees, decorations, and a special Christmas dinner; it's a celebration of children and family, a day of peace and hope, an occasion to contemplate, celebrate, and look up. This is why Christmas has become the most beloved of holidays.

Those who on this feast look up — to God — experience

something special: the world's walls tumbling down. Walls are down between male and female (because women, as well as men, are beloved by God), between saint and sinner (because Jesus said that he didn't come to call the righteous but sinners), and between races (because of the love of God for each person).

But even the best of insights require study and patience, and that's never easy. Today's first reading, for example, shows that Isaiah had gained a new awareness of human pettiness and sinfulness; of the majesty, the holiness, and the glory of the Lord; and of the enormous abyss between human beings and God. Isaiah lived and wrote in a time of intrigue and defeat for the Jews. Before the walls of the holy city of Jerusalem was the army of Sennacherib. Isaiah, in oracles of singular poetic beauty and power, constantly reminded the wayward Jews and their weak king Ahaz of Yahweh's fidelity to His promises and of their need to look up to Him for help. The weak king Ahaz instead turned for help to Assyria. As a result, the Assyrian army quickly attacked and devastated Jerusalem.

Joseph in today's Gospel was in no less a frustrating position than Isaiah and Ahaz. During his betrothal, Joseph received the mysterious news that Mary, his betrothed, was to become the mother of a child that wasn't his. He received a message that the birth of Jesus would be the work of the Holy Spirit — that Joseph was to look up, not down. With some anguish, Joseph abandoned his initial thought of quietly putting his betrothed Mary away. Thus the birth of Jesus became possible. And from Joseph and Mary, the good news went out — to the shepherds, the local populace, and the Wise Men. Jesus' re-birthing daily in our lives happens when we too look up, and through our struggle seek and find our God.

If Jesus had been born amid the splendor of a rich family, people would have been afraid to approach him, and unbelievers would surely say that the face of the world had again been influenced by the power of wealth. If he had chosen to be born in Rome, at that time the greatest of cities, they would have ascribed the same change to the power of her citizens. If he'd been the son of an emperor, they would have pointed to the advantage of authority. Imagine his father a legislator; their cry would have been, "See what you can do with the law!"

In today's second reading St. Paul makes the point that the coming of Jesus was the consummation of history. For him, history, the record of humankind, wasn't always going around in circles, as his contemporary pagans thought, nor cynical, like the modern version that says history is but the record of the sins, mistakes, and follies of people. For Paul and us, history is going somewhere, in accordance with the purposes of God, even though those purposes are at times unfathomable to us. And although some people, in their blind folly, rejected and crucified Jesus, Jesus would rise, as we will, by the invincible power of Almighty God and to His eternal glory.

The final point in the sermons of Sts. Peter and Paul is that Christ's coming is good news to all whose hearts are ready and open. In Jesus' time the Good News was received first by Jews who lived according to the Mosaic Law, and then by all people of good will. In our time the news of Jesus' coming is saving news for those who try to live according to God's law, whom Jesus's forgiving power sets free, and with whom Jesus restores real friendship between God and people.

But what is Good News for people of open heart, listening ear, and upturned eye is bad news for those who sense only empty words. They don't feel the heartbeat of the message that could pulsate life into them. Such people go on their way sad and unconverted. Jesus still speaks, and they don't hear his voice. He enters their lives and they let him go, unrecognized. Can this happen to us? Good News is ours, if we but will it. Good News is our neighbors', whatever their persuasion, if we will share it. What a precious gift at Christmas!

We wish you a Happy Christmas, and with our wish goes the hope that you today accept God's gift: the gift of the strength to respond to the Good News of Christ's birth and his message, so that you look, not only down to the world's misery, but up to God and out to your family and neighbors, and so make you and yours happy today and every day.

Feast of the Holy Family

Si 3:2-6, 12-14   Col 3:12-21 (Both in A, B, and C)   Mt 2:13-15, 19-23

The Ideal Family
The Sacredness of the Family; The Importance
of God in the Family; Family Plights Today

Outside the Church, the Christmas season is to all extents and purposes over. Unwanted gifts have been exchanged, post-Christmas sales are in vogue, and people are anticipating the New Year. Inside the Church, today's Feast of the Holy Family is a natural continuation of the Christmas season. Part of the Christmas celebration is the inspiration Jesus gives to the family, the basic unit of society all over the world.

Today's Gospel shows that not even the Holy Family was spared the trials and sufferings of every family. The baby's life was threatened and the Holy Family became displaced persons in a foreign country. No matter how many or how few of St. Matthew's details are factual, he wants to show the important phenomenon of a family open to God, yet vulnerable to the tide of fortune.

The murder of innocent children is unfortunately commonplace in human experience. The Hebrew Scriptures tell of how an Egyptian pharaoh had ordered the deaths of newborn Jewish males to limit the growing numbers of the Jews (Ex 1:15-22). Modern equivalents of Herod plot political strategies which result in the murder of children. Our world is the same one Christ entered: holy innocents still die before their time; holy families remain refugees seeking safety from murderous governments; and Herods still rely on the benign neglect of others to make innocents suffer.

Through it all, St. Joseph is the true Israelite — as devout as any Pharisee in his obedience to the Law of Moses, but able to go further and obey God's new and complete revelation. He's a courageous man of honor who wanted to protect Mary's reputation, especially because God wanted him to; a man who took Mary as his wife even though the child with whom she was pregnant wasn't his, because God told him to; a man who, to protect his family, led them into exile, because God told

---

Note: Today's homily is mostly on Matthew. For homily mostly on Luke 2:22-40,
      see Cycle B; for homily on all the readings, Cycle C.

him to. When Jesus came to speak publicly, he spoke of God as *abba*, "Daddy," and it was from the kindly Joseph that he had learned what a daddy was.

From the time of the Maccabees, Egypt was a customary place of refuge for Jews. Since it bordered on the Holy Land, many Jews were now finding refuge there beyond the jurisdiction of Herod. Alexandria, long a place of culture because — in part, at least — of the presence of Jews, had over a million of them. Joseph would be welcomed in many of these cities, and he would be able to find a livelihood in his trade of carpentry.

But the trip would be a nightmare. Traveling by night and hiding by day, the Holy Family could reach the border in three or four days; though they could then rest a bit easier, there would still remain the rigors of the broad desert. They would be exposed to cold nights and scorching daylight sand. For the more than three hundred miles between Jerusalem and Cairo, they would see not a stream of water, nor a spring, nor a blade of grass, nor the smallest shrub. Whether they walked alone or by camel in a caravan, their trip would take over three weeks. The Holy Family stayed in Egypt until the death of Herod (v. 15): perhaps as long as three years.

The Holy Family's experience of homelessness would have enhanced their sensitivity to others. When God told Joseph to go back to Israel, again he obeyed. The death of Herod "the Great" had changed things. Herod's will had divided his kingdom into three parts, one for each of his three sons Archelaus, Antipas, and Philip. Archelaus was given Judea, and was so extremely cruel that, to quell a civil war, he opened his rule with the deliberate slaughter of 3,000 of the most influential people in his area.

Because of Archelaus' cruelty, in ten years the Roman Emperor Augustus would remove him from power. But at the time of our Gospel story Archelaus still ruled Judea and Samaria, which contained Bethlehem and Jerusalem. Clearly, his presence made it unsafe for the Holy Family to return to Bethlehem or any other place in Judea. Joseph therefore guided Mary and Jesus to Galilee (v. 22), where Antipas reigned. Though Antipas was the one who would execute John the Baptist and before whom Jesus would be arraigned, it was safe, at least for now, to settle in Nazareth (v. 23).

This little town built into the unfolding limestone hills so reminded St. Jerome of the petals of a rose that he called it "the flower of

Galilee." As a boy, Jesus must have climbed the hills around Nazareth with the other boys. His views from those hills would show Nazareth to be not just a backwater town of rustics, out of touch with the world. He could look west and see the blue waters of the Mediterranean, with ships going to the ends of the earth. The plain skirting the coast contained the road from Damascus to Egypt, the land bridge to Africa. This road, called The Road of the Sea or The Way of the South, was one of the greatest caravan routes in the world: Alexander the Great had used it three hundred years before, Napoleon would use it in the nineteenth century, and the British General Allenby in World War I in the twentieth. Another road departed from the sea coast at Accre and went East, with caravans carrying silks and spices and Roman legions going back and forth to far-flung frontiers.

The town's limestone rock was honeycombed with caves. Some houses were built over or in front of these caves, giving protection against the bitter cold of the rainy season and the intense heat of the dry summer. The caves were also used as store-rooms for grain or fruit, or as stables.

As a protection against the occasional earthquakes, the houses were only one story high, and built on a solid foundation against the occasionally heavy rains. An outside stone staircase led to a flat roof, which was utilized for such domestic purposes as hanging linen and sleeping on very hot nights. Farmers used the roofs to sun wheat for the mill, and to dry figs, raisins, corn, and other produce away from animals and thieves. The natives were an outdoor people, and loved being on the roof where they could see the sun, smell the fresh air, dry their clothes, set out their flower pots, and otherwise cater to health and comfort. In fact, they spent so much time on the roof that Moses made a law requiring a railing to prevent accidents (Dt 22:8).

In every Jewish house, the woman's first duty was to grind the wheat needed for the day's consumption. Then she kneaded the flour, lighted the movable oven, and baked her bread over white-hot stones. Although the mistress of the house was never idle (Pr 31:10-31), preparations for meals weren't arduous, because the menu was simple and usually the same: eggs, milk, cheese, honey, olives and other fruits, and sometimes fish.

Joseph's workshop was separated from the living quarters, out of consideration for the peace and quiet of the family. In that workshop the tools — and the broad range of skills to use them — were not unlike those employed as late as colonial America. These were enough for making the usual carpenter things, and more: doors, door and window frames, wooden locks and bolts, pieces of furniture like beds and tables and stools and lampstands and cabinets and chests for wardrobes, winnowing forks, harrows fitted with points of flint to beat out corn sheaves, and (above all) yokes and plows. When a new house was to be built, the woodworker would be called in to square off the beams of sycamore and poplar that were to support the thatched roof and the more or less watertight layer of hard earth spread over it.

In the eyes of his compatriots, Joseph's humble position as carpenter had nothing degrading about it. The majority of famous rabbis had worked with their hands. The Rabbi Judah expressed one of the five principal duties of the father of a family: "He who does not teach his son a trade, teaches him to steal."

When Jesus was strong enough, he joined Joseph in his workshop. After Joseph died, Jesus became a full-fledged working man, having to save for food and clothes, meet an occasional dissatisfied client, and handle customers who wouldn't, or couldn't, pay their bills.

These are some of the elements which made up the daily life of the holy family, a family not unlike many from that time on to our own day and age. But something today is happening to the family. By most statistical measures, the family as an institution is in a steep decline. For many years, the divorce rate has been increasing. So has the percentage of children living in single-parent families. Out-of-wedlock births have multiplied. Parents spend increasingly less time with their children. Underlying this trend has been a profound shift in cultural values away from family commitments and toward self-fulfillment. Self-gratification has surpassed self-sacrifice, but it isn't clear that many adults have become more personally fulfilled. The value placed on children has dropped.

But human sciences continue to prove the importance of the family in molding character and facilitating people living together in peace, and to find that the best remedial program is a stable, intact family. In the face of current difficulties with children, it seems obvious that prevention is better — and cheaper —than cure. As the poet (John Malins) put it:

> So the people said something would have to be done
> But their projects did not at all tally;

Some said, "Put a fence 'round the edge of the cliff,"
Some, "An ambulance down in the valley."

* * *

Better guide well the young than reclaim them when old,
For the voice of true wisdom is calling,
"To rescue the fallen is good, but 'tis best
To prevent other people from falling."

As we shape our lives, so we shape our world. Today's children must be seen and heard — and even worried about! Let's pray that children come to appreciate the sacrifices their parents make for them and overcome the temptations which might lead them from the path of virtue. Most of all, let's remember the example of the Holy Family.

MARY, MOTHER OF GOD
Nb 6:22-27   Gal 4:4-7   Lk 2:16-21
(All A, B, and C)

Mary's Motherhood of God
God's Blessing on our New Year; True Freedom; Mary as Mother;
Mary and the Name of Jesus; Risk for God; Consecration of the New Year

Today, more than a month into our new Church year, we're still celebrating beginnings. It's appropriate that we celebrate the beginning of a new civil year, and that we do so at prayer, and in church, and together. It's also fitting, though by no means the only possibility, that today we commemorate the woman who played such an important role in the whole pageant of Christmas. Throughout the Liturgical Year, we celebrate many feasts of Mary — her Immaculate Conception, her Birth, her Visitation, her Assumption — and we have opportunities to

---

Note: This homily is on Luke. Cycle B is mostly on Numbers, Cycle C on Galatians.

revere her in other ways as well. Now we begin the year by celebrating her basic dignity, the reason for all the others: her Motherhood of God.

Today's Gospel, the conclusion of Luke's account of the birth of Jesus, renews the Christmas scene: the shepherds hastily going and finding Mary and Joseph, and the infant lying in the manger (v. 16). Already we see Christianity being topsy-turvy from the rest of the world. Those shepherds were looked down upon by their contemporaries: the demands of their flocks made it impossible for them to keep the details of the sacred Law of Moses, or even to know them. Yet they were the first, aside from Mary and Joseph, to receive the Good News. They responded in haste, and were therefore the first also to see the Lamb of God who takes away the sins of the world — appropriate indeed for those who cared for the lambs of their flocks.

Bethlehem, whose white limestone hills reflected the brightness of the first Christmas night, had a long and important history. It was famous, above all, for being the birthplace and city of David. It was from David's line that God was expected to send the Messiah, and it was in David's city that the Jews expected the Messiah to be born. The area is still honeycombed with caves, one of which, now beneath the Church of the Nativity, is still shown as Jesus' birthplace. For entry, there's a very low door. Though long ago the door was built low to prevent desecration by soldiers entering on horseback, it's fittingly symbolic that people must stoop to enter, because one should humble oneself to come into the presence of God.

Whereas the shepherds when they saw and understood God's message (v. 17) became active in spreading the good news far and wide (v. 18), Mary silently reflected upon the deeper meaning of the mystery (v. 19). Her reflection implies a searching and a wondering as well as an acceptance. Those who are mothers have an edge on the rest of us. The deep physical and mood changes over the nine months of her pregnancy can't be described; it can only be glimpsed at. As Mary pondered, the questions flooded in; the whys, the whats, and the hows — her mysterious pregnancy, the initial misgivings of Joseph, the birth in a cave-shelter for animals. And Mary pondered these things in her heart, not in her head. The theoretical answers of the head are of little use to the sufferer. Mary realized now, and throughout her life she grew in the realization, that for the follower of Jesus suffering is a problem to be explored by the human heart.

All these caused a wilderness experience — an encounter with dark loneliness. In religion, wilderness and blessing are often linked. In a wilderness we're exposed and vulnerable, and so can meet God profoundly. Through her ordeal, Mary became a true disciple of her son. Luke attaches to her only appearance later in his account of Jesus' public ministry the idea that the true response to the word of God is to be found in those who've heard the word, put it into practice, and yielded a harvest through their perseverance.

Because it was Mary who in solitude remembered all these things most deeply, we may infer that St. Luke, the writer of today's Gospel, derived his information about Jesus' infancy either directly or indirectly from her. Mary's difficulty in understanding, and at the same time her continued trust in God, are part of her message for us. As Cardinal Newman said, there is nothing more elevating and transporting than the generosity of a heart which risks everything on God's word.

Many people don't understand Mary's *virgin* motherhood. But if you were God, how would you have arranged it otherwise? Look at the alternatives. God could have arranged the coming of Jesus by sending a sort of ET, dropped out of heaven, fully grown. But that would be a Jesus who didn't come as a man — and we need a common humanity. Or Jesus, like Moses, could have been discovered in some bulrushes; then he would be fully human, but of such uncertain parentage that there would be doubts about his God nature.

Or God could have planted a seed in with Joseph's in marital intercourse and let Joseph complete the act on God's behalf. That would have eliminated any question of Jesus being an ordinary mortal. But then Joseph would be the father, and God didn't really want a surrogate. God's selecting a virgin to bear Jesus seems a quite commonsensical solution. Just look at the rest of creation. It's all virgin birth. It was all started pure and clean and innocent, in pristine beauty, from no precedent, with no intervention other than by God. C.S. Lewis expressed the beautiful thought that, because of Mary, "we are related to Jesus on his mother's side."

Mary, like Joseph, always abided by God's law. One prescription of that law was that throughout the ages, every male among the Jews, when he is eight days old, shall be circumcised (Gn 17:12). At that time he was also named. This was a very sacred ritual: God had given it to Abraham as a sign of the covenant between God and the Israelites. The Holy Family, here as elsewhere, observed the laws of the Older Covenant.

To First Testament Jews like the Holy Family, a person's name was important — almost the equivalent of one's personal character, a distinctive mark of one's personhood. When one's status changed, one at times received a new name: for instance, Abram to Abraham, Sarai to Sara, Jacob to Israel. In the New Testament, to have one's name written in heaven (Lk 10:20) or in the book of life (Rv 20:12,15) meant to be accepted as a member in the Messianic kingdom.

Today, parents choose names to retain a family tradition, or to express who their family would like them to become, or because it's the name of a celebrity, or simply because a certain name sounds good to them. At that time, the name was ordinarily suggested by the mother, but could also be suggested by friends and relatives. But it was the father who made the final decision. The angel had told Joseph that he was to name this child Jesus, because he would save his people from their sins (Mt 1:21). The angel Gabriel's advice to Mary at the annunciation had been the same (Lk 1:31). So the child was named Jesus (v. 21). The name is particularly fitting: It's of the same root as Jehovah, or Joshua, and means "Yahweh [God] saves." Saving people was the purpose of Jesus' coming into the world, and of his life and work.

Mary, who cooperated with God's saving plan, is an inspiration for disciples of Jesus who want to listen to his Good News even as it comes through the often difficult and mysterious circumstances of our lives. Whether we realize it or not, we need her for our spiritual lives. We need her tenderness, her compassion, her intuitive love. An anonymous poem tells about a magician entertaining at an orphanage. He was astounding the little children with his tricks. The children's eyes became twice their normal size as they watched him pull things out of his big black hat. The last verse of the poem describes one of the little boys questioning him:

> "But can you," asked a small boy edging nigh
> And trying hard his sobbing now to smother,
> "But can you get out anything you try?"
> "Sure, Sonny, one's as easy as the other."
> Then smiling through a mist upon each eye
> He begged, "Please, Mister, get me out a mother!"

The coming year will give many opportunities for us to live God's Good News with Mary as our inspiration. What better New Year's resolution could we make than to adopt Mary's stance before the Word-made-flesh: making her contemplative gaze our own and keeping the incarnate God constantly before our mind and heart.

EPIPHANY

Is 60:1-6   Eph 3:2f., 5f.   Mt 2:1-12
               (All A, B, and C)

Being Wise Today
All People on Earth Are Invited

Thanks to the invention of St. Francis of Assisi, during these days of Christmas we've had the crèche to help remind us attractively of what took place on the first Christmas. Today, the Feast of the Epiphany, we add the figures of new arrivals as we celebrate Jesus the Incarnate Word being revealed to all the nations of the world. This revelation was not without difficulties, especially in the person of Herod, an Idumean by tribal background, who ruled both Idumea and Judea for the Romans for more than thirty years. His ancestors, the people of ancient Edom, had been forcibly converted to Judaism long before, and their descendants such as Herod mixed their religious observances in a way that was very offensive to orthodox Jews. Although Herod began the reconstruction of the Jerusalem Temple on a magnificent scale, he also refurbished the shrines of his Idumean ancestors' gods — both for political reasons.

Today's Gospel story is a biblical and poetic meditation upon a truth, which is the manifestation of the Savior. Today's feast is called in some countries "little Christmas," and in others is the main Christmas celebration.

Because St. Matthew says these first eminent visitors to Jesus came from the east, many have thought that they were learned and wise men from Babylonia who had contact with ideas about the Jewish messiah (cf. Dn 2:2). At the very least, they were esteemed and honored

---

Note: For other homily ideas, see Cycles B and C.

persons who were consulted by people in their countries — much as the Hebrew prophets were consulted.

The word in Matthew's Gospel for these visitors — *magoi* (v. 1) — is a word that, in truth, is difficult to translate. Once they were called kings, but the original word doesn't really mean kings. That translation was occasioned by the association of these personages with the Psalmist's words that the kings of Tarshish and the Isles shall offer gifts, the kings of Arabia and Seba shall bring tribute, and all kings shall pay him homage (Ps 72:10f.).

They've also been called astrologers. They're not that in the modern sense of the word. In their time everybody believed that one could foretell one's future from the stars, and that your destiny was sealed by the star under which you had been born. This is understandable. People saw in the stars the order of the universe. And if astrologers observed some brilliant new star, in it they saw God breaking into His own order and announcing something special.

In fact, many believed that the births of great men were marked by unusual signs in the heavens. These people didn't have God's revelation, and so came to know about God through the things He had made, like the stars: "The heavens declare the glory of God," the Psalmist said (Ps 18 [19] :2). God gives all of us signs of His presence in the world, calling us to look where they point. The fact that these visitors perceived this warrants their being called wise men.

Scripture doesn't tell us how many magi there were. Early tradition put their number at twelve, but that was eventually reduced to three because of their three gifts. Gifts in the Orient were customary as signs of homage. Evidently gold, frankincense, and myrrh were the most valuable exports of the magi's native lands which they thought any foreign king would be glad to receive.

Gold, the king of metals, is *the* gift fit for a king, and so the early Fathers of the Church interpreted it mystically to typify Jesus' kingship. Frankincense, used in Temple worship, was the gift for a priest. The function of a priest is to be a mediator between God and His people. Jesus is the perfect High Priest, and so the early Church Fathers interpreted frankincense to typify Jesus' divinity. And myrrh, at that time used to embalm, was the gift for one who was to die. According to the early Church Fathers, the myrrh stood for Jesus' mortal nature as a human being.

Medieval legend added names, descriptions, various ages, and then origins befitting a representation of God's universal call of all humankind. Melchior, representing the Semitic peoples, was old, gray-haired with a long beard, and brought the gold. Gaspar, representing the other white races, was young and beardless, and brought the frankincense. Balthasar, representing the black races, was swarthy with a small beard, and brought the myrrh.

As the shepherds had been the first among the Jews outside Mary and Joseph to whom the Good News was given, the magi were the first among the Gentiles to learn of it. They were seekers of truth and — especially — wisdom. Despite the fact that our era is a time for information retrieval and data processing not noted for a search for deeper things, we, too, should be seekers of wisdom. Wisdom contains elements of understanding, foresight, discretion, and astuteness, but is different from and beyond all these. It suggests a habit of profound reflection. Wisdom indicates discernment based not only on factual knowledge but on judgment and insight. People who are so taken up with the practical business of living that they have no time for the ultimate concerns of life and death, God and man, time and eternity, are not wise.

The concept of wisdom has a noble tradition in the history of the human race that goes back to the very roots of our civilization. Civilization is a thin veneer that requires constant attention. It's also relatively modern. Were we to bring together one couple, husband and wife, for each generation of the human race since it acquired its present appearance and characteristics about 50,000 years ago, there would be only about 2,000 couples. The first 1,400 of the couples would have lived in caves, and only the last 33 would have ever seen a printed page. Throughout our history, humankind's pursuit of wisdom has remained important. It was expressly taught in our schools for over 1,000 years. Even many fairy tales speak of wisdom. In them, to "live happily ever after" means to have achieved wisdom.

When we humans named our own species, we called ourselves *homo sapiens* — "wise humankind" (deserved or undeserved). Until recently, wisdom has been one of humankind's proudest gifts. For some, it continues so today. As for the future, whether our species perishes from the face of the earth, especially by way of self-destruction, will depend on whether we achieve a greater measure of wisdom. Dr. Jonas Salk, medical pioneer who developed the first polio vaccine, said: "Metabiological evolution involves the survival of the wisest. Wisdom is becoming the new criterion of fitness."

The story of the magi is a story of the ways in which God reveals Himself, and even more about the different responses which His revelation receives. There are numerous "manifestations," or "epiphanies," of God — in our lives as well as in both the Old and New Testaments. We can learn much about how to handle God's manifestations by thinking about the magi. The magi's pursuit — no impulsive quest, and one in which they, like we, become pilgrims on the earth — was based on a sense of wonder, which is not only childlike, but also fundamentally religious. In relation to our own life-journey, they weren't wandering aimlessly. They were going in a definite direction with a specific purpose in mind. They may at times have had to alter their course slightly because of some difficulty or other, but they kept moving forward toward the aim they had in mind: to worship the new-born king. Their following their star, representing an encounter with God, can make us question our own direction in life.

They speak to us of that desire for God which is in the heart of every human being. We, like they, are called to be open to God's signs, and to go in search of a clearer vision of where those signs lead. We, too, are called to offer ourselves with whatever gifts we have. And we, like they, after returning from finding God, may, upon our return, find ourselves no longer completely at ease in our old haunts with a people now alien, clutching other gods.

We would do well to imitate their search for wisdom, which is our highest intellectual virtue and the highest gift of the Holy Spirit. To find wisdom, we may not have to travel any physical distance at all, but only the long spiritual journey to our own depths where God lives.

BAPTISM OF THE LORD
Is 42:1-4, 6f.   Ac 10:34-38 (Both in A, B, and C)   Mt 3:13-17

Time of Decision
Servant of God; True Humility;
The Baptized Christian; Jesus' Baptism and Ours

We've just come through the pleasant season of Christmas, celebrating the feasts connected with Jesus' infancy. Beginning today, the Feast of the Baptism of the Lord, the peace of the earth's holiest home is to be disturbed. For thirty years, Jesus had faithfully performed his duties to his home and family at Nazareth, though with an increasing awareness that his destiny was somehow unique. There must have been times when he thought about his future ministry and waited for the right moment to begin it. Now, Joseph had died and Jesus had grown up. Outside the family, the Jews seemed to be more keenly conscious of their need for God than before, and John the Baptist's galvanizing movement for repentance seemed to be pointing to this as the right time.

A time of decision had arrived for Jesus. All of us have to make decisions, and we never have all the information we need to make them. If we did, they would not be decisions, but foregone conclusions. All decisions involve renunciation. If we choose one thing, we thereby reject another. As a result of Jesus' decision to leave home, Mary will be left behind, Jesus will have nowhere to lay his head, the shadow of Calvary will haunt him, and he will have experiences of defeat and outright hostility.

If today we were to ask when was the exact moment that Jesus began to be what he was called to be, we would get various answers. Some would say that that moment was the Incarnation, when Mary consented to God's message. St. Paul would consider the moment to be Jesus' Resurrection. Medieval theologians might have said that the decisive moment was when Jesus suffered and died, because it was then that he gave himself for our salvation. But the primitive Gospel tradition might have said the decisive moment when Jesus became what he was

---

Note: This homily is mostly on Matthew. For homily mostly on Mark, see Cycle B; for Luke, Cycle C.

called to be was at his baptism, when he took upon himself all the sins of the entire world.

For his baptism, Jesus came from Galilee to John the Baptist at the Jordan (v. 13). But if John preached a baptism not as a sacrament but for repentance and the forgiveness of sins, why did Jesus, the sinless one, go to him for baptism? The answer is the meaning of today's feast, and can be summed up in two words: *manifestation* and *mission.*

With respect to *manifestation*, here we discern who Jesus really is: the beloved Son of the Father. That's easy for us to see, because we're heirs of two thousand years of theological development. We know that Jesus is the Eternal Word who took upon himself our human nature, that he's from all eternity God the Son, and that the Holy Spirit is the Third Person of the Triune God. But to those who at that time didn't realize the divinity of Jesus and who knew nothing of the Trinity, the coming of the Spirit was spectacular.

As for *mission*, the Spirit was seen anointing him joyfully as the Christ, sent to bring the poor the good news of salvation (Preface). The suffering Messiah steps down into our sinful world in the power of the Spirit, in order not just to experience our condition, but dramatically to become "one of us" and to transform our condition from within by the good news of salvation.

John the Baptist must have heard from his mother some of the facts about his cousin Jesus, but didn't of his own power recognize him. John's protesting observation that he needed to be baptized by Jesus rather than the other way around (v. 14) presents John's recognition of Jesus as at least a holy person, if not as the Messiah. Jesus' reply, that John permit it now, for thus "it is fitting for us to fulfill all God's will in this way" (v. 15), identified him as at least a devout Jew who observed the Law and the practices associated with good Jewish life.

Would John cooperate? As St. Peter would later experience, there was something about Jesus' face, especially the eyes, that was compelling. Eyes make no sound, yet they can speak with an eloquence that surpasses any words, and are remembered. The language of eyes begins where words leave off: the joy in the eyes of a new parent, the understanding in the eyes of a friend, the sadness in the eyes of the poor. Jesus had made his decision. He spoke these few meaningful words, and John gave in. The stern John obeyed the gentle command of the Lamb of God and baptized him.

With that, a marvelous thing happened. The heavens were opened and Jesus saw the Spirit of God descend like a dove (v. 16). The dove is a symbol of many things. In the imagery of the Jewish Scriptures, it signifies peace and love. It's also a symbol of gentleness. In today's event, the dove is preëminently a symbol of the Holy Spirit, derived perhaps from the image of the creative spirit of God hovering over the waters as mentioned in today's Responsorial Psalm. This was the same Spirit of whom Isaiah had prophesied when he said that the Spirit of God would rest upon him (Is 11:2). The implication is that Jesus, specially endowed with the Spirit, is the creator of the new people of God.

A voice from the heavens (v. 17) confirmed the scene. There are only three recorded times in the New Testament when the voice of the heavenly Father has been heard by the world. The first time was this one. The second would be at the Transfiguration, and the third at the conclusion of Jesus' ministry, when Jesus asked his heavenly Father to glorify God's name and the voice from heaven said that He *was* glorifying it (Jn 12:28).

The first part of today's heavenly message, "This is my beloved Son," came from a Psalm (2 [3]:7) and from today's reading in Isaiah, whose expression "chosen one" also means "beloved son." It was a description of the Messiah.

The second part, that the Father was pleased with Jesus, is also from today's reading in Isaiah (42:1). In Isaiah, the heavenly Father says that upon this servant He had put His Spirit (v. 1), a gift that's necessary for any redemptive work. This and the three other "Servant-of-the-Lord" oracles in Isaiah (49:1-7; 50:4-11; and 52:13 - 53:12) portray the ideal Servant of God, the perfect Israelite, whose consecration to the divine will, even in the midst of terrible suffering, shall take away the sins of many (53:12). The Isaiah of this passage is not, like his other hymns, expansive, lyrical, and exultant. He is quiet in tone to the point of being melancholy, terse, and concentrated. Whereas traditional Jewish wisdom was that God inflicted suffering only on those who deserved it, the idea that the holy and just might suffer for others was not only entirely new, but revolutionary.

The method of the Servant of the Lord would not be that of a mighty conqueror, as many thought, but the way of sacrificial love — a love that shall bring justice not only to Israel, but to all the nations of the earth. The Servant accomplishes his mission quietly, gently, transforming from within (vv. 2-3). And pagan coastlands (v. 4) shall, like exiled Israel, experience an energetic striving for spiritual life and undergo a painful period of expectancy before the new life.

In today's reading from the Acts of the Apostles, St. Peter tells Cornelius, a pagan official in Palestine, of the beginning of Jesus' ministry after John's preaching of baptism, and characterizes Jesus' ministry as endowed by the Spirit of God. Jesus' ministry was exercised, however, not only in the power of the Spirit, but also in the humility of the servant.

And, contrary to what many Jews thought, the revelation of God's choice of Israel (Hebrew *ish* + *elohim* = "man of God") doesn't mean that He withholds His graciousness from other people: God shows no partiality (v. 34). Peter refers back to Moses's assertion that God is no respecter of persons (Dt 10:17). The very fact that Peter was preaching to Cornelius, a Roman centurion, and his household, shows God's lack of partiality.

Our baptism is different from the baptism of Jesus. But, like Jesus' baptism, ours also involves *manifestation* and *mission*. With respect to *manifestation*, in virtue of our baptism we're called to show forth that the beloved Son of the Father lives in our hearts, and the presence of Jesus in our world. Our call to *mission* means that we're sent out in the power of the Spirit to proclaim the good news of the Kingdom and, with Jesus, to do good.

Both manifestation and mission call us, as Jesus was called, to be God's servants, to live in harmony with one another, to work together for that unity for which Jesus prayed, to bring God's justice to the world. All of that requires humility similar to Jesus' own; a gentleness, yet a persistence that won't permit us to cop out; a healing, yet a challenging. We may well be judged on how we meet our moments of decision. Jesus met his moment and seized it. Let's reflect on the special opportunities our particular life provides.

SECOND SUNDAY IN ORDINARY TIME
Is 49:3, 5f.   1 Cor 1:1-3   Jn 1:29-34

Testimonials to Jesus (from Salvation History)
Jesus is Lord; Confessing Christ; Light to the Nations;
The Lamb of God; We Come to Do God's Will; The Attractiveness of Jesus

When attorneys have a witness on the stand, the *Federal Rules of Evidence* provide varying rules on what they may ask. The rules depend on such circumstances as whether the attorney faces his own witness or an opposing one, a hostile or a friendly witness, and are on direct examination or cross-examination. The aim is to get the truth.

In the Fourth Gospel, John the Baptist is a truthful witness for Jesus. He shares with others the function of giving witness to Jesus before the court of world opinion: the Holy Spirit, the works Jesus performed, the Father who sent him, the Scriptures, people like the Samaritan woman, the crowds, and eventually Jesus' own disciples. The Baptist's testimony was always honest, humble, sincere, and direct.

In the Gospels' kind of "snapshot" presentations of Jesus, today the Baptist gives witness to three titles that can be given only to Jesus. One title we might call "The Greater One": He existed before me, said John (v. 30). But for the Baptist that was hindsight, and it always troubled him that he hadn't immediately recognized Jesus (v. 31). He certainly knew that Jesus was his cousin, but not what Jesus was destined to be. Enlightenment had come at Jesus' baptism, when John saw heaven pay its tribute. And the Baptist's response in word and action was: He must increase, I must decrease. Like John, we often fail to recognize Jesus when he comes hidden in others.

A second title under which the Baptist saw Jesus may be termed "The Vehicle of the Spirit" (vv. 32f.). The Baptist recounted that, even before Jesus' baptism, God had told him that one upon whom the Spirit would descend would himself be baptizing with the Holy Spirit (v. 33). At Jesus' baptism, the Baptist saw the Spirit come down like a dove (v. 32). John the Baptist in speaking of the Spirit meant the Jewish *ruach*, wind, and by extension power, life, and God — especially God. The First Testament prophets had foretold an outpouring of the Spirit in the Messianic age. The New Testament sees its fulfillment in Pentecost and in baptism.

A third title of Jesus for the Baptist is "God's Chosen One" (v. 34), an allusion to Isaiah (42:1), recognizing in Jesus the special Son of God, the chosen in whom God delights.

But all these titles, though correct, can leave us relatively cold and unresponsive. These aspects of Jesus, if presented alone, would have led to his gradual disappearance from history. But then, what image might sufficiently open up human hearts to attract the majority of people? John's answer: a young, guiltless lamb frolicking in a field, before whom children laugh and giggle, and adults smile. This image conveys notes of innocence and fragility as well as whimsy and tenderness, draws a smile from most people, and moves us to response.

Thus the most precious of all the titles the Baptist poignantly ascribed to the loving, lonesome Jesus is "Lamb of God" — the vulnerable Lamb of God, who dies that we might live. This image, which immediately captured the imagination of early Christians, is very suggestive. The Savior, the Lamb of God, surrenders his life to nourish us, his people, in love, in innocence, and at his own cost. Somewhat the same happens today as people savor eating spring lamb.

It's possible that for the Baptist the figure meant the great apocalyptic lamb in Revelation (17:14) who would destroy evil in the world, the conqueror who would bring about God's judgment. John the Evangelist, however, who wrote today's Gospel, among others undoubtedly saw in the figure a reference to the Passover (Paschal) lamb. When the Jews were in Egypt and the Angel of Death was abroad killing the first-born of every human and animal in Egypt, the Jews received instructions to smear the blood of a lamb on their doorposts so the angel would know them and pass over them (Ex 12:11-13). It was the blood of the lamb that protected them.

Ever after, the Passover lamb evoked images of the liberation of God's people. So sacred was the daily custom of sacrificing lambs at the Temple that the sacrifices never stopped, even in war and famine, until the Temple was destroyed by the Romans in 70 A.D. Even as the Baptist was giving witness, a Passover feast wasn't far off (Jn 2:13); at a following Passover, the lambs would be slain by the priests in the Temple at the very hour that Jesus was being put to death.

But the fact that the Baptist says of Jesus that he *takes away the sin of the world* (v. 29) favors the interpretation of the Lamb of God as Servant of the Lord rather than as Passover lamb. The Passover lamb had no connection with sin. And that suggests the figure of the Suffering

Servant in Isaiah (53:5-7,10), led like a lamb to the slaughter as a sacrifice to Yahweh.

Today's passage from Isaiah, which is closely connected with our Gospel, presents this mysterious Servant of God. It's the second of the four hymns called the Songs of the Servant of the Lord. All these hymns taken together give a composite picture of the servant. He has a mission from God. He sums up great figures from the past, but his mission lies in the future. He is at the same time a *real* figure, and an *ideal*. The Suffering Servant of Isaiah is God-with-Us, a beautiful person suffused with the intense caring passion of God for the world. He is lovingly inviting, vulnerably returns good for evil wherever he is, and brings out in everyone all the good that they're capable of.

If we think that our bearing witness in our particular circumstances is difficult, let's look at St. Paul. In today's passage from his First Letter to the Corinthians, he provides further thoughts on giving and receiving witness to Jesus. He wrote the letter from Ephesus around Eastertime between 52 and 57 A.D., and today's portion is the beginning of a whole series of our Sunday readings. Corinth was a seaport city, with all the evils which that image implies. The very name of Corinth was used for sexual immorality: A "Corinthianess" was a prostitute; "Corinthian's Disease" was venereal disease; to act as a Corinthian meant to engage in sexual promiscuity. When Paul preached at Corinth, these sinners — amazingly — believed. Unfortunately, though, people don't instantly change the habits of years. The Corinthians were still tempted to backslide into sexual sins; because their self-esteem was low, they had temptations to try to lord it over others; so they fought each other jealously. Paul had to write them four letters, of which only two have come down to us.

In his special kind of greeting that is a blessing in this letter, Paul wishes the Corinthians — in the midst of their mistakes, divisions, and sins — beautiful Christian gifts: grace and peace (v. 3). Grace, deeper than our perfunctory wishes for "health and happiness," means the gracious goodness of God, together with the gifts that flow from His openhandedness. Peace becomes the fruit of the reconciliation and salvation that God gives through His lamb.

As with Isaiah and the Gospel, we see in Paul's letter something outside of and larger than just ourselves: the reality of God coming to all the human community. The people of the Church in Corinth, as people in parishes anywhere, are Church, but not the whole Church. Christians may form a parish, but aren't to be parochial!

Today, God calls us again to the high caliber of John the Baptist in witnessing to Jesus. We're not to render his beautiful symbol "Lamb of God" meaningless. We can, on the one hand, elevate Jesus in such a way as to relegate him to somewhere other than where we live — to another *era*, like eternity, or to some other *place*, like heaven. Or we can diminish him, seeing in him nothing more than a compassionate human being.

Isaiah tells us that we're to be servants of God who are a light to all the nations of the world. We're to focus our light on giving convincing witness to the Lamb of God, dispelling the darkness of sin and of untruth, in our own lives when necessary and in the world always.

THIRD SUNDAY IN ORDINARY TIME
Is 8:23-9:3   1 Cor 1:10-13,17   Mt 4:12-23 (or 4:12-17)

The Lord our Light and Salvation
Jesus Begins to Preach; Beginnings of the Good News; The Good News: Ongoing, and Inviting Response; Prophetic Hope Fulfilled; Cliques in Church; A True Community of Faith; Union in Working for Community

Wise people generally put great importance on beginnings. They've coined such aphorisms as "Well begun is half done," "The end depends upon the beginning," and "Mighty things from small beginnings grow."

Today's Gospel marks some of the beginning of Jesus' ministry, a furtherance of "the dawning of the ages." In a mere few lines, St. Matthew points out some of its signs: the arrest of John the Baptist (v. 12) signals the beginning of the New Testament; Jesus' preaching in Galilee and working out of Capernaum (v. 13) presents him as the light of the nations (v. 16); the calling of the first disciples (vv. 18-22) begins the time of the Church; and the first healings by Jesus (v. 23) reveal the efficaciousness of the salvation he brings.

Galilee, where Jesus started, didn't seem a likely place for any mission to begin. The most ignorant, crass, and pagan areas of the land were the territories of Zebulun and Naphtali, where Galilee was. Matthew shared with other devout Jews the concept of Galilee as a land of darkness (vv. 15f.). And it was his mission to heathen Gentile territory that emphasized — without the Apostles' knowing it — the non-exclusive nature of Jesus' call.

The Galileans had definite characteristics. They were always ready to follow a leader into insurrection, quick in temper, and inclined to be quarrelsome. On the other hand, geographically Galilee was important. The great roads of the area passed through it. Because of its fertility, it was densely populated. Better still, its people were open to new ideas, so that Galilee could not, like Judea, keep new concepts out. If there was any place suitable for an unprecedented teacher with a novel message, Galilee was it. For Matthew, the choice of Galilee went deeper. For him it was to the people of Galilee that Isaiah had announced the Messianic light.

It's good for us to remember, as we struggle with a sense of insignificance and powerlessness, that the list of superpeople has always been short. Even Jesus found that to be true. He called Andrew, the cynic who showed a lack of a sense of risk by asking, when Jesus told him to get the boy with the loaves and fish, "What can anyone do with five loaves and two fishes?" He called Philip, the patriot who wanted Jesus to be a king, not just an ordinary Nazarene. He called Simon, the violent Zealot who thought redemption involved military and political force. He called Nathaniel, the reclining prejudiced one who, when told of Jesus, asked if anything good could come out of Nazareth.

He called Thomas, the doubter who lacked vision so much he couldn't see the obvious. He called Judas, the pragmatist who showed his desire for good business by asserting, when the woman was bathing Jesus' feet in perfume, "This perfume could be sold for a lot." He called Matthew, the tax collector who spent his life succeeding at the expense of others. He called Thaddeus, the realist looking for certification, who asked, "Why don't you just reveal yourself to the world?" He called James the Less, the chauvinist who insisted that Christianity was only for Jews. He called James the Great and John, ambitious men who were most concerned about becoming careerists in search of a good position. And he called Peter, who wanted to lead the leader often, especially when he advised Jesus, "Don't go to Jerusalem: You'll be killed."

And Jesus calls us: the thirteenth disciples, the comfortable, the fearful, the weak, the timid, the ordinary. The thirteenth disciple is to walk with the hungry, the poor, the wounded, the abused, those who aren't heard. His call is an offer, a challenge, an invitation to leadership. It calls us to help others arrive at victory, peace, joy, and equality.

If people had read the Scriptures carefully, they would have found Isaiah, as in today's first reading, speaking of the people in darkness who would see a great light — a light of good coming from Zebulun and Naphtali; Nazareth and Capernaum were there. The Responsorial Psalm is our affirmation of the hope of God's people that into the darkness of their lives light will come, expressing our hope and confidence that the Lord will give us the light we want for our lives, remove our fear, and bring us happiness.

Isaiah looked to a child, most probably Hezekiah, the successor of King Ahaz, who would fulfill the promises made about the dynasty. Isaiah said that God through this new prince would bring them out of the darkness of Assyrian oppression into a time of light and joy.

Galilee had been the first part of Israel to experience the destroying wrath of Yahweh, which was through the Assyrians in 734 B.C., Isaiah's time of writing. At that time the Assyrian ruler, Tiglath Pileser III, with his ruthlessness as a totalitarian despot, deported the local populations and dispersed them throughout his expanding empire, giving birth to the fable of the "lost tribes of Israel." Isaiah held out hope for a future restoration of "the people who walked in darkness."

In Matthew's view Jesus was the fulfillment of the prophetic words of Isaiah, and Galilee would be the first to hear of Yahweh's salvation. The sparkling pear-shaped Lake of Galilee had a warm climate and a lovely shoreline thick with fishing boats of prosperous towns. On its shores the town of Tiberias attracted tourists from the whole Greco-Roman world; it has more in common with the resorts of the Costa Brava or the Riviera today than with a sleepy fishing village in, say, Maine. This didn't help the local people's morals. That Jesus left Nazareth and went to live in Capernaum by the Lake of Galilee (v. 13) expresses a note of finality. Jesus left his home, never to live there again. It was also the beginning of something new.

Capernaum's position was ideal for reaching a larger audience. Situated on the high road from Jerusalem in the south to Damascus in the north, and serving as the frontier post of Palestine, it was a center of attraction for both Jews and foreigners. There Jesus could preach with effectiveness. His proclamation that the people repent, for the kingdom of heaven is at hand (v. 17), announced a new intervention of God. He was asking for conversion and transformation of life. That includes actively doing good works and passively being penitent, both of them toward receiving God's mercy for our sins.

To spread this message Jesus chose not the professionally religious, but tax collectors, zealots, itinerants — and salty fishermen like Peter and Andrew and James and John. These were people of no great scholarship, influence, money, or prestige (except, perhaps, Judas Iscariot). To become fishers of men (v. 19) they had to risk abandoning their former means of livelihood. Jesus went around all of Galilee, teaching in their synagogues, proclaiming the Gospel, and curing the people (v. 23).

St. Paul's First Letter to the Corinthians gives insights into one of the consequences of the dawning of God's light in Jesus. In this community of the still-immoral Corinthians that Paul had evangelized, rivalries had arisen (v. 11) and Paul had been informed by members of the household of Chloe (probably a well-off convert to Christianity who made her home available to the Christians of Corinth) that the Christians had formed into several cliques (v. 12).

One clique — probably consisting of the majority — followed Paul. These were mostly Gentiles, who accepted Paul's preaching about the end of the binding force of the Jewish Law and the beginning of the Gospel of Christian freedom. Some of them were probably trying to do what some people try to do today: turn freedom into license and do as they please. Other Christians followed Apollos, a Jew from Alexandria, which was a center of great intellectual activity. Because he was eloquent, intelligent, and learned in the Scriptures, he had made a strong impression on the better-educated minority of the Corinthian Christians; some who wanted to "be somebody" had started to follow him.

Some Jewish Christians, boasting of their attachment to St. Peter, were promoting adherence to the Jewish Law. As with Paul and Apollos, there is no evidence that Peter was personally responsible for this group that rallied around his name.

Paul's reference to a fourth clique, those who grouped around Christ, he probably meant with sarcasm as his personal protest against the other factions. If this group existed, it most likely constituted a small number who self-righteously proclaimed themselves best. Their fault would consist not in their saying that they belonged to Christ, but in their implying that Christ belonged to them alone. Such people still exist.

In this passage, Paul twice calls people who belong to cliques "brothers" (vv. 10f.), showing the kind of love Christians should have for one another. When he asks that we be united in the same mind and in the same purpose, he's saying many things. He's stating that to be united suggests a mutual adaptation, a readiness to give in to one another for harmony's sake. He's asserting that disunity among Christians is a disgraceful disruption of the expected Christian *koinonia*, or special kind of loving community, and thus a denial of the whole reality of God's saving work in Christ.

In sum, Paul's words are a realistic contrast with the idealized picture of the early Church as found in the New Testament's Acts of the Apostles, and thus an antidote to the general picture that there existed a "golden age" of the Church which later broke down. The presence of factions in the Church right from the start reminds us that the perfect state is something that we Christians must always work towards.

Today's readings are intended to stir us to action. The Gospel tells us that the spread of Christ's kingdom depends as much upon us today as it did upon the Apostles in Christ's time. Paul's letter to the Corinthians counsels us not to participate in factions within our Church and between the churches. And Isaiah reminds us that God's light is always being offered to us as it was to a people who had suffered exile, oppression, fear, and shame.

Because people who practice religion, like others, sometimes seek more their own desire for comfort and security than trying to solve strife and injustice, our non-religious brethren criticize religion, humanity's reaching out to God, as being a dangerous source of further disunity and suffering. We who practice our religion should walk, as the greatest people of old walked, allowing one's whole being to become flooded with joyous light.

Light acquires a transcendental quality. This goes beyond even the light of the bright Mediterranean known to the sacred writers; it's something more, something unfathomable, something holy. This is the light that penetrates directly to the soul, opens the doors and windows of the heart, and makes one effusive and radiant. Let's pray that we may be one small candle that may light a thousand. Well begun is half done, and mighty things from small beginnings grow.

FOURTH SUNDAY IN ORDINARY TIME
Zp 2:3; 3:12f.   1 Cor 1:26-31   Mt 5:1-12

Do Your Beatitudes Coincide with Jesus'?
Being Well-Off, Satisfied, and Content: Better than Being Humble,
Lowly, and Dependent?; Poverty: Material, Social, and Spiritual; True Riches;
Meekness, Humility, and Poverty: Do They Pay?; Meekness: Only Promises,
Promises?; Do the Poor Need God the Most?; The True Meaning of
Being "Somebody"; Christianity's Constitution; Happiness is. . . ;
Is Perfection our Goal, or Is it Happiness?; Happy the Poor?

All week long we're smoothly and slickly bombarded by values that are
different from those we hear at church on Sundays. For example, the
world teaches that power, prestige, possessions, and popularity are the
keys to happiness; or, faced with problems, we're told it's all right to
escape: escape in selfishness, escape in sexual encounters, escape in
drugs, escape in violence, escape in indifference and cynicism. Today
Jesus presents us with some opposing values. He teaches us that we can
create happiness and the capacity for joy *by ourselves* and radiate them
to others.

St. Matthew, our evangelist of the year, has Jesus put many
Christian values together at the beginning of his Sermon on the Mount
(parts of which will be our Gospel for the next six Sundays). A leading
psychiatrist once wrote that if you were to take the sum total of all the
articles ever written by the most qualified psychologists and psychiatrists on the subject of mental hygiene, if you were to combine them and
refine them and cleave out the excess verbiage, if you were to take the
whole of the meat and none of the parsley, and if you were to have these
unadulterated bits of pure scientific knowledge concisely expressed by
the most capable of living poets, you would have an awkward and
incomplete summation of the Sermon on the Mount.

The statements in today's portion are called Beatitudes, from
beati, or blessed, or happy, the opening words in each statement. All the
beatitudes speak of *this* world, not of "pie in the sky bye 'n' bye when
you die." They contain congratulations on what *is,* and promise a
reward that always consists in at least an improved relationship with
God. To view our life as blessed doesn't require us to deny our pain or
to put on a happy face no matter what. It simply demands a more all-

embracing vision. Though the list of beatitudes could be lengthened, the existing ones constitute the very foundations of the law of the Kingdom and the apex of Christian perfection.

The First Beatitude strikes the keynote of the whole sermon. Jesus is calling fortunate not the person who has nothing superfluous, but one who has nothing at all. In the eyes of the world, which pursues such symbols of material success as the right car, the right clothes, and the right neighborhood, such people are of little value. The *anawim*, as Jesus called them in Aramaic, are those who lack material goods; because poor, they have no influence; because they have no influence, they're walked over by other people; and because they have no earthly resources, they put their whole trust in God.

Jesus isn't calling material poverty a good thing. It isn't. It isn't good for people to live in slums, not to have enough to eat, and to have their health at risk. And Jesus' words aren't to condemn ambition. In fact, there should be more Christians in the academic world, the business world, the scientific world, and the technical world. What Jesus condemns is the *inordinate* love of riches, a love that makes impossible meaningful concern for the afflicted.

Though the First Beatitude teaches that it's *always* right to be detached from things, the Second Beatitude (v. 4) teaches it's *never* right to be detached from people. Here Jesus speaks of sorrow in the strongest sense: those who have a *passionate* grieving for the loss of one who's loved: for the dead, the vanished, the one who has journeyed away — or for their sins. It brings ache to the heart and tears to the eyes.

To those who think falsely that people of strong faith shouldn't have sorrow, Jesus says it's all right, and that mourners will be comforted, because adversity has its uses. An Arab proverb has it that "all sunshine makes a desert." Some flowers are brought forth only by rain, the intense color of others only by cold mountain air; some human growth requires sorrow as its seed. And some people have shown an indomitable will to survive. Some scholars believe that Dostoyevski the novelist and Van Gogh the painter probably had temporal lobe epilepsy; that Bartok the composer and Wittgenstein the philosopher were probably autistic; and that Mozart had Tourette's syndrome.

The Third Beatitude (v. 5) speaks of the lowly, a group to whom the prophet Zephaniah referred in about 620 B.C. and who deserve consideration today and all the time. Zephaniah described the religious degradation and political intrigue of his time: merchants cheating the poor, pagan worship taking place within the Holy City, and leaders looking the other way from injustice. Zephaniah called his people to a change of heart (2:1-3). Zephaniah saw a ray of hope (3:9-20), though, as in today's reading, where he promises peace and justice to a small portion of the people: the humble of the earth (2:3) who find their blessedness in God. We're to imitate their qualities of gentleness and kindness — qualities of God Himself.

Jesus' equivalent of Zephaniah's words is meekness. By it he means the self-controlled — or, better, the God-controlled. It's the mean between two extremes: excessive anger and lack of care. It's the ability to be angry with the right people about the right things at the right time to the right degree. Anger is the necessary handmaiden of sympathy and fairness, in that the most dedicated must be angry at "society," or "the ruling classes," or "meddling bureaucrats" to be motivated to do something about justice. But anger, like the moral qualities that it exists to defend, must be checked by other qualities like self-control and duty.

Meekness is the quality possessed by Moses, whom Scripture calls by far the meekest man on the face of the earth (Nb 12:3), but who nevertheless was blazingly angry when he came down from the mountain and found his people worshiping the golden calf. Meekness is the quality envisioned by the Book of Proverbs (16:32) when it says that he who rules his temper is better than he who takes a city. People can't lead others until they've controlled themselves. And so the meek will inherit the land.

They who hunger and thirst for holiness (v. 6) are those who ardently long for that goodness that is similar to God's. In ancient Palestine, hunger and thirst were real, always threatening, and terrible. It's only when we hunger and thirst as strongly for the kind of holiness that Jesus wants of us, as did the ancients for food and water, and are willing to pay its cost, that we're able spiritually to survive.

The Fifth Beatitude (v. 7) refers to a principle that runs through the New Testament: It's the merciful who shall receive mercy. Mercy isn't a sentimental wave of pity, nor is it indifference to wrongs, but is rather the ability to identify with others and be willing to suffer with them and walk in their shoes.

The clean of heart (v. 8) are those whose inner single-mindedness motivates them to serve God joyfully for His own sake and not primarily out of self-interest. In the midst of the confusion of all the complex sets of values being presented them, they're free of duplicity. The single-hearted are unadulterated (as with good wine), unalloyed (as with pure metal), and unmixed (as in flour without chaff). The clean of heart will see God in their here-and-now ability to discern His presence in the small and ordinary events of their lives.

Then (v. 9) Jesus speaks not of peace*lovers*, but of peace*makers* —those whose lives have a quality that promotes harmony within the human community. Peacemakers contrast with troublemakers and with those who without principle want an easy peace at any price. Peacemakers go out of their way to reconcile quarrels. Those who promote peace establish right relationships between person and person, and make this world a better place to live. Peacemakers will be called children of God because our heavenly Father is a God of peace, and Jesus our brother came to bring peace on earth.

Jesus' Eighth Beatitude (vv. 10-12) reminds us that fidelity to his precepts is deepened by the test of persecution. Persecution for the early Christians could mean difficulty in getting a job, ostracism in social life, the breakup of family life, and physical torture, as well as death by martyrdom. For true Christians, some degree of persecution continues to be inevitable. For one thing, true Christians are bound to be the conscience of the world. We must speak up whenever morality is offensive, and we're caught in the perpetual clash between Christ and the world. For another thing, to adhere to Christ's values sometimes means persecution by our own selfish desires.

St. Paul today gives a further contrast between Jesus' values and the world's. In the face of some haughty Christians who were putting on airs in the pagan city of Corinth, he tells his people that, by the world's standards, they may be unimportant nonentities (v. 26) — which they were — but by spiritual standards they have Christ and are therefore all-important. Paul says that we're all called — called to a new creation in Christ, who possesses everything that we yearn for.

Do we value that new creation? With all our possibilities of choice out there, do our beatitudes coincide with those of Jesus?

FIFTH SUNDAY IN ORDINARY TIME
Is 58:7-10   1 Cor 2:1-5   Mt 5:13-16

The Just Person: Salt and Light and on a Mountain
The Salt of the Earth; Light of the World; City on a Mountain;
The Truly Happy; Real Success; The World's
World-view vs. Jesus'; Giving Witness to the World

Long ago and far away, the Grand Vizier, the principal adviser to the
King, invented a new game. It was played with moving pieces on a
board of 64 squares. The most important piece was the King, the next
most important the Grand Vizier. The object of the game was to capture
the enemy king, and so the game was called, in Persian, *shahmat* —
shah for king, *mat* for dead: death to the king. In English there is an echo
of the name: the final move is called "checkmate." The game is, of
course, chess. As time passed, the game evolved. There is, for example,
no longer a piece called the Grand Vizier — it has changed into a Queen.

The King was so pleased with the original game that he asked the
Grand Vizier to name his own reward for such a splendid discovery. The
Vizier told the King that he was a humble man, and wished only for a
humble reward. Gesturing to the chess board, he asked that he be given
a single grain of wheat on the first square, twice that on the second
square, twice that on the third, and so on, until each of the 64 squares had
its complement of wheat.

No, the King remonstrated: That's too modest a prize. He offered
jewels, dancing girls, palaces. But the Vizier, his eyes lowered, refused
them all. All he wanted was the wheat. The King, marveling at his
counselor's unselfishness, graciously consented. But when the Master
of the Royal Granary began to count out the grains, the King was in for
a rude surprise. The number of grains increased: 1, 2, 4, 8, 16, 32, 64 —
and by the time he reached the 64th square the number was staggering:
nearly 18.5 quintillion grains of wheat, around 75 billion metric tons.
Unfortunately, the account of what happened next hasn't come down to
us.

A sequence of numbers like this is called a geometric progression,
and the progress is called an exponential increase. Exponentials show
up in all sorts of places. If, for example, you put one penny in a shoebox

today, doubled that tomorrow, and so on, in about a month you'd have $1 million, and you'd need about 15,000 shoe boxes, depending on the size of your feet.

Just so, there is exponential power in goodness. Although it may sometimes seem that no one is following words or examples of goodness, today's liturgy tells us that our goodness is tremendously important. In today's portion of the Sermon on the Mount, which follows directly after the Beatitudes which we meditated upon last week, Jesus is calling for us to acquire a goodness that will radiate exponentially. In homey metaphors from his time, he reveals what his people are called to be: the salt of the earth, the light of the world, and a city set on a mountain.

Today, we know much more about salt than they did in Jesus' time. With greater chemical precision, for example, we call it sodium chloride. And we know that there's enough salt in the earth's oceans and rocks to cover the continents with a blizzard of salt 500 feet deep. The amniotic fluid, in which we all prepared for birth, has the same salt content as the ocean. But what probably comes to people's minds in connection with salt are simple things, like the salt-cellars on our tables. And despite high-blood-pressure victims who have to reduce their salt intake, salt is essential to life.

In the ancient world, salt wasn't easy to get. It came from the sun evaporating pools from the sea (which you can still see in some areas). And it was highly regarded. It was traded by caravans just as people traded gems or gold, and it was offered to guests invited to share one's hearth and home. The Romans thought so much of salt that part of a legionnaire's pay was a ration of salt; to this day, our word "salary" derives from that custom.

Throughout history, as well as in our day, salt has served two purposes. One is to preserve food. Before refrigeration, meat had to be salted to keep it from going bad. Salt's second purpose is to give zest and flavor to food. The common people in Jesus' day usually put their salt, which had all kinds of chemical impurities that could cause it to be useless, in a bag; they then lowered the bag into their soup or broth. As the salt was used up and the bag had lost its flavor, only the dregs remained.

Metaphorically, we followers of Jesus are to be the pure salt that will preserve the world from moral corruption and lend flavor to life. Christians should be radiant. In a harried world, we should be the composed ones; in a despairing world, the joyful ones, because Christ is risen. But people, like salt at the time of Jesus, can go flat. And an old saying has it that *corruptio optimi pessima* — the corruption of the best is the worst. That is to say, people who are called to be the greatest constitute the worst tragedy if they fail.

Jesus paid another great compliment when he called his followers, as he elsewhere called himself, the light of the world (v. 14). Like salt, light is precious. In Jesus' time, the average home was one room with very small windows, if any at all, to prevent the loss of heat in winter and coolness in summer. Their small lamps were like gravy boats with a lighted wick floating in oil. They put them under an earthenware crate only to prevent smoke from filling the house, or for safety when they were leaving. Their major source of light was the sun.

Today, although Edison gave us light-bulbs of all shapes and sizes, all of which can be turned on and off by the flick of a switch, light it still precious. And it continues to be many things: a light in the hallway soothes a frightened child, headlights point out the road, and a small flashlight comes to the rescue of a power blackout — not to mention what the light of a lighthouse means to anyone who's been out in the black void of the ocean for days. Years ago it was the custom of pirates to set up lights along some secluded part of the shore to lure vessels to wrecking and plundering; false lights are still with us.

The image of light also shows the *public* nature of our role in the world. Discipleship can't be a merely private affair any more than light can. But spiritually we don't produce our own light; we're reflections of Jesus' light. We're like the bride who is said to be *radiant*; her radiance comes from her love.

Jesus calls us, lastly, to be a city set on a mountain (v. 14). In his time, the crown of a hill was a good place to build a city. It enabled the inhabitants both to see enemies at a distance and to defend themselves more easily. And inhabitants were proud that their city, no matter how humble, could be readily seen. In our present context, the simple Galileans to whom Jesus spoke — and we — should let God's goodness be seen through our works: not for our own pride, but so as to glorify our heavenly Father (v. 16). That's a high-wire balancing act. Whereas we're not to use deceit, tricks, and illusion to appear good, we have to have the good we do be seen; even good isn't respected unless it looks good. But that's to take place only when our good works can give glory to God.

How should we live for our light to shine? Isaiah in today's first reading explicitly tells us. The Jews, who had returned from the Babylonian exile, saw now reemerging the same social immorality which was in evidence before the exile. They thought that they would become a light for the nations if they rebuilt Jerusalem and its Temple. Isaiah said, to the contrary, that they would make a difference to the world only if they became a community of justice. With open arms they were to relieve the oppressed, share their bread with the hungry, and shelter the homeless poor; they were to do away with the clenched fist intent on violence or a demonstration of power.

Isaiah is close to the Sermon on the Mount when he concludes (v. 10) that when sharing makes the wealthy poor and the poor share their spirit of humble dependence upon God with the wealthy, the final age will have come. The Responsorial Psalm corroborates this by saying that the just person is a light in darkness to the upright.

But we may say, "I'm too small to speak of in grandiose terms of being the salt of the earth, the light of the world, and a city on a mountain. St. Paul's letter to the Corinthians provides insights into that. Paul was ill, depressed, and acutely aware that in person he was unimpressive and unable to preach with any great impact. So it was in weakness and fear and much trembling (v. 3) that he came to Corinth. Corinth was only about thirty miles from Athens, and the mostly low-class people of Corinth had ambitions to be as high and mighty as the Athenians. Paul had failed miserably in Athens, but in Corinth his fear wasn't for his own safety, nor was it a fear caused by shame. It was like the nervousness of a good artist about to perform.

With a blinding clarity he saw the paradox. The presence of God's Spirit becomes strikingly real within the humiliating context of weakness; awareness of weakness is the prerequisite condition for experiencing the power of the Spirit. Indeed, the very existence of the Corinthian church was proof of the fact that God's power can be made perfect in what human standards would regard as folly and weakness. And the open hands and vulnerable heart of Paul the Apostle were a long way from the clenched fist of Saul the Pharisee. As Paul came to realize, we draw the world to the love of God by making ourselves as attractive to this world as salt and light and a city on a mountain.

In Paul's time, Rome was a city of about two million people, among whom there were scarcely 200 Christians. But those Christians were salt and light and a magnificent mountain to the population. We, too, are to be like precious salt to a corrupt and insipid world, a vital light to a dark world, and a city set on a mountain to a jaded world. We'll be following Jesus' injunctions today if we care for the homeless, work for good marriages, reconcile families, form the young, assist those without hope, and use all other opportunities to be of help. And God will increase exponentially the goodness that we radiate.

SIXTH SUNDAY IN ORDINARY TIME
Si 15:15-20   1 Cor 2:6-10   Mt 5:17-37

Wisdom
Happiness Is Following God's Law; Spiritual Maturity; Freedom and
Responsibility; The Wisdom of Jesus vs. the Wisdom of the World;
The Spirit of the Law; Growth in Holiness; Freedom of Choice

Many people abide by fads, fashions, and custom. For example, most people today hate rats. But the ancient Romans believed that rat-keeping brought good luck. The ancient Egyptians deified rats, making them the symbol of wisdom for consistently choosing the best grains. To us, the current all-American animal is the mouse, a mascot for democratic man. Faceless, they're much like us, in the age of bureaucracy, network television, polls, mail addressed to "Occupant," store loudspeakers blaring "Attention all shoppers," Social Security numbers, traffic jams, and our immersion in larger and larger crowds. The mouse is the underdog, but it can stampede a whole herd of elephants — this being a reference to folk tales of elephants fearing that mice will run up their trunks.

That mice are viewed as "cute," rather than ugly or vicious, can perhaps be traced to Walt Disney, whose Mickey Mouse appeared in his first animated cartoon in 1928. In Disney's work, Mickey became virtually a national symbol. Mickey's name is a synonym for oppressive bureaucratic trivia, as in, "Why do we have to put up with all this mickey-mouse nonsense?"

Yet over 10 million U.S. homes have rodents as uninvited guests each year. There are mouse-borne diseases, such as salmonella, typhus, and plague. Fires are caused by mouse-gnawed wiring. Mice in our cupboards scavenge our cereals, crackers, chips, cookies, and cheese. Mice running across the floor or fleeing from suddenly opened cabinets, or night sounds from their fighting within the walls are repulsive. One study placed mice third on people's list of objects of phobias — just behind dentists and public speaking.

And many things that are true of mice are also true of rats. But in our minds, mice are timid and rats are sneaky; drab women are mousy and the men who break their hearts are rats; when our cats catch mice, we're sorry, but when they catch rats, we're proud.

There are also fads in morals, social customs, and intellectual life. These are a greater danger. It's there that we can look into the deep, far-reaching, and long-range meaning of life, and come to either foolishness or wisdom. Today's liturgy addresses an aspect of wisdom. The Gospel is from the most challenging part of the Sermon on the Mount, the keynote of a new age that wanted to supplant the Old Law with a new one.

Jesus' audience looked upon their Mosaic Law as the summary of all wisdom, human and divine: the self-revelation of God, a complete and secure guide of conduct. For most Jews, at least implicitly it was the very last revelation of God — ultimate, eternal, unchangeable.

Mary and Joseph observed all the prescriptions of the Law of Moses faithfully and performed its customary rituals. Jesus would grow to adulthood as a devout Jew living by that Law. Here in the beginning of his public ministry, he seemed to praise the Law. Throughout his ministry, the Pharisees — the most righteous of Jews — questioned him assiduously about his ideas on the Law: about the Sabbath, on taxes, on divorce, and on many other facets of the Law and life.

Jesus doesn't reject the Old Law, but clarifies its meaning. He goes to the heart of what the old commandments demand. His emphasis is on mercy, not legalistic minutiae; on far-reaching love, not destructive petty details; and on positive commitment, not prohibitions. Jesus has come to fulfill (v. 17) the Law and the Prophets, to give the Old Law all the richness that the Jews believed it had. Because Jesus saw the current leaders as blind guides, he repeatedly violated their *misinterpretations* of the Law and their burdensome regulations. He wanted a conversion of heart that goes deeper than any merely external observance of laws.

It's difficult for us to realize how shocking Jesus' teaching was to the Jews of his day. He was pointing out some inadequacies in what the leaders of the people considered to be the most sacred and wisest writings in the world. The Rabbis had standard phrases for commenting on the Law, like, "Thus says the Lord"; the implication was that no one could argue with that. Jesus put forward his own teaching instead; he spoke with an authority that held the crowds spellbound. No one had ever dared do this before.

After pointing out the correct spirit of the Law, Jesus gives four out of many possible examples of where his more demanding way of life applies: anger, adultery, divorce, and oaths — the fifth, sixth, and eighth commandments. In all, his wisdom isn't only theoretical, but practical.

First, he interprets the commandment against murder as a command against anger (v. 22): the cancerous *cause*, and not merely the *effect*. Jesus is both a good psychologist and a good theologian. He realizes what modern psychology is more and more wrestling with: for the avoidance of heart attacks and for overall good psychical health, one's basic attitude needs healing. He's pin-pointing a theological truth that's not often grasped: the sinfulness of the deeper attitude has the potential for manifesting itself in many acts unless it's revealed, claimed, and brought to the Savior. When this happens, greater intimacy can result, so that the act of sin can become a *felix culpa*, a happy fault drawing awareness to the underlying attitude of alienation.

Jesus therefore forbids the anger which broods, refuses to be subdued, and seeks revenge. To the degrees of anger, extending even to thoughts, there are corresponding degrees of punishment. Both Peter and Judas were guilty of denial and betrayal. Peter had an attitude of trust and therefore surrender. Judas, on the other hand, had an attitude of angry distrust and therefore flight from Jesus; this resulted in his ultimate ruin.

Not only must we pardon those who have offended us; we must be *the first to seek reconciliation* even when the fault seemingly has been on the other side (v. 23f.). Jesus says it's impossible to engage in worship, closely related in the Jewish mind to reconciliation with God, until you're at peace with your neighbor. He also recommends what today's lawyers advise: the settling of disagreements equitably out of court. In storms of passion, it's wise to seek a safe harbor with smoother waters, and the way to avoid an oncoming whirlwind is to step aside to safety and wait until it blows itself out. To concede today may be the best way to succeed tomorrow. Jesus is saying: Be open to talking, to listening, to risking change in your human relationships; how else can you be converted in your relationships with God?

In his second example, adultery (vv. 27-30), Jesus points to the basic attitude that leads to the offending act: namely, deliberately-entertained lustful thoughts, such as those propagated by pornographic magazines and motion pictures. The offense is best cauterized by a healthy attitude of respect for all God's people, who're made in His image. This respect for *all* persons, including women, is unique to Jesus, with no parallel known in the teaching of other rabbis. It's the basis for Jesus' attitude to his third application, divorce. The interpretation of the Law up to this time was for the benefit of males. A woman could be divorced for such trivialities as not being a good cook or not having the proper head covering. But Jesus, in declaring the inviolability of marriage as God's ultimate intent for human society, supports the position of women as well as men in the marriage contract.

Lastly, Jesus focuses on oaths (vv. 33-37), the supreme obligation to tell the truth. Too often people use sacred words, even the name of God, in an unwarranted way, and often to bolster their untruth. In Jesus' new ethics, truthfulness is assured not by oaths but by the honesty and inner integrity of persons. If we're recognized as being that way, our word is our bond. Here again he directs us to the basic inner attitude — the Kingdom is *within*.

Sirach, author of today's first reading, had a glimpse of the ideal. About 180 years before Christ, he wanted to promote the Word of God as the basis for human wisdom. Here, he gives the strongest emphasis in all Scripture on free will. We're free to choose between virtue and sin, life and death. We've inherited a tendency to evil called Original Sin, and we need God's grace if we're to triumph. It's been said, though, that we don't make big choices, but only a whole series of little ones. And this reading tells us that the fundamental choice in life is that between fire and water, life and death.

No matter how we use or abuse our freedom, God doesn't take it away. From those who choose sin and death, wisdom is withheld. If people are divided into two camps, the wise and sinners, this isn't God's work, but humankind's. God gives all of us the strength to think correctly and to behave faithfully.

St. Paul addresses that division in today's second reading. For Paul, a blunt, direct man who wanted no frills, the only genuine factor in Christian life is a vital and practical faith in God's gift of Jesus Christ.

Paul, along with St. John's Gospel, held that Jesus replaced the Torah; Jesus Christ in the flesh — not the Torah — is the eternal, ultimate, unchangeable self-revelation of God. Had Paul been an Eastern guru desirous of giving his followers a mantra to be repeated over and over, that mantra would have been "in Christ Jesus." Through the purifying trials and rapturous joys of life "in Christ Jesus," Paul wanted union with Christ in his total mystery.

Paul contrasts two groups: "material" persons who use only their natural faculties of knowledge, and "spiritual" people who allow the Holy Spirit to dwell and act within them. Some spiritual people in turn are "infants," beginners in the spiritual life, and others more full-grown in Christ: the mature. The latter are wise in the full sense.

No one would know these things better than Paul, who had walked the Grecian plain to Athens alone, with no book and no companions, and arrived to preach Christ on the Areopagus where the Athenians, the self-styled wise, were in the habit of hearing all comers. Paul tried to frame his message in terms of human eloquence and the wisdom of the world. He suffered a resounding defeat (Ac 17). From then on, he realized that you can't equate the Gospel with philosophy. If you did, the profound message of Christianity would become just another system of thought, open to fads and fashions.

The Gospel of Jesus Christ is wisdom — not the temporary mode of fads or fashion, but the way of eternal insight. Even as certain types of insight go in and out of style, eternal wisdom has an advantage: If this isn't her century, many other centuries will be. The wise have conquered the courageous more often than vice-versa.

When reflected on in prayer, God in Jesus can answer our ultimate questions about life and meaning. That, of course, means we realize that most of what's really essential is invisible to the eye. It also reminds us that true religion is something primarily for adults. There's nothing automatic about being a true Christian. And it entails facing our inner motivations, desires, and priorities, and holding them up to Jesus' new standard of honesty and love. Let's earnestly pray for the wisdom that is greater than human words.

SEVENTH SUNDAY IN ORDINARY TIME
Lv 19:1f., 17f.   1 Cor 3:16-23   Mt 5:38-48

Holiness
Expansiveness; Largeness of Mind and Heart; The Christian
Response to Violence; Reconciliation; Perfection

Infants find security in what they've learned, and cry if the world they've discovered is changed too quickly. Unfortunately, that aspect of infancy characterizes many so-called "grown-ups." In them it's called immaturity, and it has many varieties. To bring about the fullest maturity in such people, Jesus teaches largeness of heart and mind: holiness.

Today's Gospel, from the Sermon on the Mount like our previous Sundays, is the most radical section of that sermon. It presents more applications of last Sunday's basic principle that our holiness is to exceed that of the scribes and Pharisees — those who taught the Law of Moses! Jesus begins in an area that seems rooted in humankind's basic nature: violence and revenge (vv. 38-42).

He recounts the oldest written law in the world, the Law of the Talion (*Lex Talionis*, "Talion" meaning "such for such"): tit for tat, "An eye for an eye and a tooth for a tooth" (v. 38). That law had appeared as long ago as the Code of Hammurabi in Babylon over 2,000 years before. It openly differentiated between rich and poor: If a "gentleman" sustained an injury, the same injury was to be inflicted upon the perpetrator; if a worker received an injury, he was to receive only a small monetary payment.

Cruel though this may seem, historically the *Lex Talionis*, advocating proportionality of punishment to crime, was a giant humanitarian step upward from the unlimited and unregulated vengeance prior to it. Before, when a member of one tribe injured a member of another, the entire tribe of the injured person tried to wreak vengeance on that of the injurer. Often that vengeance went much beyond the injury: a life for a scratch. The Book of Genesis records (4:23f.) a terrible example of this in Lamech, who boasted to his wives that he had killed a man for wounding him, a boy for bruising him. Mahatma Gandhi is said to have remarked that if all of us were to practice the "eye for an eye" rule, the whole world would soon be blind and toothless.

Jesus' law is that for such-and such injury, we're to return such-and-such blessing. It's another giant step upward and forward. His is a law that the early Christians found as difficult as we do, a law that in two thousand years the world has proved itself unable to grow into. With it, nevertheless, a new world order has begun. Jesus says that we're to offer no resistance to one who is evil. He gives four examples of the Christian spirit in this matter.

Jesus says we're to meet the physical violence of someone who strikes us on the cheek by offering the other cheek as well (v. 39). Against litigiousness, he advised putting generosity above legal rights (v. 40). Those who are forced into labor Jesus advised going beyond the call of duty: "Should anyone press you into service for one mile, go with him for two miles" (v. 41). This "law of the second mile" is a picture from an occupied country. In any occupied country at that time, such as Palestine under Rome, the occupying soldiers could force citizens into service, like supplying food or billets. It also applied to carrying baggage: Under military law a Roman soldier could compel a Jew to carry his burden for a mile. That's what happened to Simon of Cyrene, when he was compelled to carry Jesus' cross to Calvary.

We, too, are pressed into service — not by military law, but by social life and by the practical necessity of earning a living. In the face of that, we can take one of several attitudes. We can, like the citizens of an occupied country, make clear our bitter resentment. Or we can skimpingly trudge the absolute minimum in silence. Or we can go beyond the requirements of one mile and go two, smilingly do it with a gracious courtesy and a desire to perform well. The last attitude attempts the step upward that Jesus intended.

That second mile for us consists in non-obligatory courtesies: in an unexpected present, in a surprise thoughtfulness, in a kindness that gives pleasure. It's what makes the difference between a housewife and a mother, between a breadwinner and a father, between progeny and children. The crown of all relationships is voluntary two-mile persons. Although there are no traffic jams on the second mile, among the world's heroes you will never find a one-mile person.

Jesus' fourth example of nonviolent love concerns almsgiving, which was a lovely tradition among the Jews. We find in today's reading from the "Holiness Code" of Leviticus, for example, a beautiful instruction on one's responsibility to practice justice and love in social dealings. That Holiness Code offers as a constant reason for the laws it imposes the imitation of God's unique holiness: "Be holy, for I, the Lord, your God, am holy." God is holy — totally set apart from and above everything else — and He expects His people to be holy, too.

Unfortunately, hatred seems to be a basic instinct. We don't have to turn back to the Jewish Scriptures to find evidence. Our own times give examples every day. But holiness — which is not just otherworldly —precludes any spirit of enmity, revenge, and grudge-bearing. A little child's answer about the meaning of holiness was: "Being holy means that you do what your mother asks the first time she asks." Leviticus' Holiness Code contains the most famous passage in the book: "Love your neighbor as yourself" (v. 18). That Code thus proposes self-love as the measure of all love. Perhaps a sense of possessing must necessarily come before a sense of genuine sharing. Jesus used this law, together with a Jewish prayer (Dt 6:5), to sum up the whole of the Law and the Prophets.

But it was Jesus who gave the word "neighbor" its universal meaning. In his concept, our neighbor is everyone created by God. Neither alien nor foe can be excluded. Jesus doesn't ask that we love our enemies as we love our closest friends. Our love for our enemies — those we don't like or who don't like us — isn't of the heart but of the will. Therefore to love them needn't be an *emotional* experience, but must be a decision to commit ourselves to serve the best interests of all other people.

Jesus sums it all up by saying that we should be perfect, just as our heavenly Father is perfect (v. 48). But the definition of the perfection that God expects has been argued from the beginning. It isn't to be confused with the ancient Greek notion of perfection, which is to arrive at a peak point and become changeless. As a famous epigram has it, the Greeks worshipped the holiness of beauty, while the Judeo-Christian tradition worships the beauty of holiness.

Through history, to assert the perfectibility of people has variously meant many possibilities: that there is some task in which all persons can perfect themselves technically; that we are capable of wholly subordinating ourselves to God's will; that we can attain to our natural end; that we can be entirely free of all moral defects; that we can become like self-regulating machines. There are also various kinds of misanthropes who wish to abolish the human race as it has been traditionally conceived: the infrahumanists, who would like to live with the animals; the transhumanists, who want to go beyond the finite sphere now; and the metahumanists, who have genetic dreams of "super-humanity" and other manipulations of nature.

Jesus' followers, of course, reject perfectionism in all of its naturalistic forms. We see that the apex of God's kind of perfection is compassion, a willingness to suffer with others, the object of which is always changing. Those who love in such an unconditional and non-selective way are true children of the God of limitless love.

Perhaps in the real world we can't act on this advice completely — for example, if we were a prisoner in a concentration camp toward sadistic guards — but they are ideals. And it's good to remember how non-violence has triumphed in many situations in our world: in the civil rights cause in the '60's in the United States, for example, in the Philippines revolution in the '80's, and in the bloodless revolution which brought the collapse of the Soviet Union in the '90's. It's good to remember, too, that to be a Christian isn't simply to be a genuinely good human being. Even pagans do good to those who are good to them. Machiavelli, for example, advises that, when you do good, spread it out, so people will remember; if, on the other hand, you should have to do evil, do it all at once, so that people might forget. We Christians are called to go beyond justice, and called even to the heroic charity of which Jesus speaks today.

St. Paul, never one to turn the other cheek gladly, in today's second reading presents the same call to holiness. He tells the Corinthians that they should forget their factions and pay attention to Christ — because you are the temple of God, and the Spirit of God dwells in you (v. 16). The Christian community at Corinth, or in our parish, is God's temple, one single entity. Those who foster factions destroy what God has built. Paul concludes the passage with that marvelous sentence: "Paul or Apollos or Kephas, or the world or life or death, or the present or the future: all belong to you, and you to Christ, and Christ to God" (v. 23).

It used to be said that vengeance belongs to God. In our secular times, it's the *State* that claims, "Vengeance is mine," and the State insists on the sole right to impose punishment. Is *personal* vengeance necessary when the State (or God) fails to provide justice? Should one make an exception to God's advice of kindness and mercy (Responsorial Psalm) in the case of some people whom we know as truly vile? Would mercy toward their like mock their victims? Should we be happy to see malefactors being torn at by giant birds, as in the paintings of Hieronymus Bosch and Hans Breugel, or ending in a tangle of rope dragged by the whale Moby Dick, as was the fate of Herman Melville's Captain Ahab?

In arousing feelings of hatred, in making us want to inflict pain on others, and then making us feel cheated for being unable to inflict it — in making us less human than we should be — vile people, dead or alive, provide a final touch of evil. In our dealings with other people, both friends and enemies, we're to be *magnanimous*: large-minded, wide open, generous — and holy. This is to put all smallness behind us, be it in our laws or in our hearts.

Consider the magnanimity and generosity of God in only one humble example of His gifts: the potato. Thousands of years before the Europeans adopted the potato, Andean civilizations were sustained by the many varieties that grew wild and were brought under cultivation. The true treasure of the Andes wasn't the gold the Spanish conquerors sought in the ground, but the potatoes they trampled there.

Though summarily rejected when Christopher Columbus brought it from the new world, the potato was one of the real legacies of his voyage. The current yearly value of the world's potato crop, nearly $100 billion, is three times greater than all the gold and silver ever carried out of the New World. Now the fourth most important food crop worldwide — after wheat, rice, and corn — the potato is expected to supply an even larger share of the world's essential nutrients in the next century if scientific manipulations of the potato's 230 known species and about 5,000 varieties succeed in expanding the potato's natural ability to grow almost anywhere. With research, the potato could do for many parts of the world today what it did for Europe in the 18th century, when the secure food supply it provided paved the way for the Industrial Revolution.

To imitate such generosity is to rise and soar with Christ. It's to reveal not only something of God, but what it means to be fully human. It's to be holy. This means life, not mere existence; this gives life to others, and to be a life-giver is to be a person for God, a true follower of Christ. Lord, teach us to be holy as you, our God, are holy!

EIGHTH SUNDAY IN ORDINARY TIME

Is 49:14f.   1 Cor 4:1-5   Mt 6:24-34

Christian Priorities

The Providence of God; How to Avoid Work; The Real Wealth;
Counting your Money; Trust in God; God as Father, Mother, and Rock

We hear a lot these days about security. While its pursuit is praiseworthy, it's sometimes a common excuse for the undue quest of worldly
goods. Proper priorities in that respect is what today's liturgical message is about.

In the Gospel, we're still in the Sermon on the Mount, dealing with
the essence of Christianity. As was his custom, Jesus at the outset stated
the basic principle on which the rest of the passage is commentary and
application. The Christian principle is that you can't serve God and
material possessions (v. 24). Then, as now, some considered wealth a
sign of divine favor. Jesus denies this and shows that wealth may even
be a barrier to God's will (though not necessarily). One who serves has
an allegiance to his master. Our possessions have a way of possessing
us. All things belong to God. We can buy and sell things, rearrange
them, and change them, but we can't create them. That's God's
prerogative. No one can say absolutely, "This is completely mine"; all
we can say is, "This is God's, and I'll use it as the owner intends."

The history of wealth, especially in industrial societies, teaches
that the Christian principle of considering people as always more
important than things has frequently been abandoned by those engaged
in the undue pursuit of money. The excessive pursuit of wealth is so
time-consuming as to cause the neglect of God. It has victimized needy
fathers of families; forced children to work in factories, shops, and
mines; manipulated women; and shamefully taken advantage of workers.

Regretfully, this same history also shows that it's the Christian
portion of the world's population that controls most of the world's
wealth. It doesn't seem to have dawned on some Christians that God
intends the blessings of creation for *all*, that there's presently enough for
each person's need but not enough for each person's greed, and that
many of us must live more simply so that others may simply live.

In getting our Christian priorities straight, we have to address many moral problems. The world population, now almost six billion, is double that of the late 1950's. In a century or so, the global population is likely to double, and the grim question is: Will all those people — nearly 12 billion of them — be able to provide decent lives for themselves without doing irreversible damage to the croplands, water resources, forests, fisheries, and other ecological resources on which life ultimately depends?

The debate on the subject has historically been divided into two camps. Neo-Malthusians, principally ecologists and biologists, predicted general disaster unless the population surge is contained. Cornucopians, mainly economists, argued conversely that as scarcity develops, it will surely be defeated by human inventiveness in raising crop yields and coping with diminishing resources.

These are now joined by a third view, which holds that products of human ingenuity like the science-based Green Revolution, in which the development of high-yield grains enabled food production to keep pace with the population explosion of the last quarter-century, do indeed hold the key to supporting an expanding populace. But ingenuity of this sort, some experts say, has been sputtering in recent years because of complacency and lack of support.

In the twenty-first century, one expert says, some countries will win the race between need and ingenuity, while others will fail and sink into varying degrees of poverty, violence, and environmental degradation. These failures will touch off national and regional crises.

The global projections for the future understate the problem in the Third World. According to the United Nations, Third World populations will nearly double in 30 years and increase by two and a half times before stabilizing. In some countries, a threefold or fourfold increase is expected.

Another problem to be addressed by Christian priorities is that a combination of rapid population growth and rural unemployment is leading to massive urbanization in areas which have never before seen such concentrations, including the creation of numerous megacities of over 10 million inhabitants in the developing countries. These cities impose serious environmental strains on the hinterlands — including the clearing of forests and savannas for fuel, shelter, and food production. The problem is exacerbated by rich countries' overconsumption of third world resources like timber.

If the optimists are wrong, we will have burned our bridges. The soils, waters, and forests will be irreversibly damaged, and our societies, especially the poorest ones, will be so riven with discord that even heroic efforts at social renovation will fail.

Material possessions are intrinsically good — but merely if used properly, like a row of zeros that have value only when a number is put in front of them. The number represents God. Wealth is a good that is, like the zeros, always subordinate to Him. It was by the deliberate idea of starting from zero that St. Francis of Assisi, who gave up his father's wealth for a life of poverty, came to enjoy earthly things as few people have enjoyed them.

When we find in money or other material possessions a rival salvation, we've found an idol — as hard, cold, and irrational as the golden calf worshipped by the Israelites under Moses, and as ineffective as the military power, national security, and political alliances for which they forsook the Lord. A bullish Dow-Jones industrial average, a rising Gross National Product, and designer clothes don't give eternal life. And there's no way in which anyone can earn a star or deserve a sunset.

If people want money to help their family, or to secure a decent independence, or to help others, it's praiseworthy. Certainly we should do our Christian utmost to overcome unemployment and alleviate poverty. Many people aren't in church today because they don't have decent clothes or haven't eaten properly for days. Many are getting their food from garbage cans and sleeping on sidewalk grates. In all the world, the distance between the rich and the poor is too great. Too often, people who spend a lot of time amassing wealth have allowed their money to become not their servant, but their god — a god which dominates but doesn't delight.

Jesus tells us (v. 25) not to *worry* about material things. He's not against advance planning or Social Security; he isn't advocating a shiftless, improvident attitude. He's warning against undue cares which make life colorless and joyless. He wants us to live in this universe detached, free, and serene because of confidence in our God. A sure measure of the depth of a loving relationship is, after all, the extent to which we put our trust in the other.

In terms of the basic needs, food and clothing, Jesus reminds us that life is more than food (v. 25), and that the God who gave us life will give whatever is necessary to support it. So worry is *needless*. Again, birds and other animals fascinatingly live day by day, fed by the heavenly Father (v. 26). But Jesus isn't recommending indolence. Birds work hard — but they don't *worry*. Worry is a *blindness* — a blindness to God's bounty, which provides so generously for the life even of birds, and is usually a blindness to God's love. Can any of us by worrying add a single moment to our life-span (v. 27)? But our lives are held in loving, all-powerful, and caring hands.

As for clothing, Jesus gives a lesson from the scarlet poppies and anemones and other wild flowers which bloom in profusion in the Holy Land Spring. Even the splendor of Solomon couldn't compare with them (v. 29). Their beauty and their peace contrast sharply with up-tight worriers who have the highest rates of ulcers, high blood pressure, and heart disease. What Jesus advocates for religious reasons, medical science now substantiates: laughing helps health.

Thomas Edison tried two thousand experiments in search of a filament for the light bulb. When none worked to his satisfaction, his assistant complained, "All our work is in vain. We've gotten nowhere!" "On the contrary," Edison replied, "we've come a long way and we've learned a lot. We now know that there are two thousand materials which will not make a good light bulb." The assistant was a worrier, Edison a doer who learned from setbacks.

All earthly attractions are fleeting. Even the resplendent Holy Land landscape lasts but a short time. Everything shrivels in the sun, the hills quickly turn brown after the rainy season, and needy peasants burn the dried-up flowers to heat their ovens. Even the luster of Solomon — that wise ruler, diplomat, military genius, and enormously wealthy king who rebuilt the Temple and a magnificent palace — lasted but a short time.

We have to have faith that God, who loves us more than He loves the flowers and the birds, will provide for us. For Matthew, who often deplores those of little faith (v. 30), faith means a confident trust in a loving and providing God. Matters of resplendent material possessions and worry about them are characteristic of unbelievers who don't know what God is like (v. 32). Worry is, therefore, essentially irreligious. It's not understandable among people whose heart is in their belief. The priorities of Jesus' advice to seek first the Kingdom of God (v. 33) are the same as in the Lord's Prayer, where *first* we pray for God's Kingdom to come, and then we ask for bread. God is central to our lives, all else is peripheral.

Blessed is the person who's too busy to worry in the daytime and too sleepy to worry at night. To avoid worry, live one day at a time. That motto has been adopted successfully by people with problems, with pain, and with diseases like alcoholism. The Lord's Prayer, in which we're taught to say, "Give us this day our *daily* bread," provides us with the secret of all internal peace. If our savings of material possessions become an unneeded *accumulation*, they're subject to the teachings here. If we're to avoid worry, we must live today fully, leaving our tomorrow to God's care in a spirit of faith. As someone has written:

> Yesterday is history.
> Tomorrow is a mystery.
> Today is a gift.
> That's why we call it "the present."

That's essentially what today's first reading says. Its message, the absolute trustworthiness of God, parallels the Gospel. From a selection of poems addressed to Zion (Jerusalem) in Isaiah, this passage is a profoundly consoling statement of God's tender love for Zion, and resembles a dialogue between loving parents and children. In the first verse (v. 14) Zion, like a child, expresses her despair. Jerusalem has been taken into exile, and is now facing the discouraging work of rebuilding. Jerusalem feels, as many people do, forsaken and forgotten.

Isaiah is the first to touchingly identify God's love as being like the tender love of a mother for her infant child (v. 15). Matthew, on the other hand, shows God as a loving and provident father, and today's Responsorial Psalm presents God as a rock. The Song of Songs presents God as a marriage partner. The most adequate images of God are based on intimate human relationships. The totality of the images is that God is our all.

St. Paul in today's second reading (our last this year from his First Letter to the Corinthians) is aware that the Corinthians have already decided as a human tribunal (v. 3) that he was not as eloquent nor as clever as some of the other leaders. That doesn't concern him. He's mindful of having to answer to his people, to himself, and to God — as must we all. Paul is like a civil servant whose position as administrator of an estate increases his degree of responsibility. Paul makes the point, however, that, even with this superior position, he's still only administering his master's property, not his own. What's most confidence-inspiring to Paul is that it's the Lord who's the one to judge him (v. 4).

We can leave church today with many questions. Do my priorities correspond with the Gospel's? Should I rethink them? Do I worry overmuch? About the wrong things? Am I too security-minded? Does my idea of God include His having a mother's tender love, a father's providing care, the stability of a rock, and the intimacy of a marriage partner? Are my material possessions consonant with my spiritual outlook and a proper set of values? Now and again it's worthwhile to do a spiritual "Spring cleaning," no matter what the time of year.

NINTH SUNDAY IN ORDINARY TIME
Dt 11:18, 26-28   Rm 3:21-25, 28   Mt 7:21-27

Faith Is as Faith Does
Faith and Practice; The Confidence Born of Faith;
How Can You Get Right with God?; What's God's Will for Me?

Who is the most dangerous person in the world? The burglar? The drug addict? The sex fiend? The homicidal maniac? The person who maligns you at every opportunity? In the long run, it's more likely the person who, with attractive personality and shiny countenance, sets out to deceive others by seductive ways of thinking and acting. This person fulfills the observation of *Hamlet*, that "one may smile, and smile, and be a villain."

Today's readings denounce this type of person and demand that our lives and our faith be consistent with each other. The first part of today's Gospel (vv. 21-23), the end of the Sermon on the Mount, echoes the first section of the Lord's Prayer. In the Lord's Prayer we pray, "Hallowed be Thy name"; here we learn that not everybody who cries the name of the Lord is acceptable. Lip service isn't enough; faith must be alive and effective. In the Lord's Prayer we pray, "Thy Kingdom come"; here we learn of those who will enter the Kingdom. In the Lord's Prayer we ask that God's will be done; here we learn that, to enter God's Kingdom, we must *do* the will of our heavenly Father. That's the test: doing the will of our Father in heaven (v. 21).

St. Paul's letter to the Romans adds that, for all who have used

Jesus' name under false pretenses, the day of reckoning will come and they will be exposed (v. 23). The saved will be those who have been both hearers and doers (vv. 24-27). Jesus' words are a *call to action*, not mere understanding or fine words: "Everyone who listens to these words of mine *and acts on them* will be like a wise man" (v. 24). Many people — all of us at one time or other — confess God with our lips and deny Him with our lives. It's seldom hard to recite the creed, but it's often hard to live the Christian life.

It's important for us to remember that the judgment, the rainy season (v. 25), will come. Jesus the woodworker knew what he was talking about in the building of houses. His illustration isn't that of a theoretician, but of a practical man. In Palestine the torrential rains of November to April often destroy houses that aren't solidly built. Jesus asks that we not only *hear*, or *assent*, but that we *perform* as well. Even non-Christian students can pass examinations with distinction in Christian doctrine; it happens all the time. But our religion isn't simply a matter of knowledge, but of commitment. Knowledge must be translated into action, theory into practice, and theology (the study of God) into theophily (the love of God).

It's with some of us as it was with some of the leaders of the people in Our Lord's time: many prefer the outward symbols to the inner reality. In today's first reading, Moses told the people to bind God's words at their wrist and let them be a pendant on their forehead (v. 18). We're not sure whether this was purely figurative, to symbolize thinking correctly and doing right actions, but later interpretation resulted in the phylacteries, as they're called, being tied by leather straps to the left arm and the forehead. The phylacteries were little boxes that contained sacred texts, especially the *Shema* (Dt 6:4), the great Jewish prayer which Jesus cited as part of the greatest commandment in the Law. But Jesus condemned certain Pharisees for widening their phylacteries to call attention to their being persons of prayer.

Another outward sign that was meant to express inward acceptance of God's word still exists among religious Jews: the *mezuzah*, a small container at one's doorway which holds little parchments on which are written Scripture texts. It recalls God's promise to bless His people in their coming in and in their going out of their homes (Dt 28:6). We, too, have outward symbols that are supposed to represent inner realities. One is our custom, when the Gospel is announced at Mass, of tracing the cross upon our forehead, lips, and breast, to remind ourselves that the Gospel must be on our minds, upon our lips, and in our hearts, always available to be acted upon.

In today's reading from St. Paul's letter to the Romans, we learn that part of the reason for the hostility between the Jews and the Gentiles was the differences in their answers to the question, "How can a person get right with God?" The Jews answered that it could be accomplished by one's doing scrupulously all that was demanded by the Law of Moses. But the Jews, having broken the Law time and time again, had nothing with which to defend their cause. And the Gentiles through the many philosophies that guided them were also unable to please God and do His will.

For the Jews, God Himself broke the impasse. The righteousness of God (v. 21) is shown to be apart from the Mosaic Law. The Christian dispensation ushers in a new era, is independent of the Mosaic Law, and is destined to take its place. The concrete showing of divine uprightness is Jesus Christ. He is fully comprehended only by those who have faith in him, which faith is the beginning of salvation. All have sinned (v. 23), and the advantage of the Mosaic Law is that it made people aware of personal, individual actions by which they do wrong. Humankind by these actions has fallen short of its moral goal and estranged itself from the intimate presence of God.

God's coming to the rescue has nothing to do with anything that humankind earned. People are justified freely by God's *grace* (v. 24). Jesus' death on the cross made possible the establishment of a right relationship between us and God that nothing else could do (v. 25). The only way anyone can understand that is through Jesus' teachings, life, and death. Many of the Jews simply couldn't accept this.

The basic way for us to establish a right relationship with God is to tie our humble performance to the love and the grace which God offers us in Jesus. We're to try to do good not because we're afraid of God, but because we love Him: not because sin is breaking God's law, but because it's breaking God's heart. God loved us so much that He gave us Jesus as an expiation (v. 25) — not in the sense of placating an angry God, but in the sense of enabling God's forgiveness of our sins. The benefits of Jesus' expiation are shared by all who have faith.

There are only two forbidden "F" words in much of today's culture. One is "Failure." The other is "Faith." We're not to be "street angels, house devils" — those who hypocritically profess their faith in public, but in private act in ways that contradict it. Those are the kind

of people who, as we said in the beginning, are dangerous. Let's pray
that we may in both faith and action be true imitators of Jesus, one of
whose chief glories is that his actions were consonant with his faith. If
we act upon that, we will be like the wise person in today's Gospel who
built his house upon rock. Then when the rains of temptation fall, and
the floods of evil come, and the winds of suffering and doubt blow and
buffet the spiritual house, neither we nor our house will fall.

FIRST SUNDAY OF LENT
Gn 2:7-9; 3:1-7   Rm 5:12-19   Mt 4:1-11

Is Humankind Evil?
Temptation — Putting God and Us "To the Test"; A New Beginning;
Men like Gods; Naked Human Nature; Sin and Grace; Reality of the Devil;
God's Permission of Temptations; Be Merciful, O Lord!

Many modern inventions make it increasingly difficult to get away
alone to think out the problems of our life: for example, the noise of
portable radios (other peoples' if not our own) and television. Yet there
are some things we can work out only alone. At times we have to stop
doing and start thinking. For this we need to get away, especially at a
time like Lent.

That's the way it was with Jesus. Shortly after his baptism, he got
away to fast, to pray, and to think. At his baptism, the voice from heaven
had said that he is God's beloved son, and that God's favor rests on him.
That provided part of the reason why the forces of evil were interested
in testing his power. There are several reasons why Jesus would have
been willing to allow such a test. One is provided by the whole salvation
history of humankind given in today's first two readings.

Today's portion of Genesis, a book of humankind's salvation
history, comes in two parts. The first tells how God created us from the
earth and breathed life into us. God, in making humankind, made
something very special. Then God placed us in a garden, among whose
fruit trees was the tree of life, a symbol of immortality, and the tree of

the knowledge of good and evil, a symbol of God's right to determine what's good and what's bad.

The second part of the reading presents the mythic drama of the "original" sin. The exact meaning of "original sin" has many interpretations. One is that Eve, the woman, was the responsible one for committing it. Before Jesus and after, throughout history the story of Adam and Eve in Genesis has had a more profoundly negative impact on women than any other biblical story. It has led writers to depict Eve as subordinate and inferior to Adam, because she was created after and from him, and as weak, seductive, and evil, because she fell and tempted Adam to fall too. Many women, ancient and modern, find such misogynist views unacceptable.

In the matter of the serpent speaking only to Eve, for example, some commentators have interpreted this to mean that woman is morally weaker than man and thus an easier prey. But this is mere speculation. The text itself doesn't say why the serpent spoke to the woman. The text could allow speculation instead that the serpent questioned her because she was the more intelligent of the two, or because she had a better understanding of the divine command, or because she was more independent. Likewise, Eve's so-called "temptation" of Adam is deduced from the fact that, after she herself had eaten the forbidden fruit, she gave some of it to Adam who was quick to blame her for the fact. The tree of the knowledge of good and evil represented moral autonomy. The temptation for us to "be like gods" — a proud reliance on self rather than on God — is still with us.

Genesis chooses the serpent (3:1) to represent evil because of the snake's powerful grip on the human imagination. Found everywhere — not only on the ground, but also in the depths of the sea as well as in trees — snakes have been a worldwide obsession of humankind then and now. The snake symbolizes many things, at the same time — paradoxically — eternal life and agonizing death. With regard to eternal life, early peoples, finding snakes' cast-off skins and their bright new scales and not knowing that in truth snakes shed their old skin when they outgrow it, thought the snake had been born again, and thus that the snake knows the secret of immortality. With regard to agonizing death, people have always been fascinated by the snake's cunning in hunting its prey, and by its ability to kill with a single bite.

Because of their hinged jaws, many snakes can consume meals

double their own body weight and three times the width of their heads. From early times, therefore, people have endowed snakes with cosmic powers. Egg-eating snakes are especially symbolic: primitives explained a lunar eclipse by a cosmic serpent engulfing the moon. People in Cambodia to this day warn the disappearing moon of danger; they try to drive away the attacking evil serpent by gunfire, drums, and other noise.

In India, the snake is associated with the god Shiva and his wife. It is one of Shiva's symbols of fertility, a symbol aided by the snake's number of offspring; snakes often lay sixty eggs at a time. It's easy to see, therefore, that many people who worship the serpent show cautious admiration rather than fear and loathing.

The Genesis story describes well the lure, the deceit, and the deviousness of all temptation. Temptation is like the snake called the South American "Bushmaster," which is utterly enticing. Its multicolored scales reflect the sunlight and, as the snake glides along, those scales dance and flash with all the colors of the rainbow. Those who've seen the snake marvel at its beauty; they talk about being mesmerized! Yet that snake is so deadly that its venom can kill a person in twenty minutes!

In Genesis, distortion follows on distortion on the part of the woman, the serpent, and the man, so that God's truth is forgotten and the serpent's lies prevail. Both Adam (Hebrew word for "humankind") and Eve (Hebrew for "life") were jointly responsible. With the couple's failure, they realize their nakedness — a nakedness greater than the merely physical. They now know that they're exposed, frail, and vulnerable.

St. Paul, in today's section of his letter to the Romans, reveals what's basic to the dogma of original sin. Through one person sin entered the world, he says (v. 12), and through sin death came to all. The death brought about by original sin is both biological and spiritual, being the separation of people from God, Who is the unique source of life. Into this decay comes Jesus. As Adam was at the root of all sin and death, Jesus, the new Adam, is at the root of all pardon and life. His righteousness outweighs all that Adam and Eve had done and gives humankind a new lease on life. One way in which he proved that is the way he handled temptation.

For Jesus' temptation, the scene changes from the watered Garden of Eden to the desert west of Jericho in Judea. This scene follows the account of Jesus' baptism and the coming of the Spirit upon him with the voice of the Father declaring him to be beloved.

In any desert, with its boundless vista and majestic sky, there is an awesome silence, seemingly magnified by the uninhabited horizon. Its forms are bold and suggestive. The mind is beset by light and space. The desert sky is encircling, majestic, terrible, infinitely vaster than that of rolling countryside and forest lands. In the unobstructed sky the clouds appear more massive, and seem to measure the enormous distances by a stately progression toward the horizon.

But there are drawbacks. In the desert, the basic algebra of the existence of every traveler or nomad is: water equals life. During the day, the sun tightens into a glowing white fireball, until the solid wall of noonday heat stops people from traveling. People then take shelter anywhere they can, their head full of dreams of cool water.

And there are animals that eke out an existence in the desert. The Souf Museum in Egypt exhibits some of them. There's a collection of venomous snakes the size of earthworms, intestinal worms almost the size of boa constrictors, scorpions the size of huge lobsters, horned beetles as big as Princess telephones, hairy spiders, bristling lizards, and blood-sucking centipedes. The museum's real spectacle, though, is a formaldehyde-filled glass in which fat gray blobs float around like rotten grapes; beneath it a typewritten card in three languages identifies the blobs as "Blood-Engorged Ticks."

Beetles scurry across the dunes, pursued by lizards that spend most of their time burrowed under the sand. After sunset, hyenas leave their holes, announcing their presence with bloodcurdling cries. They often kill livestock and people traveling alone. At night, the stars seem to leap out of the clear sky, and there's a wide range of contrasting vistas from mountains to plains, colors across the spectrum, and living things from the primitive to the intricate.

For people in the desert, there's a terrible emptiness. At night, the solitude and fear seem magnified many times over, broken only by the distant barking of jackals. And the worst enemy is yourself. The nomads who live in the desert say there are evil spirits (*jinn*) that live there, and can spin your head around until you can't tell west from east. Alone, in an unchanging landscape of sand and rock, you begin to lose touch with reality. You enter a surreal dimension where grim figures seem to follow you, only to disappear when you turn your head. At night you hear spectral footsteps, and the shadows that flick among the rocks seem to be alive with malevolent power. Worse than that, you sense inside yourself the presence of strange, primitive, violent beings you hardly know. A wife traveling through a desert with her husband said to him, "I keep thinking that I might change into a werewolf or a vampire, and cut your throat while you're asleep!"

Jesus' experience, though it came from an external source, was this struggle within. Matthew tells us that he fasted for forty days and forty nights (v. 2). The sacred number forty is frequent in Scripture: Israel wandered in the desert for forty years, and Moses spent forty days and nights on Sinai. It simply means a long time.

The central theme of Jesus' tests is basically the same as for Adam and Eve: obedience to God. The first temptation is, "If you are the Son of God, command that these stones become loaves of bread" (v. 3). The phrase, "Son of God," refers to the messianic king. It will be repeated by the leaders and the crowds at the crucifixion. The enticement to change stones into bread is a temptation to lose confidence in God's providence for ordinary material needs. It's a temptation for Jesus to use his power with the people in the time-honored way of political bribery: the "bread and circuses" of ancient Rome, today's pork-barrel give-aways. Jesus' answer from Deuteronomy (8:3) indicates that most of humanity's needs are spiritual, not material.

That temptation, that Jesus *distrust* divine providence by taking power into his own hands, doesn't work, and so it's followed by another: to *presume* on God's providence. From the parapet of the Temple (v. 5) where there's a sheer drop of several hundred feet to a populous area below, Satan tempts Jesus to throw himself down (v. 6), with the pious assurance from Scripture (Ps 91:11) that God will protect the just. It was consonant with the expectation of a Messiah who could never suffer or be defeated, and certainly not die. Besides, it would be thrilling for the crowds in the Temple courts to see a man throwing himself down from the dizzy Temple height into the Cedron Valley below, and live. This vain ostentation would not, however, glorify God. Jesus' reply, again from Deuteronomy (6:16), is admirably to this point: No one should demand miracles of God as evidence of God's care for His people (v. 7).

The third temptation is to *compromise*. Don't aim so high! Come to terms! Don't try to change the world — become like it! Go "halvesies": there's plenty of territory for all; just give a little; live and let live; don't be too absolute. Then people will serve you, and we'll all get along just fine. It's the most subtle of all three temptations. Delivered when Jesus is lonely, weak, and friendless, it tries to play upon the human craving for power, fame, and wealth. Taking Jesus in imagination to a mountain (v. 8), it presents him with a picture of Egyptian wonders, Grecian loveliness, Roman power, the wealth of Indian princes.

Satan says, "All these I shall give you" (v. 9). He could say this because, after the fall, all humankind is, in a certain sense, under his power. Jesus meets Satan's audacity with sternness: "The Lord, your God, shall you worship, and him alone shall you serve" (v. 10). Jesus had won! A river of grace had sprung up in the desert.

He reversed the sin in the Garden! In the Garden, people had wanted to become God, and here God in Jesus entrusted his frail humanity to overcome humanity's pretensions to divinity. His vanquished enemy left him (v. 11), but only for a while. The devil will return at such times as when Peter tried to persuade Jesus not to take the way of suffering. Perhaps the worst time of all was in the Garden of Gethsemane, when the tempter tried to get him to give up the idea of the cross — that cross which in the end meant Jesus' victory and Satan's defeat.

The temptations of Adam and Eve had been the exaltation of self. The temptations of Israel were to abandon God. The temptations of Jesus were to abuse his identity and mission. Unlike the others, Jesus used his freedom to choose the good. Temptations now assail us, in ways known best to each of us. All are based on various ways of sinning against the great commandment to love God with all our heart, soul, and might. As with Jesus, many of our temptations come through our gifts: if good looks, to use them to get away with things; if brains, to look with disdain on the efforts of others; if a facility with words, to use them for selfish gain.

Jesus has already shown how we must overcome our root temptations: through doing penance, engaging in prayer, and giving extra attention to the word of God. We have an opportunity for all this, in addition to giving more attention to the commitment of our baptism, especially during Lent.

SECOND SUNDAY OF LENT
Gn 12:1-4   2 Tm 1:8-10   Mt 17:1-9

God Still Speaks: Listen to Him!
Our Call to Holiness; True Greatness; Faith; Joy and Hardship; Perspective on
Suffering; Suffering and Leadership; Trust in the Lord; Let Go, and Let God!

When the preacher's car broke down on a country road, he walked to a
nearby roadhouse to use the phone. After calling for a tow truck, he
spotted his old friend, Frank, drunk and shabbily dressed at the bar.
"What happened to you, Frank?" asked the good reverend. "You used
to be rich."

Frank told a sad tale of bad investments that had led to his
downfall. "Go home," the preacher said. "Open your Bible at random,
stick your finger on the page and there will be God's answer."

Some time later, the preacher bumped into Frank, who was
wearing a Gucci suit, sporting a Rolex watch, and had just stepped out
of a Mercedes. "Frank," said the preacher, "I'm glad to see things really
turned around for you."

"Yes, preacher, and I owe it all to you," said Frank. I opened my
Bible, put my finger down on the page, and there was the answer —
Chapter 11."

Aside from misuses of the Bible, the scriptural readings in the
liturgies of Lent contain many lessons. We must reflect deeply on what
seems helpful to our personal situation. Today's readings speak of our
call to holiness, of true greatness, of faith and trust, of the loneliness of
leadership, of hardship in joy, of suffering seen in perspective, and
much more. Of them all, let's ponder the idea that God still speaks to
people, and we should listen to Him.

Our first reading — the first historical passage in the Bible, the
previous chapters of Genesis having dealt with pre-history — begins a
family photo-album of our forefathers in faith to be shown on the next
three Sundays: Abraham, Moses, and David. Today we see the seventy-
five-year-old Abram, to whom God appeared in his home town of Haran
in Mesopotamia to tell him to travel to Canaan to fulfill the destiny God
had in mind for him there.

Although the possessions of this nomad weren't many, it's not difficult for us to imagine Abram's hardships in having to leave his home, his family, and all the things that made up his world, to face the perils and uncertainty of the unknown. But Abram loved God and lived his life searching for God's voice and, being a good man, when he heard it he took the risk of letting go of all that was secure and familiar, to journey by faith into the completely unknown. Striking as it is that he obeyed, even more striking is his swiftness. There's no sense of self-protection of the kind that too often characterizes our world. Today's Responsorial Psalm echoes this response of faith.

A couple of thousand years later, Jesus likewise listened and obeyed. It had become obvious that he was going to suffer and die at the hands of the leaders of the people, whom he had challenged and deprived of income. Now, as he was preparing for the ultimate letting go, he needed to listen to his heavenly Father to learn whether he was right in setting his face to Jerusalem for further confrontation with worldly power. For all those subjects of prayer, he went up a mountain, mountains being associated in the Bible with experiencing God, receiving revelations, places of prayer, and favorite retreats for Jesus.

He took with him the three who would be closest to him in the scandal of his passion: Peter, James, and John. The prayer of Jesus with his heavenly Father also involved two men cherished by all Jews: Moses and Elijah. Moses represented the Law given to him on Mount Sinai, Elijah the prophets who spoke bluntly in God's name.

The ways in which their experiences paralleled Jesus' experience is fascinating. Moses found God on a mountain-top and his face shone from the glory of that meeting. Elijah found God in a still small voice, on the same mountain-top. This place, apart from and above the turmoil, was important for Moses and Elijah — a place called Horeb (or Sinai) — because there they met God and forgot themselves. God's voice came to Jesus on the mountain to strengthen him to take the hard road. God spoke from a cloud — no ordinary cloud, but the luminous and mysterious *shekinah*, familiar to believing Jews as the saving presence of God. A "pillar of cloud" had led the Jews out of Egypt. When their tabernacle was completed, a cloud had covered it, and the glory of the Lord had filled it. It was in a cloud that God had given the tables of the Law to Moses. And a cloud had filled Solomon's temple at its dedication.

Jesus' experience of God wasn't only for him but for his followers. God's voice tells us all to listen to Jesus. Anyone who does that can be initiated more deeply into the life of Jesus. Peter, the man of action, glimpsed in this meeting with God the first steps of contemplation. He experienced, without really understanding, the wonder of God, and he longed to stay there. This is the magic, the mystery of God in our lives. Whenever God's almighty Power and Presence touch us in ways beyond our normal experience, we're struck with awe and wonder. At such times words fail us; like Peter, we can only babble; the babbling makes little sense — except to God — who understands because He reads our heart.

Peter succumbed to it all. He babbled foolishly about building three tents, alluding to the annual Jewish feast of Succoth (or Tabernacles, or booths, or tents). Originally an agricultural feast which commemorated the Israelites' having made little huts to spend the night in the fields during harvest, it developed into a commemoration of their living in tents during their desert journey from Egypt. One of their most joyous feasts, it was often called simply the Feast of God. The huts came to be lined with presents for the children. Peter was comparing the joy of today's scene with the most joyful setting he could imagine.

Hidden within his babbling was the germ of his real desire: "I want to stay with you." God read the desire and granted it — but later, and in God's own way. Peter had opened his heart and had risked being spontaneous and seemingly foolish, but it was a true response of a child of God to the almighty and loving Father, and it bore fruit. We have the beginning of wisdom when we risk letting the coming of God into our lives cause us to wonder, to be awe-struck, and perhaps even to babble.

Today's reading from the Second Letter to Timothy looks back to the first reading and forward to the Gospel. It reminds us that God hasn't stopped speaking to people. As Abram was called by God, and as Jesus listened to his heavenly Father, people of all time are called to become holy. But the Good News whereby God speaks to us can entail hardship. The timid and fearful Timothy is being asked to preach the Gospel despite the fact that Paul is now in jail for doing just that. But Paul and Timothy recognize that God's word is a Gospel of power, of salvation, of the expression of God's eternal purpose, of immortal life, of service, and — above all — it's the Good News of Jesus Christ.

Jesus speaks to us, of course, through the Gospel. He speaks also through members of his Body, his Church, because "where two or three are gathered together in my name, there am I in the midst of them." He speaks through the Sacraments: for example, nourishing our life with his life in Communion; in the Sacrament of Reconciliation, harmonizing us with God and with all Jesus' people; and in the Sacrament of Marriage, ministering His grace in and through hardships and joys to growth into the fullness of life. During Lent, he speaks to us most especially through the Sacrament of Baptism, for which many candidates are now preparing.

A story is told to illustrate the fact that God is always with us. One night a man had a dream. He dreamed he was walking along the beach with the Lord. Across the sky flashed scenes from his life. In each scene he noticed two sets of footprints in the sand — one belonging to him and the other to the Lord. When the last scene flashed before him he looked back at the footprints and noticed that many times along the path there was only one set of footprints.

He also noted that this happened during the lowest and saddest times in his life. This bothered him, and he questioned the Lord: "Lord, you said that if I decided to follow you, you would walk beside me all the way. But I notice that during the most troublesome times of my life, there was only one set of footprints. I don't understand why, when I needed you most, you deserted me." The Lord replied, "My precious one, I love you and would never leave you. During your times of trial and suffering when you saw only one set of footprints, I was carrying you."

In God's calling Abram, in His making Jesus known, and in His calling us, there are similarities. With all, God takes the initiative. For all, God made promises that at times seem outlandish: to the seventy-five-year-old childless Abram, that his descendants would become a great nation; to the scared disciples, that Jesus is God's beloved Son; to the fearful Timothy, that Jesus has destroyed death and restored life; to us, that God is with us through thick and thin. All know that life involves hardship: for Abram, an uprooting from his native land; for Jesus, his passion and death; for all disciples, adversities; for us, troubles that seem sometimes to be without measure.

Our Lenten journey is a symbol of the total road of our lives: sometimes marked by monotony ("Most people lead lives of quiet desperation"), sometimes by changes, and sometimes by the need to move on in order to grow. That's often difficult. We've grown into the persons we are and acquired much baggage on the way — habits, opinions, peculiarities — just as we clutter up our rooms and houses with all kinds of bits and pieces which we don't think about until we have to move elsewhere. Abram didn't want to move, and neither did Peter. Lent is a time to examine our situation. The Gospel is to comfort the afflicted and afflict the comfortable.

At times the road seems to stretch far ahead of us, and we're tempted to speed down it without much thought, or to stray on the way, or just to stay put and not go anywhere. Lent is an opportunity to go forward to an open-bordered land that God will show us. We'll find God not in noise or distractions, but in prayer to God, in communion with one another, and in deep quiet with ourselves. Having found God's voice, we listen, and having truly listened we obey: We "let go, and let God."

THIRD SUNDAY OF LENT
Ex 17:3-7   Rm 5:1f., 5-8   Jn 4:5-42 (or 4:4-15, 19-26, 39, 40-42)

Insights into Yourself
Recognizing Jesus as God's Gift; Drinking Water and Living Water (Grace);
Testing God; The Waters of Salvation; Reminders of Baptism;
Who Jesus Is for Us and Who We Are for Him; Don't Harden Your Heart;
Our Thirst for Life; Jesus' Thirst for Us; Awakening our Faith

Life is rich in meaning, but it takes a poet's vision to plumb its mysterious depth and wonder. Too often the beauty which the poet longs to share is lost on leaden souls. When Jesus had this problem, he took people where they were, patiently teaching them and ultimately bringing them to a share of his vision.

The elevation of the Samaritan woman in today's Gospel story is one of the greatest encounter texts in St. John's Gospel, and gives expression to one of John's central themes: that Jesus communicates divine life to believers. This can also happen to us, if we too stay with Jesus and let him reveal in love who we are and who we can become. For reasons that went way back in history Samaria was hostile territory for Jews. But it was there that Jesus, weary from his day's travel, sat down (v. 6) on the coping of Jacob's well, while his disciples went off into the nearby town to buy provisions (v. 8).

It wasn't bad enough that the person Jesus encountered at the well was a Samaritan: she was also a woman. A man wasn't to greet any woman in the street, even his wife or daughter. For any offense against these proprieties a married woman was liable to divorce, an unmarried woman open to the worst suspicions. In his morning prayer, a man blessed God "who hath not made me a Gentile, a slave, or a woman."

Jesus went against all that. He associated with women regularly: to Martha he confessed his divinity, to Mary Magdalene he would confide his resurrection victory, and to this Samaritan woman he speaks of his mission. Here, Jesus faced the added obstacle that this was a woman of bad reputation. Because of the heat of the day, women usually came for water in the cool of the dawn or evening. But, to avoid encounters, this Samaritan woman came at noon, a fact that marked her isolation as a result of her ill repute. Her loneliness would speak strongly to the Savior of all people in need.

How did Jesus meet her need? How does he meet the needs of all of us? He first recognized the privation — in this case the need for grace. Then, as a poet with vision, he took ordinary objects that are near at hand — in this case, water — to lead from the obvious, which is present and visible, to the spiritual and less obvious. The gentle one lowered the race barrier and overturned the accepted male superiority. And he overcame her aloofness by doing the woman a service. That *service* was *not* to do *her* a favor, for that might make her feel inferior and under obligation, but to ask her to do *him* a favor: the favor of a drink of water on this hot day. That would make her feel good, as doing a favor does.

The dialogue between Jesus and the Samaritan woman is instructive about Jesus' belief in women's ability to respond generously with all their heart if they're convinced of the integrity of another person. When Jesus made the first move, the woman, accustomed to disrespect from men, was defensive. She sought to put Jesus in the wrong by reminding him of the enmity between their respective races. Jesus didn't meet her aggressiveness with more aggression, as people often tend to do, but calmly led on from an ordinary request for a drink of water to a higher level, by his reference to God and to himself, which stimulated her curiosity: "If you knew the gift of God and who is saying to you, 'Give me a drink,' you would have asked him and he would have given you living [running] water" (v. 10).

Suffering from lack of water is also what today's reading from Exodus is about. The Jews' journey through the desert is filled with griping and grumbling. Just after they left Egypt, when they heard that the Egyptians were pursuing them, they complained that they would be better off as slaves of the Egyptians than dead; God delivered them. Later they complained that they had no food; God sent them quail.

Today's passage tells of their complaining about their thirst, a figure of human longing for spiritual satisfaction. The place was called Massah and Meribah, two words commemorated in our Responsorial Psalm which sound very much like "place of testing" and "place of quarreling." When God told Moses to strike the rock, and the water would flow (v. 6), again there is deeper meaning: namely, that water — so essential for life — comes from God. And, just as Jesus speaks in today's Gospel of God's *gift* of running water, the emphasis of old was also upon the gift.

The woman, though not understanding exactly what Jesus was talking about, heard his veiled reference to his being somebody special. Something about him — perhaps his gentleness, or maybe his sincerity — kept her seeking in the only way she knew. That was by a defensive scorn which begged to be convinced that maybe here was a unique someone who could satisfy *her own* heart's well-repressed longing to be special to someone — special for who she *is* rather than for what she can *give*. Jesus understood her hidden longing even better than she did, and so he began to lead her to where he, the healer, could astound her by the truth that indeed he is the Christ.

As he did with others, in the face of misunderstandings Jesus the teacher repeated his idea in different words. Here, he wanted to teach a lesson about grace. He told her that whoever drinks the water he would give would never thirst (v. 14), words from the Jewish Scriptures (Si 24:29) which anyone with spiritual insight would have recognized. Jesus, knowing that every human being has a thirst so vast that only things eternal can slake it, continued that the water which he would give would become a spring *within* every person who receives him. The woman expressed — perhaps with a sneer — her wish for this water, if only for the practical reason that if she had it she wouldn't be thirsty or have to keep coming here to draw water (v. 15).

At this point, when Jesus thought she could take it, he boldly went to a real problem: her immorality. He did it by abruptly changing the subject — "Go call your husband" (v. 16) — and this caught her off guard. She was quick to parry that she didn't have a husband (v. 17). She told the truth, but not the whole truth. Jesus proceeded to challenge her by telling her the whole truth: that she had had five husbands, and the man she had now was not her husband (v. 18). What kind of woman would have practiced the serial polyandry of our time in those days of intense disapproval? A woman no doubt of great passion, despite her faults — and a woman in need.

That he tell this passionate, loving, needing woman things about herself without anyone telling him, things that she wouldn't want known, was scary. The effect was magnificent. "Sir," she began (v. 19), indicating a possible move toward faith, and continued, "I can see that you are a prophet." Pointing to Mt. Gerizim with a trembling hand and referring to the dispute between the Jews and the Samaritans about where God should be worshiped (v. 20), what she *really* wanted to ask was where she could find God. He answered that she didn't have to go anywhere special to find God: He's everywhere (vv. 21f.).

The woman was no longer contentious. So, with an incomprehensible concession, Jesus rewarded her with his first open declaration of the great and staggering truth that he is the Messiah (v. 26). Here in Samaria it was possible to reveal it, and she was ready for it. His procedure reaped marvelous results: a changed life for the woman and an apostle in a hurry to share her experience. She left her water jar: she was coming back, and in the meantime she wanted Jesus to drink. She broke out of the disabilities imposed on her as a woman and a Samaritan, and brought her townspeople to Jesus.

As a result, the people wanted his company, so they invited him to stay with them (v. 40). After they saw for themselves for two days, they completely surrendered to him. The Samaritan woman had come a long way. She had initially identified Jesus as a Jew, then as a prophet, then as possibly the long-awaited Messiah, and finally with her townspeople she proclaimed him to be the Savior of the world (v. 42). She was the first missionary in John's Gospel and the first woman to proclaim the Good News.

St. Paul in today's second reading provides a beautiful reflection on the other readings. Whereas God in the desert and Jesus at the well offered water to slake *physical* thirst, in bringing about salvation through Jesus God offers to slake *spiritual* thirst by presenting us with peace and hope. Peace (v. 1), the Hebrew *Shalom*, means all the blessings of God. Jesus offers hope that never fails (v. 5), because through him we have gained access to God (v. 2). In short, God's new gift is grace — water with a difference: living water, life-giving water.

The procedure begins with our baptism, of which today's water images remind us. All over the world at this moment, people are preparing for commitment to Jesus in baptism at Easter. The Spirit of God, given to Jesus at his baptism in the Jordan and conferred on us at ours, is the bond uniting us with the triune God: making us heirs of heaven, sharers of God's life, children of the Father, and brothers and sisters of Jesus. Baptism also unites us in love with one another, urging us to be generous with one another, urging and enabling us to love even those who injure us. Whereas in the theology of St. Thomas Aquinas all the Sacraments are ordered toward the Eucharist, in the theology of St. John and St. Paul all the Sacraments are ordered toward baptism. To them, all the other Sacraments are to augment baptism or to impart a new aspect to our baptism.

We, like the Samaritan woman, should be acquiring insights into ourselves and unfolding our faith slowly to full realization. Lent is a journey toward self-authenticity. We can't master ourselves into that or anything else, though, if we don't understand ourself. There are mirrors for the face, but the only mirror for the spirit is wise self-reflection. In order to undertake any Lenten program wisely, we need understanding: either our own, or borrowed. Many people, like the Samaritan woman, are unaware that they don't know, and others think they know when they don't.

Just as Jesus chose in the Samaritan woman a seemingly unsuitable and unexpected apostle in an undreamt-of place, so too he wills to find generous apostles in us. Like the Samaritan woman, we must get insights into ourselves. We must stay with Jesus, listen to what he says and, if we don't understand, keep asking questions. He will teach. He will explain. But to be insightful, we must be honest, open, generous, and trusting in God. And, as today's Responsorial Psalm says, "If today you hear his voice, harden not your hearts."

Fourth Sunday of Lent

1 S 16:1, 6f., 10-13   Eph 5:8-14;   Jn 9:1-41 (or 9:1, 6-9, 13-17, 34-38)

Confronting Jesus with the Problem of Suffering

Overcoming Spiritual Blindness; Growth in Faith and Love; Called to Light and Life; The Blindness of Seeing and the Seeing of the Blind; From Darkness to Light; From Death to Life; Sight and Insight; Humility Over Pride

The No. 1 pickpocket of New York was riding in the subway when he felt a hand on his wallet. He whirled about and confronted a pretty female face which, it turned out, belonged to the No. 1 pickpocket of Chicago. The discovery of their respective identities provoked a lot of technical talk, and she admitted that her technique had been bungling.

One thing led to another. They had dates, and finally they married. Pretty soon a child was expected. Of course, coming from such distinguished forebears, this child couldn't miss being the No. 1 pickpocket of America. But, alas, the baby was born with a deformity. Its right hand was tightly clasped, and nothing would make it open. Obviously, with such a handicap it could never become a great pickpocket. The best medical people could do nothing.

In desperation, the parents took the child to a psychiatrist. After trying all of the conventional methods, he took a gold watch on the end of a gold chain and, holding it six inches or so over the closed little hand, swung it back and forth. Gradually, the hand commenced to open, bit by bit. Written on the faces of all was amazement, for in the hand was an object — the midwife's wedding ring!

Heredity, environment, or both have been held responsible for many problems, including suffering in the world. There have also been other explanations for this vexing problem the world has wrestled with. Can it be an all-good God? Sin? Responsibility for suffering is the problem of today's Gospel story. Everyone knew that the beggar who accosted Jesus had been blind from birth. If the all-good God and an innocent beggar-baby aren't responsible, is it the sins of the parents? Indeed, there can at times be a connection between sin and suffering. In Jesus' time, that was an accepted interpretation.

Suffering is a mystery, and so it can't be completely understood. A poet (Shelley, "To a Skylark") once said that "our sweetest songs are those that tell of saddest thought." That observation is correct. In drama, we made one of the greatest plays of all time Shakespeare's stirring tragedy of young love, "Romeo and Juliet."We made one of the best-selling novels in the history of the United States "Uncle Tom's Cabin," a tale of pitiful slavery. In poetry, one of the most popular pieces of English literature is Gray's "Elegy Written in a Country Churchyard"; two lines of the Epitaph of that poem state:

> He gave to misery all he had, a tear,
> He gained from Heaven ('twas all he wished) a friend.

Yet these sad but sweet songs of life are far more enjoyable in a book or on the screen than they are in personal experience. Were we made to sacrifice what we love or desire as were Shakespeare's lovers, we become miserable. If we were forced into the wretchedness of the "Uncle Tom's Cabin" we love so much in literature, many of us would despise life and its Maker. When we realize that death will snatch us from our pleasures as surely as it ended the misery of the person in Gray's "Elegy," we feel resentful.

It may seem cruel to slap and shove a freezing person on to the warmth of the nearest fireside when all he wants is to lie down and sleep, but to allow him his wish would spell his death. And so it goes: for the comfort of a proposed building, the mason must go through the intermediary hardship of hardened palms and misshapen fingernails; the musician to be able to produce the spark that will enthrall an audience must have at least a bowing acquaintance with mourning; the author to present fully the well-springs of life must drink well of the cup of suffering.

What's true of the natural order is also true of the spiritual order. The saints knew this; in fact, God often afflicts His closest friends with the most mourning. They tell the story of St. Teresa of Avila who, after having certain troubles, cried, "O Lord, why do you put such difficulties in our way?" She heard an inward reply, "Don't complain, my daughter, this is the way I treat my friends." To which she said, "Yes, "Lord, and that's why you have so few."

Jesus gives the comfort of his example. Instead of the splendor with which he could have surrounded himself, he chose a stable, persecution, obscurity, and finally abandonment. He "went about doing good," even when he was weary and hadn't a place to lay his head. *Once* the Gospels record that the impulsive woman in the crowd called out her commendation. *Once* they said, "Never did man speak as this man," and *once* they wanted to make him king. But what were these to the cruel taunts and bitter criticisms: "You have a devil"; "You are a Samaritan"; "They took up stones to cast at him," and the sight of the tears streaming down his mother's face as she watched him suffering all these things.

By the end of Jesus' life, Mary and the Apostles had fully-realized knowledge of suffering that they had learned from him. Suffering is to be prayerfully endured, yet mercifully and constantly relieved in others. Suffering was to be their lot in what is, after all, a period of trial, in order that their joy might one day be full; the way of the cross, for all its sorrows, was a road leading to perpetual fullness.

So there are Christian insights which may help all whose eyes are wet with tears, the desolate, the abandoned, and all to whom life is hard and whose hearts are bleeding. From the lives of Jesus, his mother, and the saints, we know that God can and does draw good out of suffering: For example, suffering borne as Jesus and his mother bore it can be redemptive for the world. Suffering can both *purify* and *beautify*, so that the sufferer who keeps in touch with Jesus has an opportunity to grow in virtues like endurance, patience, understanding, selflessness, gratitude, compassion, kindness, mercy, pity, empathy, and concern. And those who suffer are assured of the tender compassion of a God whose own life on earth was a story of suffering from beginning to end. Further, suffering may be the only place where some of us will ever truly meet God.

Too often people are the cause of their own suffering by abusing God's gift of freedom. The violence of our age, with its consequent suffering, is witness to this. Nevertheless, we must all fight against suffering.

Suffering has been put to good use by people even from prehistoric times. In what is now the Southwestern United States, in wet times — with plentiful fish and game and grass — food was easy to come by and pre-archaic life was very good. But during bad times of warmer and drier intervals, there was less fresh water, fewer grasses, and more scrub. Resources were sparser and more widely distributed, and life went from poor to desperate. But these were the times of innovation, invention, and change. It was then that prehistoric people increased the variety of plants and animals they used, made more intense use of what was already available, and developed newer and better means of processing and preparing food.

The blind man of the Gospel story seems to have acquired many of the virtues that can come through suffering. He was trusting of others, and willing to be dependent upon them. Through injustice, harshness, and abuse of power at the hands of the Pharisees, he remained open enough to be able to grow in his contact with Jesus. Even his cure brought its own form of suffering, in the Pharisees' attempts to get him to admit that Jesus didn't heal him, and in his parents' desertion because of their fear of being expelled from the worshipping community in their synagogue.

Although the healing of his physical blindness was instantaneous, his growth in spiritual sight was gradual. He grew from the vague perception of the Savior as the man called Jesus (v. 11) to boldly proclaiming Jesus as a prophet, and finally to turning his back on his lack of parental support and the hostility of the religious leadership to recognize Jesus — whom he had never actually seen face to face — as the Lord whom he worshipped.

While the blind man came to see, the seeing became more blind. The Pharisees saw the same miracle, but to their spiritual loss. The Pharisees met Jesus, without really meeting him. Their spiritual blindness deepened because of their smugness, self-centredness, and general hardness of heart — qualities that often characterize people who haven't sufficiently suffered. They heard Jesus and they saw him, but they neither saw nor heard the salvation that was at hand. They were expert at preaching the word of God to others, but they were blind to the words of their own Scriptures, such as that if you would hear God's voice, harden not your hearts (Ps 95 [94]:7f.).

The correct heart is the dwelling-place where God lives. The heart is our hidden center, beyond the grasp of our reason and of others. It's the place of decision, deeper than our psychic drives. It's the place of truth, where we choose life or death. It's the place of encounter, because as image of God we live in relationships (*Catechism of the Catholic Church*, 2563).

For those whose hearts are not properly formed, like the Pharisees, suffering can be a barren waste, but for the person of true heart who is seeking God it can be, as for the blind man, the way to heaven. Suffering may be inevitable in life, but misery is optional. Of course, wisdom doesn't come only from suffering, but from suffering reflected on, accepted, assimilated. If one is so busy doing and experiencing that there's no time for reflection, life becomes not a connected whole, but a mound of beads without a string.

The young David in today's first reading suffered from his own father's not recognizing his worth. Judging from mere outward appearances, David's father recommended his son Eliab for the kingship because he was tall and strong. Since his son David was only a shepherd-boy, his father didn't even think of presenting him as a candidate. But whereas humans are often swayed by appearances while the Lord looks into the heart (1 S 16:7), it was David whom God chose as His servant. He became the greatest of Israel's kings. As with the Pharisees and with David's father, so with us. Though God sees people's inner being and wants to illumine our darkest selves, most of us most of the time see only outward appearances. Because the world sees only faces, plastic surgeons earn fortunes making them pleasing.

Paul's letter to the Ephesians repeats the Gospel's talk of light and darkness, which is as good a symbol as any to illustrate what we've been saying about suffering. While, as the letter says, light produces every kind of goodness and righteousness and truth (v. 9), the differences between light and darkness are frequently subtle, and it's often more difficult to choose light than darkness. Sometimes, the light of suffering appears as unacceptable as the darkness of self-indulgence.

The forms of blindness in the Gospel are varied: the blindness of faithful disciples, who speak in trite slogans and couch their theology of illness in terms of blame; the blindness of neighbors and family, who won't be involved in the new vision, either out of discomfort or fear; the blindness of a religious establishment, which couldn't see anything good happening outside its own system.

We, too, suffer from various forms of blindness. For that reason and more, we need the penances and sacrifices of Lent. Lent is a time of preparation for, and reflection on, baptism and the sacrifices entailed in its promised allegiances. Though for many of us penances and sacrifices may at times appear to be unnecessary and unacceptable suffering, they can help make us as trusting of God, open, humble, strong, and beneficially pliable in God's hands as the blind man was. Self-denial can purify us into becoming a ray of that blessed light which broke the darkness of Calvary and heralded the glorious Resurrection; it can beautify us before God who is looking into our hearts and seeing goodness that people can't see; and it can change the sinful part of our lives from the blindness and darkness of appearances into seeing the way God sees.

FIFTH SUNDAY OF LENT
Ezk 37:12-14   Rm 8:8-11   Jn 11:1-45 (or 11:3-7, 17, 20-27, 33-45)

The Best of Both Worlds: Earthly Life and Eternal Life
Back from the Grave; Flesh and Spirit; Jesus the Life of the
Believer; Eternal Life to Believers; The Fullness of Redemption;
Conversion and New Life; God as our Center

When Jesus left Nazareth with the dear memories that always cling to
our concept of home, he had nowhere to rest his head. At times Mary,
Martha, and Lazarus — his second family — offered him hospitality in
their home at Bethany.

When, therefore, Lazarus's sisters sent word to Jesus about their
brother's illness (v. 3), the message contained no request to come. They
didn't consider it necessary. As St. Augustine said later, it's impossible
that a person at one and the same time love someone and desert him. The
message simply stated the facts, as had Jesus' mother's message at
Cana. And, as at Cana, Jesus seemed at first to reject the request (v. 4).

Jesus wasn't making light of Lazarus's illness. There is here, as
so often, a deeper meaning: the glory of God, not death, will be served
through this illness (v. 5). Though his love for Martha and Mary pulled
at Jesus to hurry to their side, his known will of his heavenly Father
made him remain where he was for two days (vv. 5f.). By the time he
arrived at Bethany, Lazarus, whose funeral was held in accord with
custom on the day of his death, had been dead four days (v. 17).

Because everyone wanted to show their respect during the seven
days of mourning rites (sitting *shiva*), the house was full of friends and
sympathetic acquaintances — many from Jerusalem, only two miles
away. The mourning of the entire group would be an almost hysterical
shrieking. The ancient Jews, like some moderns, had the notion that the
more unrestrained the mourning the greater the honor paid the dead.
Martha, anxious and wanting to be alone with Jesus, went out to meet
him (v. 20).

Martha's grief tore her between anger for his not coming sooner
and trust in him. What she was really saying at first (v. 21) was, "When
you received our message, why didn't you come right away?" But no
sooner were these words of impatient reproach out than, even through

her sorrow, she spoke words of faith: "I know that whatever you ask of God, He will give you" (v. 22). Jesus' reply, that her brother would rise (v. 23), was a contradiction of the current rabbinical teaching. Even the *holy* people during most of the Older Covenant didn't believe in a life after death. Most of them believed that the souls of both the good and the bad went to *sheol*, a vague place of shadowy life.

Today's reading from Ezekiel, though it at first seems to speak of resurrection, is actually a prediction of the renewed vitality of the whole people Israel after their exile from Jerusalem starting in 587 B.C. The people seemed dead: the Temple had been destroyed, the land wasted, and the leaders taken into custody. The passage contains no reference to the resurrection of individuals.

In the passage before this, Ezekiel painted a picture of dry bones, as in the spiritual, "Them bones, them bones, them dry bones will rise again." The bones of warriors who had fallen in battle and remained unburied littered the plains of some battlefields. For Ezekiel, that Death Valley scene represented Israel's dashed hopes. Dry bones are without life. Today's passage shifts the metaphor from bones to graves (v. 12), but the idea is the same: God's life-giving breath will restore His people as a group, and will give them His own life in resettling them upon their land (v. 14). For the Jewish community, this action of the Lord of re-creating, restoring, and raising up his people reminded them of the creating Spirit with Adam in the beginning, the restoring Spirit at the time of the flood, and the powerful Spirit in the words of the prophets.

By the time of Jesus the majority of Jews, except for the Sadducees, did believe in a life after death. Martha, in replying that she believed in her brother's resurrection on the last day (v. 24), was expressing one of the highest achievements of her nation's faith. In his response, Jesus' profound assertion that "I am the resurrection and the life" (v. 25) was another of Jesus' "I am" statements in John's Gospel which allude to the meaning of the name God gave to Moses: "I am who am." It reminds us of a Persian word used in northern India by Hindu and Muslims alike — *Khuda* — which means "that which exists of itself": that which is self-sufficient, and exists without needs.

From the fact that Jesus was God, we can stake our lives on the fact that everyone who lives and believes in him will never die (v. 26). Faith in him means that we too are truly resurrected: freed from the fears that characterize the godless life, from the frustration of the sin-laden life, from the meaninglessness of the Christless life.

Martha's reply showed a deep faith. She hadn't yet been told that Lazarus would physically rise, and yet she believed in Jesus as Messiah and Lord. When Mary and the mourners from the house joined Martha and Jesus, Jesus entered into a fierce struggle with the power of death: He became perturbed and deeply troubled (v. 33).

And the shortest verse in the Bible (v. 35) shows Jesus the fine human being: It tells us that "Jesus wept."

For the Greeks, for whom St. John's Gospel was written, weeping was incredible for any eminent person, and most especially for a god. They believed in a god who had *apatheia*, a complete inability to feel any emotions. They reasoned that one who feels deep emotions — joy, grief, love — has allowed an outside influence to enter. That in turn means that someone or something, at least for that time, had power over him or her — in other words, that someone or something else is greater. These things simply couldn't be true of a god. Jesus demonstrates a completely different picture of God: as One who cares.

Jesus' request that the gravestone be taken away (v. 39) was another trial of faith. The horrified faces of the onlookers reflected their belief that it was a sacrilege to violate a dead person's tomb. The practical Martha could think of only one reason why he would want the stone removed — to look at his beloved Lazarus' face for the last time. But, in view of the four days that Lazarus was dead, in that climate Jesus would be looking upon the face of a putrefying corpse. Nevertheless, upon Jesus' reassurance, they removed the stone. As on all important occasions, Jesus then prayed — no doubt in a lower tone. He wasn't play-acting for the sake of the crowd, but seeking the heavenly Father's glory (vv. 41f.).

Now Jesus became the drama's central figure, who challenged each participant by clarifying the central issue: the real meaning of death and life. Then Jesus arrived at the climactic moment: He called loudly, "Lazarus, come out!" (v. 43). Dramatically, Lazarus, still wrapped in linen but alive and well, hobbled out. Paradoxically, Lazarus's restoration to life would lead to Jesus' death (vv. 46-53). There had been a build-up of opposition to Jesus among the Jewish leaders, and the Lazarus incident made them more determined to kill him. And ironically, the death of Jesus gives true life to the world.

In today's second reading, St. Paul continues the theme of resurrection which is common to the other readings. Many consider the chapter from which this reading comes to be the second most beautiful chapter in the entire Bible, next to the thirteenth chapter of his First Letter to the Corinthians, on love. It should be read and meditated on when we're feeling discouraged.

This selection considers what wonders we can do when we put God in the center of things. Paul distinguishes between two widely contrasting kinds of life: the life of the flesh and the life of the spirit. Flesh for Paul didn't mean the body; Paul didn't despise the body. Flesh for him meant pretty much the same as what Ezekiel meant by dry bones and graves. The life of the flesh — which is the life of nature — is dominated by the self; it has no future; it's on its way to death; it's ultimately self-destroying. People who live according to the flesh are spiritually dead and cut off from Christ (v. 9). People who espouse the Spirit, on the other hand — in other words, the life of grace — have God as their center and are spiritually alive. They die like the first, but die to rise again. They have a future, are on a path of true life, and are self-fulfilling. They believe firmly in our creed's phrase about "the Lord, the giver of life."

Our reflections as we approach the end of Lent show us many truths, but especially three. First, the body is mortal. The loss of loved ones powerfully reminds us of the profound wrenching, the finality of death, and the emptiness despite the comforting presence of friends. But, in all of that dark night through which everyone must pass, today's liturgy reminds us that the darkness is reversed by the Spirit of the Lord. The Spirit offers us a new vision of all that's created, so that like St. Francis of Assisi we're able to accept sun, moon, stars, and even death, as brothers and sisters whom we love.

Secondly, we reflect on the significance of our baptism, which leads us into the life of the Holy Spirit. It's most important that parents nourish their faith in this sacrament so that when they request that their children be baptized they are sincere in accepting the responsibilities flowing from it. The same responsibilities apply to adults being baptized. And all of us are called to sincerely renew our baptismal commitment to Jesus and his commandments — a commitment which will be formalized at Easter.

Lastly, Paul reminds us to convert from the ways of the flesh and become alive in holiness. That's the kind of new life we should be resolving to find today.

PASSION (PALM) SUNDAY
Is 50:4-7   Ph 2:6-11 (both in A, B, and C)   Mt 26:14 - 27:66

Looking at Our Response to Christ
Emptying Yourself through Suffering, Filling Yourself with Joy;
It's Always Darkest before the Dawn; Fickleness; Be a Servant when
You Grow Up; The Role of Suffering; Suffering and Fulfillment;
How to Suffer; Humble Service; Emptying Yourself of Self

Today, with the beginning of Holy Week, we begin to focus intently on the heart of the mystery of salvation. It's the mystery of dying and rising, the mystery of humiliation and exaltation, the mystery of suffering and glorification, the mystery of death in order to live eternally, the mystery of defeat which is crowned with victory.

It's a story of the fickleness of the crowd that we hear shout "Hosanna" today and "Crucify him" on Good Friday. It's a story in which agony and ecstasy are combined. It's a story full of contradictions: to call today "Passion Sunday," for example, emphasizes suffering and death, while the words "Palm Sunday" emphasize glory and victory. To the extent that the word "Passion" might imply that Jesus was a passive victim, the word is a misnomer: Jesus was a willing and active partner with his heavenly Father in the work of salvation.

As told in today's Gospel by St. Matthew, whose account is probably the most authentic representation of what happened, it's the story of a man whose loneliness and being misunderstood lasted to the end of his life. At the Last Supper, for instance, the self-seeking Judas, who loved money, joined the other Apostles. Unlike the others, who addressed Jesus as "Lord," Judas used the title normally used in Matthew's Gospel by the faithless: "Rabbi."

To Judas's inquiry about whether he would be the one to betray Jesus, Jesus replied with studied reserve: "You have said so" (26:25). Jesus had accused Judas of nothing, but Judas, and only Judas, knew what he meant. Caiaphas the high priest ordered Jesus to tell under oath whether he was the Messiah, the Son of God (v. 64). Caiaphas, who was mad for power and hence blindly eager to please the Roman procurator Pontius Pilate, had weakened the power of the Sanhedrin by removing

---

Note: This homily is on Matthew. For Philippians, see Cycle B; for Luke 22, Cycle C.

them from the Temple Mount, and had strengthened his control of trade by encouraging the moneychangers and the sellers of animals to enter the main court of the Temple.

In Jerusalem he was powerful enough to protect Jesus success-fully from death if that were politically expedient for him. But Caiaphas saw in Jesus a danger for the Romans, for the Jews, and for his rule. What he did was not one of the noblest acts of history, but — for a man of his caliber — understandable.

The Sanhedrin, the supreme Jewish judicial body, knowing that the charge of blasphemy (26:65f.) would be meaningless to the Roman court under Pilate, trumped up three political charges which a Roman authority like Pilate couldn't ignore: (1) that Jesus was a revolutionary, (2) that he had urged the people not to pay taxes, and (3) that he claimed to be king. Pilate didn't like the Jews, and they knew it. Unlike his more diplomatic predecessors, he had offended their sensibilities by a blatant display of the Roman eagle and images of the emperor. Although he had had a much-needed aqueduct built, his plundering of the Temple treasury to meet its cost was a gross violation of the Jews' rights. And the fact that he was always subject to Jewish report to Rome made him feel insecure. Conflicts were inevitable.

This wary representative of Roman domination suspected a hidden agenda at the Jews' presentation of Jesus: it could well be a Jewish intrigue to lead him into a trap and disgrace him in Rome. He checked things out up front by bluntly asking Jesus if he were the king of the Jews. Again Jesus quietly answered with his enigmatic turning the question back to Pilate (27:11). Pilate's "magnanimous" offer to release a prisoner in honor of the Jewish national holiday was more to escape a possible trap than an effort to save Jesus. He tried to load the deck by presenting what he considered the least welcome alternative to Jesus: a notorious prisoner. That backfired. The mob, driven wild by their leaders, rejected Jesus and chose for release the villainous Barabbas. Evil had one of its moments of triumph as the incited crowd persisted in crying for Jesus' crucifixion (27:22f.).

Pilate, to signify that he was innocent of Jesus' blood (v. 24), accommodated himself to a Jewish custom by washing his hands. His plea was a futile gesture of unloading personal responsibility, a gesture that many of us indulge in: "I'm not my brother's keeper!" But it's our business to be involved in the Passion of Christ our brother wherever it's happening today, and "washing our hands" of responsibility won't cleanse our guilt.

The scourging to appease the crowd and excite pity was indicative of the injustice of the whole trial. A man was declared innocent and then lashed on his bare back with a thong of bone and lead until his flesh was raw. The horseplay of the ignorant and barbarous conscript-soldiers who mocked him added psychological torture to the physical torment of the scourging and the crowning with thorns.

For the route to Calvary, the soldiers took the longest route there was, so that as many people as possible might view the scene and be deterred from crime. Jerusalem was at that time an excited oriental city on the eve of a great festival. People were arriving by the thousands. Hawkers were shouting their wares to earn for themselves months of earnings in a short time: water carriers with goatskin gourds, sellers of fresh and dried fruits and sugared almonds, merchants of lemonade from portable tanks. Purveyors of goats, sheep, doves, and cattle for the Temple sacrifices were driving their herds toward the Temple enclosure. The festival would soon begin, so everyone was in a hurry. There were no police keeping order: the mounted centurion at the head of this procession had to make the pathetic group's way with the point of his lance through the beasts and the people. Jesus frequently fell on the unseen crowded steps in the terraced street.

Crucifixion was so horrible that the Romans wouldn't permit it for a Roman citizen. They adopted it from crueler nations, for the lowest type of criminal: runaway slaves, bandits, rebels. The crucified usually hung on the cross to die slowly from the long time without food, and of thirst from the loss of blood, pain from his wounds, and the torture of the gnats and flies attracted in this semi-tropical climate to his sweat and blood.

The inscription over Jesus (v. 37) read, "This is Jesus, the King of the Jews." It was in Greek, the language of culture; Latin, the language of the government; and Hebrew, the language of the country. While Jesus hung between heaven and earth, darkness came over the whole land (v. 45). As a symbol of the power of darkness (Lk 22:53), this was fitting: as heavenly light had shown upon his cradle, darkness should characterize his terrible death.

Look at Jesus at this point. His skin and flesh had been shredded on his thighs and back, his rib cage torn into massive wounds. His shoulder was bruised, its skin broken, raw, and torn from the weight of the cross. His chest was pierced by a sword up into his heart's left ventricle. His abdomen, ripped by the scourge, was encrusted with blood serum and shredded by the tearing off of his robe which had become stuck to his skin during the hot and painful walk to Golgotha. His head was entirely scarred from the weave of thorns that were beaten into his head as a crown for his kingship. The thorns' deep pressure into his skull caused blood from the ruptured vessels to flow into the sinuses under his eyes. His hands, scarred with gaping nail wounds, were drained of their blood, discolored and blotched from the lack of oxygen. His feet were black from the dust of the way, blue and swollen from the settling of the venous blood, the tissues mottled. The nail through both feet tore wide from the weight of his dying body.

As if his physical condition weren't enough, his desperate feeling of loneliness and desertion was worse. Toward midafternoon, Jesus cried out, "My God, my God, why have you forsaken me?" (v. 46). If it were a cry of despair, it would be understandable: He had, after all, been rejected by his country's leaders as a blasphemer, handed over to strangers, had had a revolutionary preferred over him for freedom, was treated by the Romans as a criminal, spurned by his own people, jeered at by a brigand, and forsaken by his friends. Abandonment by his Father, if that were to happen, would be the deepest pain of all.

His words are the beginning of Psalm 21 [22]. Like Jesus' agony, the psalm begins in dejection, but ends in triumph. His suffering was the worst kind that a person must endure: not the suffering which is inherent in our human condition like disease, or part and parcel of this fragile planet like earthquakes, but the unjust suffering inflicted by other people. Jesus had unflinchingly borne all the lethal mixture of evil of which human beings are capable: betrayal, prejudice, denial, fickleness, misunderstanding, indifference, hardness, avarice, jealousy, ignorance, and brutality. He had fully experienced sadness, loneliness, abandonment, and physical pain. In this low point he met his heavenly Father. He had endured suffering for God's sake; he was now liberated from it and was able to thank God for it.

When it was Jesus' time to surrender his spirit to his Father, he died — the world's most celebrated case of capital punishment. Then the soldiers divided his garments by casting lots (v. 35), while they kept watch over him (v.36) to ensure that no one rescued him. His agonizing death was as the "Servant of God" who had emptied himself at the service of his heavenly Father and of us his brothers and sisters. Accompanying Jesus' death were many hard-to-understand phenomena: his cry in a loud voice (v. 50), the rending of the huge Temple veil

(v. 51), the earthquake splitting the rock of Golgotha (v. 52). After his resurrection many of those who had been buried were coming forth from their tombs (v. 53) — not only symbolizing Jesus' victory over death, but portending the resurrection of all people, the final cosmic event of human history. Perhaps the greatest wonder is that even a hard-bitten Roman soldier was terror-stricken at it all to the point of confessing that this was truly the Son of God! (v. 54).

Jesus' passion is, as we said in the beginning, a paradox. It's the story of a suffering servant who is at the same time a royal figure — a story of both servanthood and glory. If we emphasize one at the expense of the other, we misinterpret the story. If we emphasize the servanthood, we may come to think that God loves most those who grovel. If on the other hand we focus on the victory of a royal figure, we may degenerate into self-congratulation and false pride.

Each of us stands alone before Christ. Like Judas, Caiaphas, Pilate, Pilate's wife, Simon the Cyrenean, the Roman centurion, and all the others who had a role in the drama of the passion and death of Jesus, each of us must declare where we stand by our attitudes and actions. The best test of that is whether we're faithful to Christian principles: principles of justice, of peace, of married life, of human existence. Jesus didn't suffer and die to exempt others from suffering and dying, but to redeem us and to show us how to suffer and die.

EASTER SUNDAY

Ac 10:34, 37-43   Col 3:1-4 (or 1 Cor 5:6-8)   Jn 20:1-9
(All in A, B, & C)

The Original "Good News"

The Three Main Characters of the First Easter; This Is the Day the Lord Has Made; Testimony to the Resurrection; Seeing Isn't Necessarily Believing

A criminal lawyer once discredited a witness whose testimony had a critical bearing in the case against his client. The witness was a man who throughout his testimony spoke of "dese" people doing "dose tings" on

---

Note: Today's homily is on John. For homily on Colossians, see Cycle B;
on Acts, Cycle C.

"Toity-Toid Street." In the course of his long testimony, however, there were two occasions when he popped up with phrases that were unusual for him, like "I heard a weird, uncanny sound — like a gasp," and "The suspect was all a-flutter." In his summation before the jury, the defense lawyer claimed that nothing but the work of a coach or an animal trainer could have put phrases like that in such a witness's mouth. He thus demonstrated perjury and the collusive repeating of a prepared story.

In the four evangelists' witness to Jesus' resurrection, and in the testimony of witnesses such as those in today's Gospel, there's no collusion. Considering the importance of Jesus' resurrection, that's remarkable. Although the story is essentially the same in all of them, they all tell it with different emphases.

Today's Gospel from St. John draws our attention to something of probative importance: the empty tomb. It was the first day of the Christian week when Mary Magdalene came to the tomb (v. 1). It was Jewish custom to visit the tomb of a beloved departed for at least three days after burial. Jesus' friends couldn't visit on the Sabbath, because that would be breaking the law, so by Sunday Mary Magdalene's overpowering love for Jesus could wait no longer: early in the morning, when it was still dark, she went to the tomb.

There was enough light for her to notice that the huge stone, which opened and closed Jewish graves of the time, had been moved, and the body was gone. To her, that could mean either grave robbers, or the desecration of Jesus' body by his enemies' moving it somewhere else. Both were easily possible. Grave robbers weren't uncommon, and the Jewish leaders themselves were afraid of Jesus' followers' stealing the body and then saying Jesus had risen from the dead.

Mary excitedly ran back to the city to get support and help from Peter, the leader of the disciples, and John, the disciple Jesus loved (v. 2). Why Peter? By now everyone surely knew of Peter's denial of Jesus, which had shown his weak and cowardly side. But there was another side to Peter. Despite that momentary lapse, Peter had the quality of charismatic leadership. Jesus' confidence in him wasn't misplaced. Shortly, we now know, Jesus would place further confidence in him by telling him to feed his flock. And why John? He was the "Beloved Disciple": he had had a place of great honor at the Last Supper; on that occasion, Peter had asked him to identify the traitor; during Jesus' trial, he had helped get Peter entry to the court of the High Priest; and at the foot of the cross, Jesus had entrusted the care of his mother to him.

By the time Peter and John arrived at the tomb, there was enough light to see better into the inner of the two burial chambers. They sensed something strange about the burial cloths. The cloth that had covered his head had been set apart (v. 7), but the rest of the clothes didn't look as though Jesus had taken them off or as though they had been removed by anyone else. The intact folds appeared almost as though the body had evaporated out of them. Putting everything together, the amazing truth seemed to be that Jesus had risen! Initially, that thought hadn't occurred to any of them.

In retrospect, one might say that some First Testament passages had suggested the resurrection (for example, Ps 16:10; Ho 6:2; Jon 1:17; 2:1), and that the Apostles should have understood. But, while it may be true that life may be fully understood only backwards, it must be lived forwards. The Gospel frankly admits that the Apostles didn't yet understand the Scripture (v. 9) about Jesus rising from the dead. So it wasn't the Scriptures that convinced the Apostles.

Both Peter and John *saw*, but the Gospel records that only John saw *and* believed (v. 8). Seeing isn't necessarily believing. Seeing, plus a lot of loving — these are what it takes to enable one to understand what others cannot. To know other people in their uniqueness, as other persons and not merely as objects, love — not only intellection — is necessary. Love is the quality that will enable us to recognize the Lord in our family, in our parish, and in other people. So the Beloved Disciple believed without a major sign — so important that Jesus later commented in the form of a beatitude that it's those who have not seen and have believed who are blessed (Jn 20:29). John's faith, his trust, and his love were three dimensions of one reality: total commitment to Jesus.

For Peter, as for everyone, growth in faith and trust and love is slow, but the fascinating thing is that growth in any one of these increases, in a remarkable way, growth in all three. This holds true in human relations as well as in our relationship with God. When we love others our trust in them grows, so that we believe in them and hope for great things for them. Our faith tells us that the Risen Jesus lives in and loves every person, and he accepts as done to himself whatever we do to one another.

When we say or sing, "Jesus Christ is risen today," we don't mean only "Jesus Christ was risen once upon a time." We mean that the risen Christ is all around us, in the eyes and faces of those sitting beside us, in the bread and wine of the altar, in the newly baptized, and in the people we meet all the time. He walks the earth today — teaching, healing, touching, suffering, dying, and rising. If we go seeking the risen Jesus with faith and hope and love we will find him. Seek him, find him, love him in every person by serving their needs. Then truly not only is Christ risen but we, too, are already living a risen life by his power and grace.

In contemplating Jesus' Resurrection, this central mystery of our faith, we may profitably ask ourselves which of the three witnesses we personally identify with, and why. Do we identify with Mary Magdalene, whose love and compassion couldn't wait to arrive at the complete truth about Jesus? Or do we identify with Peter, who acted impetuously but wholeheartedly, was a born leader but was painfully aware of his shortcomings, and who, on this occasion, had no insight into the meaning of the event? Or do we identify with John, whose young heart saw, loved greatly in a special way, and generously believed?

We have the opportunity to ask ourselves those questions as we now stand and renew our baptismal promises. As we renew these promises, we should be mindful not only of the extent of our belief, but also of the extent of our love. In the words of the poet (Roy Croft), we can say to Jesus, as we can say to anyone in whom we believe and whom we love:

> I love you
> not only for what you are
> but for what I am
> when I am with you.
> I love you, ...
> for what you are making of me.
> I love you, for the part of me you bring out.
> I love you, for putting your hand into my heaped-up heart,
> and passing over all the foolish, weak things
> that you can't help dimly seeing there,
> and drawing out into the light
> all the beautiful belongings
> that no one else looked far enough to find.
> I love you because you helped me to make
> of the lumber of my life
> not a tavern, but a temple;
> out of my works, of my every day,

> not a reproach, but a song.
> You have done it
> with your touch, with your words,
> with yourself.

May the Risen Lord provide us with the grace to grow in love, and may the joy of Easter cast its glow on our efforts.

SECOND SUNDAY OF EASTER
Ac 2:42-47   1 P 1:3-9   Jn 20:19-31

People Made Whole
Our New Birth; New Life in Jesus; Quality of Life; The Life We Share;
The Start of Something Big; God's Life in Us; My Lord and My God

The patient went to his doctor for a checkup, and the doctor wrote out a prescription for him in his usual illegible handwriting. The patient put it in his pocket, but he forgot to have it filled. Every morning for two years he showed it to the conductor as a railroad pass. Twice it got him into the movies, once into the baseball park, and once into the symphony. He got a raise at work by showing it as a note from the boss. One day he mislaid it. His daughter picked it up, played it on the piano and won a scholarship to a conservatory of music.

Even more versatile than that prescription is today's Gospel. It takes us from fear to joy, seclusion to mission, absence to presence, disbelief to faith, mere existence to new life. It shows Jesus breathing on the Apostles, reminiscent of the first creation when God breathed His Spirit into a living being (Gn 2:7). This second creation, like the first, was the start of something big. Through baptism it made it possible for us to be born again in Jesus, into the life of holiness and the Spirit, and to renew that life through the forgiveness of sin. This Easter season constitutes a special time of celebration of that new life.

Part of today's Gospel deals with "doubting Thomas." He had his own preconceived ideas of what God was like, and didn't want to part from them. He was not unlike a man who met another at a convention.

"Gee whiz, Max," he said, "I haven't seen you in years. Gosh, you've changed. You used to be fat, now you're skinny; you used to have hair, now you're bald; you never had a moustache, now you have one; you were short, but now you seem taller — gosh, how you've changed, Max." The other man said, "But my name isn't Max!" "Oh!" replied our friend, "you changed your name too, eh, Max?"

Thomas, a complex person of courage, ignorance, doubt, and faith, isn't unlike ourselves and our own preconceived ideas. From dealing with our own doubts, we think no less of Thomas for his. And Thomas had other characteristics, ones we could be proud to have. When, for example, everybody knew that for Jesus to enter Judea presented a serious danger of death because his enemies had been plotting against him there, Thomas, with full knowledge of the danger, courageously said to the others, "Let us also go to die with him" (Jn 11:16).

And when, at the Last Supper, Jesus spoke of the way to salvation, it all seemed too vague for Thomas. He needed to have everything in its place and a place for everything. That's how he was made. Jesus knew that, and accepted him, while trying to draw Thomas to risk having more faith. Here, too, Thomas seems to have had the same characteristics as many moderns: problems with faith and with obedience, but an openness and an honesty whereby, once committed, one is wholeheartedly involved. This is better than an easy but shallow faith and a meaningless compliance.

Jesus made his entrance into the room where the Apostles were gathered in the same way as he had on Easter Sunday: through the locked doors, and with the same beautiful greeting of "Peace" (v. 26). He accommodated himself to Thomas's doubts by inviting him to examine his hands and his side. Through the suspenseful contrasts of fear and peace, doubt and faith, and seeing and believing, the climactic moment arrived when Thomas came to believe as strongly as he had disbelieved.

Overcome, Thomas the "doubter," the one "slow to believe," was given the outstanding grace by the Risen Lord to turn unbelief on its head, to make the most complete affirmation of Christ's nature to be found in anyone in the Gospels, and to proclaim the truth of Christ for all generations to come. Using two Older Covenant titles of God, he exclaimed, "My Lord and my God!" (v. 28). Thomas applied them to Jesus. In that moment of the triumph of faith over unbelief Jesus remembered each of *us* with his beatitude, "Blessed are those who have not seen and have believed" (v. 29).

During the Easter season, our first reading is from the Acts of the Apostles rather than the Jewish Scriptures, because we're to see the life of the young Christian Church as a continuation of the wonderful redeeming work of Jesus. In today's reading from that work, its author St. Luke presents four characteristics of the early community that continued the Easter spirit of Thomas: the Church. It was a *faithful* Church, devoted to teachings from the Apostles (v. 42); a *communal* Church (vv. 42, 44), where all members shared and cared for the poor; a *praying* Church, devoted to the breaking of the bread and to the prayers (v. 42); and a *happy* Church, enjoying favor with all the people (v. 47). Although these inspirational verses, along with others in the Acts of the Apostles (4:32-35; 5:12-16), remind us of what we're called to be as an Easter people, they are a picture of what *should* be more than of what, in many instances, was the case. Not all those who were baptized became instant saints.

It was because of abuses and problems in the Church that Paul wrote to the Thessalonians to correct their wrong message about Jesus' Second Coming, to the Corinthians to end their factionalism, to the Galatians to proclaim that they weren't going to be saved by keeping the Torah, and so on. And it was because of problems that today's reading from the First Letter of St. Peter came about. It's a counterbalance for those who think that the joy and enthusiasm of the early Christians is easily come by. The letter was written from Rome to Christian converts either by Peter shortly before his death, or by a group of leaders who knew Peter and his thought well and wrote shortly after his death. It presents the reality of authentic Christian life which, harshly, must be tested by fire in situations that transcend all cultural experiences, political situations, and time.

Our life, says Peter, is patterned, in an unbelieving world, on the death and resurrection of Jesus. God's saving action begins in a big way with new birth through baptism. Because our new birth is the theme of the Easter season, we will read sections of this letter at Mass in the next six weeks. When you think about it, the entire New Testament is about the new birth emphasized in this passage. Our new birth is a birth to many things. It's a birth to true *hope* (v. 3), a hope which draws its life from what happened to Jesus in his rising from the dead. Sophocles encapsulated the contrasting despairful pagan viewpoint for all time when he wrote: "Not to be born is best. . . but once a man has seen the light the next best thing, by far, is to go back. . . where he came from, as quickly as he can."

Our rebirth is also a birth to an *inheritance* (v. 4). For the Jews, the Promised Land had been their inheritance. For Christians, the inheritance is the heavenly kingdom. Whereas nonbelievers see the world as a place where everything decays and where one ultimately winds up in endless darkness, Christians see themselves as reborn of the incorruptible seed of God Himself.

Best of all, we're reborn to *salvation* (v. 5). In the New Testament, salvation can mean many things: deliverance from danger, emancipation from sin, release from the shackles of personal limitations, freedom to grow. Like our hope and our inheritance, our salvation isn't something remote, but here and now. As we view our hope, our inheritance, and our salvation — our eternal life bestowed in baptism — there is cause for rejoicing (v. 6). Through it all, Peter is reminiscent of Jesus' words to Thomas: "Although you have not seen him you love him; even though you do not see him now yet believe in him, you rejoice with an indescribably and glorious joy" (v. 8).

All of us find ourselves in the situation of Thomas, non-eyewitnesses of the Resurrection who have to put our faith in the testimony of our brothers and sisters in the community of faith. The New Testament is the written record of that testimony at the end of the first century A.D. and the beginning of the second. The Church that wrote the New Testament for us is the same community of forgiven sinners in which we keep faith with God and with Jesus in the Spirit to the present day. The Church, at times as vacillating as Peter, as stubborn as Thomas, as irascible as Paul, and always as faithful as Mary Magdalene, continues to proclaim saving truth generation after generation.

Can we say that as members we contribute to making the Church the same today as it was when it came from Jesus' hands? How strong is our faith when we don't see? Do we take personal responsibility to keep on learning about our faith? Do we see ourselves as a *community*, having responsibilities for justice and charity? Do we see prayer as not only a duty but a privilege? No matter what our past, we should show that Christ is truly risen, alleluia, and lives in his Church today — in each of us individually and in all of us communally.

Signs and miracles make an impression, but generosity in times of need, and sharing as a believing community, are at least as attractive.

Our inexpressible joy in ourselves and glory toward God for our faith membership in our Church and for our new birth to hope should motivate us to give evidence that Jesus is for each of us "my Lord and my God!"

THIRD SUNDAY OF EASTER
Ac 2:14, 22-28   1 P 1:17-21   Lk 24:13-35

Life Out of Death
Love Changes People; Recognizing the Lord in Life's Events; Openness, to Change, Growth, Love, and (especially) Joy; Our Path of Life

An old novel tells the story of a wealthy woman who traveled the world over, visiting museums and art galleries, meeting people, and viewing the sights. She became completely bored. Then she met a man who had none of this world's goods, but a great love of beauty and a sincere appreciation of it. In his company, the world looked entirely different to her. At one point she told him, "I never knew what things were like, until you taught me how to look at them." In every love story, there comes a point when the lover says that to the beloved, either directly or indirectly.

The story in today's Gospel, told by that expert story-teller St. Luke, confirms this. The story is probably the greatest of the post-Easter accounts of encounters with the risen Lord. Cleopas and his companion were disciples of Jesus — not Apostles or intimate friends, but disciples, which means simply that they were followers. This may help to explain why they didn't recognize Jesus. They'd left Jerusalem downcast because of their disappointment that Jesus their hope had been crucified — the end of their dream, they thought.

What went wrong, they wondered. They'd stayed in Jerusalem long enough to hear some of the women's tales of an empty grave and of angels, but they didn't put much stock in that. Perhaps the women were a bit emotionally overwrought. The atmosphere in Jerusalem was gloomy, sad, and heavy. So they took to the road, and on the way a stranger joined them. Jesus — for the stranger was he — started up a conversation with them. The conversation is a model for prayer. The stranger understood that people who are caught in their own little world of discouragement and depression don't bother to look out to see others. He understood their anger, frustration, and pent-up feelings. He knew that the two must vent all of this before they would be ready to listen to him. And he took them exactly where they were.

Jesus' inquiry into their discussion (v. 17) drew the ironical, yet exasperated, response, "Are you the only visitor to Jerusalem who does not know of the things that have taken place there in these days?" (v. 18). "What sort of things?" inquired the remarkable stranger, asking the one question which touched on the open wound and drew out the hurtful poison. The disciples revealed the false expectations they had of the Messiah. That's what Jesus was waiting for.

That's what he waits for with us. He knows that we set our hearts on persons and projects that frequently fail us. Frustration sets in when we try something good and it ends in disaster. We know ourselves to be disillusioned, and God seems dead. That's what prayer is about. Jesus is with us in the midst of our problems; he knows about them, but we need to get in touch with them and express them. Then, when we're rid of a lot of blinding obstacles, Jesus can begin to speak to us.

We can see that happening with the disciples. Very soon Jesus had their full attention as he assured them that nothing had gone wrong; rather, they had been unable to see the saving hand of God in Jesus' sufferings and death, as shown in all the Scriptures beginning with Moses (v. 27). How much more satisfied we would feel if only Luke had given us an account of precisely *which* Scriptures Jesus used, and Jesus' exact comments on them!

An educated guess tells us that what Jesus spoke of was the constant scriptural theme that's also the theme of the Easter season: that God reveals Himself unceasingly as the One whose characteristic work is to bring life out of death. The first scriptural note of this theme is in God's promise to Abraham that he and his wife Sarah — whose hope of bearing children had, because of old age, long since died — would receive life through a son in whose descendants all peoples were to find a blessing. Because Sarah laughed at the idea, their son when he was born was named Isaac, a wordplay on the Hebrew verb "to laugh."

The Hebrew Scriptures continue to present the idea of God raising up the lowly, of bringing joy out of sorrow, of the vocation of Israel as a "Suffering Servant" constantly defeated and yet always raised up again by the Lord. The Exodus contains a death-resurrection motif. The Psalms speak of the stone rejected by the builders which becomes the cornerstone, and of one who is beaten down being vindicated.

These and other stories of God's bringing life out of death show common patterns. In every case God acted *unexpectedly* and *unimaginably*. And each time He did the *impossible*, restoring to life people who were either dead or as good as dead. And a *leitmotif* throughout is God's question to the doubting Abraham, "Is anything too marvelous for the Lord to do?" Applied to Jesus' Resurrection, who could imagine that his tomb was empty Easter morning because the Lord had gone to a new and higher life, beyond death? Too hard to believe? Impossible? Exactly! Such deeds are characteristic of God! And, said Jesus (v. 25), the two gentlemen now before him were too foolishly slow to believe these lessons of Scripture.

When Jesus pretended he was leaving them, he gave them a further opportunity to reveal themselves. Their now-responsive hearts begged him to stay, which he was — and is — only too willing to do. Then, as he had nourished them on the word of God in Scripture, as in the Mass he nourished them on the bread of life, which he is; that's how they recognized him.

Thus he left them. The disciples, renewed and invigorated — as we can be after prayer — hurried back to the city. They wanted to tell their good news to the others. They found their thunder stolen by the news that the others had, but meeting Jesus had changed them. Now they were willing to listen. When they got their chance, without any frustration at the delay they told their story of how Jesus was made known to them in the breaking of the bread (v. 35).

Among the things the Jerusalem group told *them* was one of the greatest untold stories of the ages: that Jesus had appeared to Peter! *There* was a man brought from death to life! Peter had during Jesus' lifetime shown his participation in spiritual death on many occasions — right up to his threefold denial at the end. Now Jesus, with divine compassion, gave Peter, as he does with all repentant sinners, the chance to redeem himself in God's eyes and regain his self-respect. Peter now had the chance to know the complete Jesus — not only Jesus of suffering and death, but of the risen life and the Mystical Body; not only the pain, but also the joy, the unspeakable joy, which Jesus had said should be present among his followers.

And that's why we can read today in the Acts of the Apostles about so gleeful a Peter. Despite its title, the Acts of the Apostles is at least one-quarter speeches, and of the speeches recorded there Peter gave five. What we heard today is a masterpiece of condensation of the first recorded Christian sermon. Peter gave it fearlessly on the first Pentecost, and it contained all the elements of his other speeches. His sermon is in a nutshell what we believe. It contains the idea that if we are loyal to the Lord, he will see us through, even though we may not see him physically. Peter proclaimed Jesus in the beautiful words of the sixteenth Psalm, which he saw as having foretold Jesus' passion, death, and resurrection. The psalm is given more fully in today's Responsorial Psalm. In its words, God indeed shows us the path of *life*.

Today's portion of the first letter of Peter provides the fitting advice that we're to conduct ourselves with reverence (v. 17) during our sojourn in this strange land of earth. If the author of that letter knew philosophy, he would have remembered that Plato, when referring to the heyday of Athens, had written that "reverence was then our queen and mistress"; Plato made it clear that his great city fell into decadence when its citizens became arrogant and irreverent.

We, in contrast, are an Easter people and alleluia is our song. Even in our nuclear age God remains the One whose characteristic work continues to be to bring life out of death. But there are barriers that sometimes cause people to fail to recognize the Lord even though he may be walking with us as we journey through life. Some seemingly upright people don't believe, or ridicule religion — perhaps because they've had problems in their family, or scandal over controversy in the Church, or suffering, or death, and take it out on God.

We speak of physical death being caused by high blood pressure, cancer, heart disease. What's the cause of our personal participation in spiritual death: envy? self-centredness? lust? coldness? arrogance? Faithful sensitivity to the Scriptures and prayer can make our hearts burn within us as they bring us to recognize the presence of the Lord. Let these understandings work in us as they work in every love story, so that we can see the world broad-screen, in full color, with a new freshness, unprecedented meaning, and sheer joy, like everyone else in love in the whole world.

Fourth Sunday of Easter
Ac 2:14, 36-41   1 P 2:20-25   Jn 10:1-10

Our Shepherd and Guardian
What a Good Shepherd Is; Attitudes Towards Pastors; Repent!

One of the chief ways in which people are different from the rest of creation is our ability to communicate in detail and with precision. Yet some people are often careless about words. Take, for example, the Episcopalian vicar in a remote corner of England who, one Friday, telegraphed his bishop: "My wife just passed away. Please dispatch a substitute for the weekend."

Two important words used carefully in today's readings are "shepherd" and "guardian." The term shepherd contains within it the meaning of guardian, but it's more tender. It occurs frequently in the Jewish Scriptures, perhaps the most striking being in Isaiah (40:11). Psalm 23, today's Responsorial Psalm, describes all of the things that the Lord our Shepherd does for us His sheep. Jesus, too, used the tender image of the shepherd. He applied it to himself.

In today's Gospel, which is the only parable in St. John's entire Gospel, Jesus adds to his previous images of himself his being both the Good Shepherd and the Gate to Life. As Good Shepherd, he calls his own sheep by name (v. 3). Among the Hebrews, sheep were most often raised for wool and for milk, and not for meat; so, like our domesticated animals, they became almost pets to the shepherd. Palestinian shepherds didn't use dogs to herd their sheep and nip at their heels; rather the shepherd led his sheep. And they would respond to the voice of their own shepherd, but not to another's. The true sheep of God are able to discern the one who speaks with God's voice (v. 5).

Jesus also calls himself the Gate for the sheep (v. 7). "Gate" is also what we mean by door. In our time of electric and automatic entrances and keys and locks we think of doors mostly as territorial barriers against being robbed or otherwise violated. Doors stand between public and private, between mine and yours. Doors signal hospitable greeting or blatant rejection, the last barrier across which guards throw themselves against an invading enemy. Even in our space age, doors haven't lost those meanings.

But Jesus had more in mind. Imagine yourself a cosmonaut walking in outer space, umbilically attached to your craft. Seeing that your air reserve is almost gone, you realize that it's time for you to return to your ship. You reach for the hatch lever and find the door locked. You desperately claw the bolted door. When the door is thrown open from within and you're pulled through it to escape into life, you realize the importance of a door and the meaning of the gate of life.

Jesus adds the warning that all who climb into the sheepfold in some other way than himself is a thief and a marauder. He wasn't necessarily directing such imagery only at the Temple priesthood or the professionally upright lay elite, the Pharisees, or the Herodian quisling invaders of God's sheepfold. Nor are his words applicable to such modern invaders as Hitler, Stalin, or Mao tse-Tung. He includes also all those in the Church responsible for bad leadership or foolish followership and all of us who have a little of the shepherd and a little of the thief in us. John Milton in his poem *Lycidas* included "such as for their bellies' sake,/ Creep and intrude, and climb into the fold." That means all politicians and church-goers who try to use the Church for their own ends.

Thinking about all those things brings us to the dramatic climax of St. Peter's Pentecost sermon in today's reading from the Acts of the Apostles, where Peter contrasts what God did to Jesus with what people do to him. God raised Jesus, exalted him, and made him both Lord and Messiah (v. 36). People crucify him. So awakened were the drowsy hearts of Peter's hearers to a sense of guilt that they asked what we should ask: "What are we to do?" (v. 37).

Peter's answer was to reform, to repent and be baptized (v. 38). Reforming and repentance are *positive* concepts, a recipe for salvation. It's a change of heart, a conversion, a *metanoia*, a turning toward God. We must look at our lifestyles to decide our besetting sins from which we must convert to risen life in Christ.

Lest our ideas about shepherds be too romantic and our notion of repentance too far off, the letter in the tradition of Peter in today's second reading brings us down to earth. It's addressed to slaves. In the Roman Empire in the early 60's when this letter was written, there may have been as many as 60 million slaves. People became slaves by having been the victims of kidnapping, or hostages of war, or prisoners brought back by the conquering Roman armies, or debtors unable to pay, or even the children of slaves. They included physicians, teachers, musicians, and actors. These men and women were considered the property of a master, no different from his sheep or his fields.

They did manual labor, worked the farms, manned the ships, and dug the mines. But the majority were the household slaves (v. 18) addressed here. They served as maids and servants, or managed the estate. Some rose to high positions. The Roman attitude was that it made no sense for Rome to be ruler of the world if its citizens had to do their own work. Slaves weren't necessarily treated poorly, but they weren't treated as persons. They weren't allowed to marry, so they cohabited. Their children became as much the property of the master as lambs, kids, or colts.

Christianity came into that kind of world not to demean people by calling them sheep, but to elevate them with the good news that every human being is created in God's image, that all persons are precious because all are so loved by God that He gave His only Son. New Testament Christianity could go no further — by teaching the wrongness of slavery, for example — until the small Church communities became a larger entity whose principles penetrated society.

The importance of God's sheep to the divine shepherd resulted in the notion of the sacredness of persons. This in turn led to new relationships and conditions: democracy, for example. Democracy — "government of the people, by the people and for the people," in Abraham Lincoln's definition — is not only a form of government, but a spirit. It consists largely in assumptions — one person about another, one nation about another. In our civilization these assumptions are Christian assumptions. Nevertheless we, torn to shreds by media that are alien to our values, by counter-cultures, and by leaders who are sometimes blind, must seek a shepherd's guidance through God's voice in Jesus. We can't even go to our nation to find the shepherd or the gate.

Is the United States a Christian nation? That's a bone of contention. Our country is Christian in the sense that the basic teachings of Christianity are in its bloodstream. The central doctrine of our political system — the inviolability of the individual — is inherited from two millennia of Christian insistence upon the sacredness of persons. Christian idealism is manifest in the arguments that politicians use in public, in the popular ideas of good taste, and in the laws and manners of our people.

John Adams, who proclaimed himself a Christian in his inaugural address as second president of the United States, blamed his defeat for re-election on his calling for a day of fasting and prayers to Christ. After his defeat, presidents kept Christ out of their inaugural addresses, confining themselves to phrases like "the Almighty Being." It wasn't until after the election of 1840 that Christ again made a major appearance in a presidential inaugural address, when William Henry Harrison expressed "a profound reverence for the Christian religion."

In 1911, the year before he was elected president, the historian Woodrow Wilson told 12,000 listeners: "America was born a Christian nation." Jimmy Carter, a born-again Christian, told a campaign crowd in North Carolina in 1976 how important prayer was in his life.

Some presidents also have referred to the need for religion. George Washington did that many times. Harry S. Truman said in 1950: "The fundamental basis of our Bill of Rights comes from the teachings which we get from Exodus and St. Matthew, from Isaiah and St. Paul. ... If we don't have the proper fundamental moral background, we will finally wind up with a totalitarian government which does not believe in right for anybody except the state." Franklin D. Roosevelt said: "No greater thing could come to our land today than a revival of the spirit of religion."

Even the Supreme Court, so unpredictable in the area of religion, has occasionally given tribute to its benefits. For example, in 1892 it said that "we are a Christian people, and the morality of the country is deeply engrafted upon Christianity" (*Church of the Holy Trinity v. United States*, 143 U.S. 457 at 471). In 1952, Justice William O. Douglas, speaking for the Court, wrote: "We are a religious people whose institutions presuppose a Supreme Being" (*Zorach v. Clauson*, 343 U.S. 306 at 313). And in 1961 Justice Felix Frankfurter declared of the United States that our "religious institutions have traditionally regulated virtually all human activity" (*McGowan v. Maryland*, 366 U.S. 420 at 461).

Unfortunately, however, the United States isn't Christian in any formal sense. Our citizens transgress Christianity's precepts freely. And our citizenship doesn't in any way imply any relationship of sheep and shepherd or of any door to God.

Let's discover the meanings and implications of such important words as "shepherd" and "sheep" and "gateway." The leaders of Christ's Church are called pastor, which means shepherd. May our pastors always lead us by example as well as words. May those who have wandered far from the flock of God, whether through hurt or through apathy, rediscover their gateway to God. May we be open to the call for repentance, attune our minds to the sound of Jesus' voice in more than just our immediate concerns, and allow him to shepherd us through life.

FIFTH SUNDAY OF EASTER
Ac 6:1-7   1 P 2:4-9   Jn 14:1-12

Leading a Full Life
No Faceless God; A Map of Life; "Through Jesus Christ, Our Lord";
The Glory of Jesus; The Way, the Truth, and the Life; Involvement;
Commitment; God's Presence in Time of Adversity

An unschooled man watched from the curb as a large funeral went by with a half-block-long hearse, ten flower cars, and twenty-five limousines filled with mourners. Finally, unable to contain his wonderment, he said to the man next to him, "Man, that's livin'!"

True living comes from developing ourselves to become all that we can be. To the extent that we do less, and are undereducated, we're dead. Some may consider Plato to have been overeducated. If he hadn't spent all that time asking questions about a lot of intellectual matters, he might have been able to go into the wine business and retire on a nice annuity instead of changing the course of civilization. "What's the difference," someone once asked Aristotle, "between an educated and an uneducated man?" "The same difference," he replied, "as between being alive and being dead." And many consider Abraham Lincoln to have been overeducated. Surely, the opinion goes, he didn't need to spend all those hours studying the Bible and Shakespeare in order to become President of the United States — many have made it without even bothering to take thought.

Today's liturgy tells us what the *fullest* living is about. The Gospel — appropriately for this Paschal season — is from a part of Jesus' profound farewell discourse, which is tinged with glory. "Don't let your hearts be troubled" (v. 1), Jesus says, remembering perhaps especially his own troubled emotions at the death of Lazarus and, moments before his present conversation, the betrayal of Judas. His advice is that we center an untroubled heart in a living faith in the Father and in himself.

Jesus is about to leave them, but his death shall result in victory. In his Father's house there are many dwelling places (v. 2), where he and his faithful followers can be together. Jesus' departure is in order that he might prepare a place for us, a place where we will be eternally at home. We all know the comfort, peace, and well-being of being together "at home," especially at family feasts like Christmas, Thanksgiving, and Easter. For further reassurance comes the promise that he will return from death (v. 3) and give new life to those who are baptized.

"You know the way" (v. 4), he says, the way to the Father. The "way" is obedience to the teachings Jesus gave and the manner in which he'd lived his life. The earliest name the Christian community gave itself was "The Way"; it wasn't until later, at Antioch, that they were called Christians. The Chinese Taoists also have a "Way"; it uses an attractive image that is not dissimilar from what Jesus meant. "The highest good," says their *Tao Tê Ching* (ch. viii), "is like that of water. The goodness of water is that it benefits the ten thousand creatures; yet itself does not scramble." Jesus' way is both a method of reaching our goal and the goal itself.

But the Apostles know how to "forget" unwelcome truths, just as we do! In reply to Thomas' question, "How can we know the way?" (v. 5), Jesus declares who he is, in a memorable summary of the good news: "I am the way and the truth and the life" (v. 6). "I AM" is Yahweh's own name and so Jesus, subtly but definitely, states his sonship to his heavenly Father. Jesus therefore is for us, his people, as he had said so often, the *way* to the Father, both by example and by identification with the Father. He's our unique means of salvation. He's the *truth*, since in Jewish usage the *true* signifies the divine order, as distinguished from the deceptive disorder of humankind. He reveals the Father. He's the *life* — that is, not mere existence, but sharing in the very life of God and communicating that life.

Because the disciples' understanding was as poor as that of Jesus' opponents, Jesus considers it not insulting to repeat the words he had uttered against his opponents: that if we know *him*, then we will also know his heavenly Father (v. 7). In other words, if anyone wants to know what God is like, one has only to know Jesus. And by to "know" Jesus means to have a deep, warm, personal relationship with him.

Philip, totally nonplused and showing the same lack of comprehension as Thomas did, demands, "Show us the Father" (v. 8), hoping for some extraordinary vision. And Jesus answers that whoever has seen him has seen the Father (v. 9). Truly a fantastic statement! To the Greeks, God was, by definition, invisible. The Jews believed that no human being has seen God at any time. And many people at that time, like many today, emphasized the distance between God and the world of people. Yet here is a calm statement that stuns: In Jesus we see the heavenly Father.

The apostles have yet to learn that the vision of God given to this world is through Jesus Christ. He alone reveals the Father, in the *way* he lives, in the *truth* of his word, and in the quality of new *life* that he brings. Yet he's close to us. He lived an ordinary life, worked as we all do, was tempted, experienced the joy and the pain of loving, and died on a cross. He reveals the Father in the "ordinary" things of life, where you and I can meet him.

The passage ends as it began, with Jesus' call to deepened faith. He prefers to be believed for the *words* that he spoke (v. 10), which elevate ordinary language to the heights of poetry. If that's not enough for them, his *works* should convince (v. 11). And yet we remember in prayer those troubled souls who seem to experience the absence rather than the presence of Jesus. Jesus concludes by combining the call to deepened faith with the theme of departure (v. 12).

Jesus says that the person of faith will do greater works than he did. When the promise and the struggle appear vain, it's good to recall that where Jesus fed a few thousand, believers can feed millions; that where Jesus cured a few, believers can now support enterprises which relieve millions of disease and pain; that where Jesus raised two or three from the dead, believers by their generosity can give life to millions.

His tremendous work of salvation takes place all over the world, beginning with the events recalled in today's reading from the Acts of the Apostles. Sad to think, this salvation history of the Church, then as now, was fraught with internal discord. But it's consoling to realize that divisions within the Church are not just something of our own time, or dating from the Protestant Revolt of the sixteenth century. The first converts came from two groups of Jews, the Hellenists and the Hebrews. The Hellenistic Jews were Greek-speaking, and had returned to Jerusalem from all over the Mediterranean region. The Hebrews were native Palestinian Jews who spoke Aramaic.

Today's reading from Acts demonstrates one of the tensions

between them: the Hellenistic group complaining that their poor widows were being neglected in the daily distribution of food from the common store (v. 1) by the majority group, the local Hebrews. Another problem was that some of the members were so overworked in the service of the community that they were neglecting other important duties.

The solution, arrived at by prayer and discernment, showed flexibility and growth, optimism and imagination. It showed the Church as an organization with an atmosphere of love, consideration, and enthusiasm. It showed a Church with each person treated equally with love, in the forefront of breaking down ethnic and racial barriers.

Many of these qualities of the early Church were embodied in a new office: that of deacon. Though these assistants aren't called "deacons" here, their office is "deaconing": that is, service. Deacons were, however, to meet more than the immediate material need. Later (Ac 6:8 and 8:5) we see two of the deacons involved in evangelization. All the faithful are called to serve with comitment. We are the lifeblood of the Church.

That's addressed in today's letter from St. Peter. When you and I are faithful to our obligations — to God and to other people — despite the possible pain of monotony, or a seeming lack of success, or rejection, or financial reverses, or social problems, then Peter's words about growth to the full life come alive. One can't participate in spreading the faith or in any other spiritual activity without first growing in personal holiness. And that can only happen when we let Jesus become the foundation stone (v. 4) of our life. If and when anything seems lacking, we pray with today's Responsorial Psalm, "Lord, let your mercy be upon us, as we place our trust in you."

As living stones in the Church, we become, by Jesus' power and love, members of a chosen race (v. 9), sharing "a royal priesthood." Like the Israelites of old, we become "a holy nation": that is, through baptism we are set apart and reserved for God. Lastly, from being "no people," deprived of all mercy, we become God's people, the chosen recipients of His mercy. Though from different races, nations, and social backgrounds, we're united in Christ. We should deeply realize our dignity as members of the Church, and live our vision to the full.

That's real life — *our* life, the life that is Christ, the life in its fullness in which "I live, now not I, but Christ lives in me." It's a life of involvement, of sharing in a life which always calls us beyond ourselves. What a vast difference from the full life as understood by the man watching the funeral cortege from the curb!

SIXTH SUNDAY OF EASTER
Ac 8:5-8, 14-17   1 P 3:15-18   Jn 14:15-21

Be an Apologist and a Protestant for Jesus
How to Apologize for Jesus; Let All the Earth Sing Out with Joy;
The Life of the Spirit; Actions Speak Louder than Words;
Stop, Look, and Listen; An Authentic Christian Life Can
Make an Impact; Hope; Baptism and Life in the Spirit

A man said to a counselor: "My wife and I just don't have the same feelings for each other we used to have. I guess I just don't love her anymore and she doesn't love me. What can I do?"

The counselor asked, "The feeling isn't there anymore?"

"That's right," he affirmed. "And we have three children we're really concerned about. What do you suggest?"

"Love her," the counselor replied.

"I told you, the feeling just isn't there anymore."

"Love her."

"You don't understand. The feeling of love just isn't there."

"Then love her. If the feeling isn't there, that's a good reason to love her."

"But how do you love when you don't love?"

"My friend, love is a verb. Love — the feeling — is a fruit of love, the verb. So love her. Serve her. Sacrifice. Listen to her. Empathize. Appreciate. Affirm her. Are you willing to do that?"

"Love" is a four-letter word, written about in the world's greatest literature, spoken often by many people (especially young lovers, but less so — unfortunately — by man and wife), and yet difficult. To quote Dostoevsky, love is "as hard as hell." Part of the explanation for its being so hard is Jesus' farewell talk in today's Gospel. If we love, we obey the commands and wishes of our beloved. That applies to our relations with other people and with us and God. Though reasonable and for our betterment, that sometimes goes against our grain.

God's love causes Jesus to promise to give us another Advocate (v. 16). He said "another" because he himself was an advocate, but he would soon no longer be with his followers physically and this other advocate would continue Jesus' work. "Advocate" in modern terms connotes a combination of intercessor, witness for the accused, defense attorney, best friend, and comforter in distress. While in modern speech an attorney has the dignity of being called an advocate, perhaps the most appropriate symbol for the conveying of the Spirit is the embrace of compassion and love and the joining of hands in unity.

A child falls down and skins a knee, and immediately runs to a parent for comfort. The injury continues to hurt, but someone else has joined in feeling it. The child is no longer alone, and is comforted. Adults, too, have a need to be helped by someone willing to join in the trying experiences of life. Perhaps you experienced the urgency at a time of serious illness, or at the death of someone close, or when you were so desperate that you didn't know where to turn, or you were being lied about or ridiculed, or were in need of a job or money. In these human situations we experience the ache for one another, and for the power and comfort of the Holy Spirit.

The Holy Spirit — the best gift in love God can give — stands beside us, comforts us when we ask, helps us in difficult times, and speaks in our behalf when we're in need. Although people with no religious faith comfort one another, our fellowship with the Spirit is deeper and more awesome. That doesn't mean ecstatic speech or luminous visions. The Holy Spirit is most often more quiet and simple — and more available — than some people believe.

All spiritual life, all holiness comes from the Father through Jesus by the action of the Holy Spirit. From time to time, if we have the sensitivity to perceive it, we're aware of what's happening as we truly share the Spirit with one another. The Spirit is present in our common kindnesses, loving concern for one another, and bursts of inspiration.

Sometimes, though, we're fearful of those touching experiences, not knowing how to handle the emotion that often surrounds them. In other words, we sometimes give the Spirit a difficult time breaking through. But the Spirit's coming will happen whenever we love God enough to keep His commands.

Take, for example, the story of today's first reading. Stephen had been put to death for his faith, and Saul was carrying out his campaign of persecution against the church in Jerusalem. Because of the persecution, although the Gospel was spreading, believers were scattered. So the Apostle Philip set off on a one-man mission to preach the good news of Jesus to the Samaritans.

How extraordinary! The Samaritans hated the Jews, and the Jews —even the Jewish Christians — still thought that salvation was only for themselves. To the Jews, the Samaritans were the "disposables," the "throw-away" people — somewhat like today's runaway children, pregnant teens, drug addicts, streetpeople, and those who stay alive by selling their bodies. This mission to the Samaritans is the first crossing of the threshold into the non-Jewish world, indicating that God's gift is not merited by race, prior religious commitment, or deserving deeds.

Because Philip loved enough to sacrifice himself for God, many crippled of mind and body were cured, and more importantly the people in Samaria received the Holy Spirit. And there was great joy in that city (v. 8). As happens all the time, love had worked miracles among people who hungered for it. The joy and surprise of the Jerusalem Church that the Gospel should be well received by the Samaritans is reflected in today's Responsorial Psalm, that all the peoples of the earth (not just the Jews) are to cry out with joy to God.

The Apostles in Jerusalem sent Peter and John to help formally to incorporate the Samaritan converts into the Church (v. 14). They imposed hands on the people, a symbol which they understood as a conveying of power. Christians still use that potent symbol — at baptism, at confirmation, as people are blessed in the name of Jesus, and as priests and bishops are ordained. It still symbolizes the giving and receiving of the Holy Spirit.

How are we to show that the abundance of life which the Holy Spirit gives has truly come to us? Today's excerpt from the first letter of Peter tells us, stressing the essential dimensions of Christian commitment and highlighting the cost of living virtuously. It's addressed to Christian converts who were suffering for their beliefs as a minority in a pagan society. The advice on how to relate to a disbelieving culture still has relevance. We still have a responsibility to bring God in Christ to our world today, a world often more hostile to Christ and his values than were Samaritans and Jews to each other. We do this by being ever ready to reply. Our reply can be summed up in two words: "apologize" and "protest."

To apologize can mean, of course, to say we're sorry for our behavior, but its original meaning is "to speak on behalf of" someone. God chooses to allow His word to be spoken by those whose hearts are open to receive the outpouring, in love, of His Spirit. The second word is "protest," whose original Latin form, *pro-testificare*, has a deeper, more positive meaning than it has today: that is, to give witness, to testify for another. In giving witness by the way we live and by the values we hold, we can protest for Jesus' quality of life.

This is to be done, the letter says, with gentleness and respect (v. 16). Too often when people try to give witness to their love of God by their lives, they appear to be smug, proud, conceited, and closed to points of view differing from their own. They erect barriers. Gentleness doesn't mean groveling Casper Milquetoast-ishness. No, we show our love even in the way we differ from others. True love manifests itself in a selfless radiance of joy. We can try, with Christ's Spirit, even to suffer gladly, if that be the will of God (v. 17). And inasmuch as everyone must suffer to some extent, it's far better to suffer for doing right than for doing wrong. We're to show that, even if we're put to death in the flesh, as "resurrection people" we've been brought to life in the Spirit (v. 18).

Our world needs the discipline of love and the life of the Spirit as much as did the disciples to whom Jesus spoke, the Samaritans Philip met, and the converts to whom Peter wrote. There are many painful lives affected by broken relationships, shattered dreams, disappointments, physical and mental ills, and torturing guilt. We must let such people know that they needn't be alone in their pain.

In the face of a contrary world that wants us to take the easy way of keeping quiet and making no waves, we need the Spirit for ourselves as well, because we, too, have "been there." So let's not be faint-hearted in receiving the Spirit and in communicating Him to others by the witness of our lives. All of today's readings — John's Gospel, Luke's Acts of the Apostles, and Peter's letter — tell us that to be an apologist and a protestant out of love for Jesus befits a resurrection people.

FEAST OF THE ASCENSION
Ac 1:1-11   Eph 1:17-23   Mt 28:16-20

Christ Still Present with Us
Your Commission; Christ above the Universe; The Wealth of
Christ's Heritage for You; The Life of Grace; Sharing the Divine Life;
Our Hope and Our Joy; Achieving Immortality

We come together on this feast of our Lord's Ascension not to
commemorate a departure, but to celebrate the living and lasting
presence of him who at his birth was called "Emmanuel" — "God with
us." Jesus, the living head of his body the Church, remains always with
us as he promised — now in a new way. In fact, by this celebration we
proclaim that the risen Jesus enters into the fullness of the glory given
him by his Father. For those who follow him, his presence with us can
make our earth, our daily life, a heaven.

Where did the Ascension take place? St. Matthew tells us that it
was on the mountain to which Jesus had ordered them (v. 16). The
mountain, however, is as yet geographically undeterminable. It possibly belongs to the same *theological* category as the mountain of
temptation, the mountain of the sermon, and the mountain of the
transfiguration.

When and *how* did the Ascension happen? According to St. John
(20:17), Jesus' ascension took place on the day of his resurrection. But
for John the ascension means primarily the risen Jesus' new existence
with the Father. St. Luke in the Acts of the Apostles doesn't intend to
date the event. For him, the ascension marks simply the end of the
appearances of Jesus, except for the extraordinary appearance to St.
Paul. Christian traditions considered especially sacred the interval in
which the appearances of the risen Christ occurred, and expressed it
therefore in terms of the sacred number forty (cf. Dt 8:2). But that
tradition didn't solidify until around the fourth century.

Of one thing, however, we're sure: Jesus' ascension took place.
There had to be one final moment when Jesus entered the fullness of
glory that was his. The resurrection appearances couldn't go on forever.

Note: This homily is mostly on Matthew. For mostly Ephesians, see Cycle B;
        for an amalgam of all the readings, Cycle C.

And they couldn't just taper off; their end had to be definite. For the people of Jesus' time, including the Apostles, there was an added reason for a definite time for a specific ascension. Their view of the cosmos was that over the flat earth was a solid vault of sky, above which was God's throne. Whereas we regard heaven as a state of blessedness with God in a place that's cosmologically undeterminable, for them heaven was up: somewhere in the great beyond. For them, it was necessary for Jesus to go "up there," either by simply vanishing or by some kind of visible ascension.

The atheist Russian leader Nikita Khrushchev once ridiculed Christianity by remarking that his cosmonauts, on their journeys in space, had never reported seeing Jesus passing by. What he in his poor humor didn't know is that all stories about outer space, including that of Jesus' ascension, are based on cosmological assumptions of a particular time and place.

Whereas the science fiction of our time expresses our fear of the universe as forbidding and alien to human life if not positively hostile to it, the biblical accounts of Jesus' ascension employ bits and pieces of a cosmological picture which views the universe as truly awesome. It's the work of God, and it's run according to God's mysterious purposes. Human beings are far from aliens in it.

Today's celebration doesn't have to do with speculations about the universe, however, and with whether heaven is "up there" and we "down here"; our celebration deals with two other matters. One is God's involvement with human life, and the conflict of human wills — personal, social, national, and even cosmic — which threaten to overwhelm God's involvement. We must realize that heaven isn't up and out and away, and the Lord is with us. The other is our confidence in the ultimate triumph of the new human life which God is bringing into existence through the death and resurrection of Jesus.

No matter where, when, or how Jesus ascended, before he left he commissioned his followers to go and make disciples of all the nations (v. 19). Brief as this commission is, it's a communication of the authority that Jesus mentions as being his, both in heaven and on earth (v. 18). And it contains the conditions of membership in Christ's Church: faith in him, baptism, and observance of his commandments (v.20). The Chinese proverb says that a picture is worth a thousand words. But the one word that's worth a thousand pictures is that word "go." It brings to our mind's eye ardent missioners in kayaks, on donkeys, in primitive carts, in worn automobiles, and on foot to bring Jesus to hidden corners of this planet earth.

It must have been simply overwhelming for eleven humble Galileans to receive a commission to go out and conquer the world. The command applies with equal force to all who call themselves disciples of Christ. Our mission is not to an abstract world. Our social contacts, personal experience, and communications media keep us aware of the real world of sin and problems to which we're sent.

Our assignment, like that of the first apostles, is to all the nations. Our work is to baptize (v. 19) and to teach (v. 20). Baptism literally involves being plunged into the life of God. This rite of initiation is performed "in the name of the Father, and of the Son, and of the Holy Spirit." To do anything to someone "in the name of" another is to signify that one belongs to the person or persons named. Our participation in the divine life entails all that Jesus has commanded us (v. 20) — all the teaching of Jesus contained in the Gospel. What Jesus commanded isn't just the establishment of a new Law, but the beginning of a new way of life.

This amazing command is possible of fulfillment because of Jesus' concluding words: "I am with you always." Matthew had begun his Gospel with the promise of "God-with-us" (1:23); now he concludes with this strengthening assurance of Jesus. A more magnificent conclusion couldn't be found.

Jesus' ascension wasn't an ending of Jesus' presence on earth, but a constant testimonial to the fact that Jesus lives. In the face of all the wonder which today's feast represents, silence in the face of evil and inertia in the face of what must be done doesn't fit the true follower of Christ. In the face of all the current difficulties of the Church, we who believe in Christ's ascension mustn't just passively sit and wait. We must have an urgency in our waiting, an urgency which leads to active commitment on our part to work for our hoped-for future. Let's remember the words of today's Preface, that Christ has passed beyond our sight, not to abandon us but to be our hope, and where he has gone, we hope to follow.

SEVENTH SUNDAY OF EASTER
Ac 1:12-14   1 P 4:13-16   Jn 17:1-11

Quality of Life
Discipleship of Christ; Prayer; Joy; Glorifying God; Unity; Waiting;
Reminiscing; Knowing God; Suffering; The Mission of Disciples

People in the military joke that their way of life is, "Hurry up and wait."
But we all spend much of our life in waiting: for someone to arrive,
traffic to move, a loved one to return, life to be better. Today we
commemorate an important waiting: the early Church after Jesus'
Ascension waiting for the promised coming of the Holy Spirit.

Can you imagine yourself being present in the scene of today's
Gospel? It's the night before Jesus died. Aware of his fate on the next
day, he prayed. He prayed both to be heard and to be overheard — heard
by his heavenly Father, overheard by his Apostles and us. His prayer
was essentially for his Church, asking his Father to complete within it
what he had begun. It's a eucharistic prayer, because it expresses
gratitude for what the Father had given Jesus, and a priestly prayer
because, as mediator, he intercedes with the Father.

It's also a prayer structured as the Lord's Prayer, and therefore is
a model. Jesus first places his whole being before God. Then he prays
that through him God may bestow eternal life on all who accept him. By
eternal life Jesus means not the *duration* of life, but the *quality* of life.
This consists in knowing the true God (v. 3). In our age of facts, ideas,
research, and information on every subject imaginable, what does it
mean "to *know*"? There's no doubt that intellectual grasp of Christian
teachings plays a role in faith — but, alone, that doesn't lead to eternal
life. To know in the biblical sense denotes intimate experience of
someone: "Adam knew Eve his wife, and she conceived" (Gn 4:1).

What does it mean, especially, to know God? Jesus speaks of the
God whom he had taught us to call "Father." In fact, Jesus had
intimately called him "abba" — "daddy." Jesus prays that all who call
themselves Christian will come to know himself — with all his
compassion, courage, and other superb qualities. The person who really
knows that God is Father, and recognizes Jesus as the one who reveals
Him, enjoys life.

What Jesus means here is that a life of quality is a life of intimate experience of God. And the context in which Jesus speaks shows that he also means by knowing God being a part of the community of believers, having a share in the life of God's people. And it means giving glory to God on earth by joining with Jesus in finishing the work that the heavenly Father has given us to do (v. 4). An old poster said, "Be patient with me — God isn't finished with me yet!" And the earth in many places doesn't look like the finished homeland of those who love God and each other.

Today's reading from the Acts of the Apostles tells us that the first Christian community had learned Jesus' lesson and was at prayer between Jesus' Ascension into heaven and the coming of the Holy Spirit on the first Pentecost: They devoted themselves *with one accord* to prayer (v. 14). By their prayer, the *whole community* directed itself in *oneness* toward and opened itself to God.

In other words, it wasn't an individualism which many in our time prefer, attempting to get away from responsibility for one another; it was a shouldering of responsibility for one another, especially in such substantial parts of prayer life as Mass and the Sacraments. At every Mass, we're the assembled disciples of the risen Jesus waiting for the promised Holy Spirit to come to us and form us more fully into Christ's Church. It's by our participation in the Eucharist, the greatest prayer of the Church, that we both show that we are the Church and continually prepare ourselves to receive the gift of the Holy Spirit.

Whereas in the reading from the Acts of the Apostles the Church was embryonic and relatively safe, today's reading from the First Letter of Peter, the last of our six weeks of excerpts from the letter, makes a slight jump in time. Now we're probably in the time of one of the persecuting emperors, Nero or Trajan, when Christianity was outlawed and martyrdom was more than just a possibility. The letter shows the ambivalence of trying to live the Christian life. On one hand we're to rejoice in our giving glory to God. On the other hand, we're to be aware that we, like the rest of humanity, will suffer. That means organizations, too, including the Church. We may at times like to think of the Church, the "barque of Peter," as a sleek, modern, polished, beautiful ocean vessel cutting its way effortlessly through the seas. Actually, the barque of Peter is more like a leaky old tub in which everyone must just keep bailing — and rowing.

Does suffering detract from the quality of life? True suffering is to be seen not as what we bring upon ourselves through our own character weaknesses, but as meeting the unconquerable. Paradoxically, it's through the courage of enduring and accepting sufferings for Christ's sake that the disciple grows. One author (Anne Morrow Lindbergh) wrote:

> Courage is a first step,
> but simply to bear the blow is not enough.
> Stoicism is courageous,
> but it is only a half-way house on a long road.
> It is a shield permissible for a short time only.
> In the end, one has to discard shields,
> and remain open and vulnerable.
> Otherwise, scar tissue will seal off the wound
> and no growth will follow.
> To grow, to be reborn,
> one must remain vulnerable — open to love,
> but also hideously open
> to the possibility of more suffering.

Peter's letter tells us to rejoice to the extent that we share in the sufferings of Christ. Since Christians are called to suffer *for Christ*, they give witness to their faith in him by the way they face suffering.

When our suffering seems intolerably intense or unbearably long, we may find food for thought in a tale about a powerful Eastern king of long ago. He was in a position of such magnificence that wise men were his mere employees — even wise men. One day he felt himself confused and called the sages to him. He said: "I don't know why, but something impels me to seek a certain ring, one that will enable me to stabilize my condition. This ring must be one which, when I am unhappy, will make me joyful. At the same time, if I am happy and look upon it, I must be made sad." After deep contemplation and consultation, the wise men eventually came to a decision as to the character of the ring to suit their king. The ring they devised was one upon which was inscribed the legend: THIS, TOO, SHALL PASS.

A study has shown that an estimated 90 million Americans suffer from chronic pain, and thirty thousand tons of aspirin are produced every year. But what is pain? Some see three views of it in the annals of Western culture: the classical idea that pain is ennobling, the romantic idea that it's the source of art and truth, and the modern idea that it's nothing but an electrochemical disturbance in some neurological pathway for which relief should be found as soon as possible.

We're not to be indifferent to pain and suffering brought on by injustice: political tyranny, for example, or the corruption and prejudice which starves two-thirds of the human race and brutalizes millions. In that connection, we must also think of environmental justice. It's no longer possible to be religious without being an environmentalist; the ecological crisis is a moral issue. Justice, peace, and the integrity of creation all go together (*Catechism of the Catholic Church*, 2415 and *The Gospel of Life*, 3 & 42). Poisoned water crosses borders freely. Acid rain pours on countries that don't create it. Greenhouse gases affect the earth's atmosphere for many decades regardless of where they're produced.

And what about the way we treat the animal world? We're the recipients of two old traditions. The mainstream Western tradition has been that animal nature is not like ours, so animals simply don't matter, and people can do what they like with them. The other tradition, more subordinate, treats animals as our fellow-creatures, conscious beings like ourselves. This latter tradition, like the other, has had many impressive spokesmen: St. Francis, Montaigne, Voltaire, Plutarch, Blake, and John Stuart Mill, among others.

In our religious tradition, hostility to animals grew out of the preoccupation with establishing monotheism and avoiding nature-worship. Pagan religions had made much use of animal symbolism, and had often revered particular animals and plants as sacred. The gods had them as companions. Jove had his eagle, Athene her owl, Odin his ravens and his eight-legged horse. Moreover, pagan writers such as Plutarch who had championed animals had sometimes used arguments from the reincarnation of souls — that the souls of deceased people who proved themselves unworthy went into animals — which was contrary to Christian doctrine.

So the defense of animals smelled of heresy. St. Francis' influence in this respect — despite today's blessing of animals on his feastday — wasn't widespread. At the time when people like Montaigne had begun to suggest kindness to animals — the beginning of the seventeenth century — animals were hit by another piece of bad luck. Descartes, in laying the foundation of modern science, exalted human reason as the only genuine form of consciousness. Animals, having no reason, are just automata. This convenient doctrine was invoked to justify crude vivisections which even the conscience of the age found shocking. But Descartes' distinction became harder to swallow, because the difference between human nervous systems and those of other animals simply didn't turn out large enough to make it plausible.

What prevailed in general, however, was Spinoza's notion that animals, though conscious, can't concern us, because they're simply too different from us to warrant consideration. This kind of Enlightenment rationalism went far beyond Christianity. Exalting reason as humankind's link with God, self-worship by reason of human intelligence became to some extent an overt religion, as when the French revolutionaries enthroned the Goddess of Reason on the altar of Notre Dame cathedral in Paris. Similarly, the idea of humanism came to be given a religious dimension. Auguste Comte, the founder of Positivism, set up a formal Religion of Humanity.

Upsetting the general body of scientists as much as Christianity was Charles Darwin. A minority of his followers spoke of a unified physical world which was all God's continuous kingdom. For them, God's dignity was not at all damaged by the news that His creation had been slow and complex. But what worried many scientists about Darwin was not God's dignity but humankind's. For them, Darwin's idea that human dignity is compatible with an earthly origin was unbearable.

The romantic idea of the human being as conqueror is today largely replaced by a more realistic picture, based in particular on a better grasp of animal behavior. We now know, for example, that wolves don't spend their whole lives trying to devour each other, nor people. We live here surrounded by our animal relatives. In order to understand ourselves, we need to take animal parallels seriously, though of course not simplistically. Today, the Church distinguishes between the sin of worshipping animals and having some consideration for them.

Just as Jesus restored life by healing, so too are Christians called upon to heal the earth. Personal, social, and earth healing are essential for the survival of human societies and of planet Earth itself. Contemplation of God as being active and present in creation needs to be strongly encouraged; it's practiced in many Asian religious traditions.

We must also confront the world's growing population crisis. The strain on the earth's life-support systems by the doubling of the world's population (from 2.6 billion in 1950 to about 6 billion today) can't be ignored. The crisis will intensify as 90 percent of future population growth takes place in Asia, Africa, and Latin America, while the affluent nations maintain low population growth and dominate world resources. What's needed to lower the fertility rate are fundamental changes that improve women's lives, including education and increased control over money, credit, and other resources.

We shouldn't dismiss the trials of the oppressed with airy remarks about being better off "later on" in another life. God never sanctions the removal of dignity and worth from the creatures He's made. He's intimately interested in them: in the inadequate plumbing of the poor, in their welfare allowance, in our need for good police.

As we wait for Jesus' next coming, let's examine the quality of our lives as Christians, primarily in those areas we thought about today. Overall, let's go home with one important question that derives from the letter of Peter: If being a Christian were against the law in our country, and I were indicted for being a Christian, would there be enough evidence to convict me?

Pentecost Sunday
Ac 2:1-11   1 Cor 12:3-7, 12f.   Jn 20:19-23

Little Pentecosts
The Holy Spirit in the Church; Welcoming the
Holy Spirit; The Church, A New Creation

Originally, Pentecost was a Jewish feast called Shavuot or the Feast of Weeks. A week of weeks is forty-nine days, but if you count both ends (as the Semites did), it comes to fifty. It was celebrated on the fiftieth day after the Feast of Harvest or the Feast of the First-Fruits. It was a major feast and a very popular one on which Jews came to Jerusalem from all over the world to celebrate.

The awesome story of the first Christian Pentecost, fifty days after

---

Note: This homily is on Acts. Cycle B is mostly on John, Cycle C mostly on
1 Corinthians.

Jesus' resurrection, is told in today's reading from the Acts of the Apostles. St. Luke, its author, initiates this new creation in the same way in which he tends to highlight important events like the birth of Mary's child (2:6) and Jesus' resolute determination to go to Jerusalem to fulfill his mission and die (9:51). He now introduces the dawning of the age of the Holy Spirit as the dominant reality in the life of humankind. In Hebrew, Greek, and Latin, the word for "spirit" is the same as the word for "breath" and for "life."

As symbols of the coming of the Holy Spirit, Luke uses a driving wind, sound, fire, and tongues (vv. 2, 3). These symbols wouldn't have been strange to Jews who knew their Scriptures. The Spirit of God blew over the waters at creation and rushed upon David on the occasion of his anointing as king (1 S 16:13). And God appeared frequently in the Jewish Scriptures in the form of fire, the best symbol to the Jews of the brightness and intensity of the activity of God — as, for example, God appearing to Moses in a burning bush and on Mt. Sinai in the form of lightning.

The familiar symbol of tongues is easily grasped as communicating a heavenly gift. Tongues of fire came to rest on each one of the Apostles (v. 3) — due, as Luke points out (v. 4), to the activity of the Holy Spirit. The phenomenon of the people from many nations understanding the Apostles is the countertype of the confusion of tongues at the Tower of Babel (Gn 11).

The activity of the Spirit is the subject-matter of the rest of the Acts of the Apostles. The Spirit instructs the early missioners, is the driving force in proclaiming the message of salvation, is responsible for conversions to the new faith, gives strength in persecution, is the inspiration for St. Paul's journeys, and is responsible for the inclusion of non-Jews in the early Church. And all of God's saving activity until the end of time is due to the loving action of the Holy Spirit.

But perhaps the greatest marvel was the fact that weak, timid and shallow men were changed into bold and wise men who would reach the ends of the earth to proclaim Jesus. Four of these men were fishermen. Because of the fiery tempers of two of them — James and John — Jesus had nicknamed them the "Sons of Thunder." Another of these fishermen, Peter — who was called impetuous, but who a less benevolent interpreter might call thoughtless — was fast to speak, and slow to hear. Jesus had alternately called him "the Rock" and "Satan."

The group contained a reformed tax collector, Matthew, at least one member of an outlawed party of violence (Simon the Zealot), a skeptic (Thomas), and a no-nonsense sophisticate (Judas). When the crowds saw the fullness of joy in the Apostles and the wonders they were working, they were amazed. The phenomenon of the proclamation of the Gospel message in all languages seemed to point to the beginning of a universal experience — the Church — that would reach all humankind.

But what is the Church? In a religiously monolithic society in which there is one dominant religion — Spain with Roman Catholicism, England with Anglicanism, Sweden with Lutheranism, Israel with Judaism — a church has a relatively clear identity. In a pluralistic society professing religious freedom and in which there are many churches, sects, cults, and denominations, as in the United States, the definition of church — as, for example, in "Church-State relations" — is difficult.

The U.S. Congress, which exempts churches from some tax and other obligations, has in studied silence left the word undefined. The courts usually define "church" functionally, often as a building, because they have to settle property disputes between members or decide zoning regulations and variances. Although the Internal Revenue Service has admitted its inability to formulate a definition, it has loosely used fourteen criteria which it derived from the practices of recognized churches.

Even among us there are confusions of definition of the Catholic Church. Aside from the church building ("Let's go to church"), people often use such expressions as "The Church says," "The Church forbids," and so on. To be accurate they should rather say, "The Code of Canon Law says," or "According to Vatican Council II," or "the statutes of our diocese state." In other words, people sometimes say "Church" when they mean the hierarchy, or the proclamations of law, or the Church's administration.

The titles of Vatican Council II's two documents on the Church tell what the Church should be: a light to the nations and joy and hope to the world. The Pastoral Constitution on the Church in the Modern World (*Gaudium et Spes*), asserts that the Church must consider itself as part of the human family, sharing the same concerns as the rest of humankind. It says (Arts. 3, 92) that just as Christ came into the world not to be served but to serve, so the Church, carrying on his mission, seeks to serve the world. In the Church's dialogue with the world, the

Church has important things to say to the world, as well as the world to the Church.

Of the 95 images in Scripture for the Church, Vatican II picked four, each for a reason, and each with its own difficulties. The first is the Church as the *New People of God*. Vatican II chose this image from Paul to counterbalance the view of the Church as being only the hierarchy. Obviously, the image emphasizes *God the Father*. The Christian community is the *new* People of God profoundly linked with the Older Covenant. By using this image for the Church, the Council wanted to stress that the Church has to be seen as involved in history and therefore affected by the weaknesses and infidelities of its members who constantly stand in need of God's mercy and forgiveness.

The concept of the Church as the New People of God likewise emphasizes the notion of equality in the Church, and the democratic element of participatory democracy. The knowledge that "the Church is us" gives a solid sense of unity as well as the realization that the mission of the Church is essentially concerned with the penetration of God's dominion in *this* world as well as with life hereafter.

The Vatican Council's second image is that the Church is the *Body of Christ*. This emphasizes *God the Son*, expressing our intimate union with the risen and glorified Lord as his continuing presence in the world. This image never enjoyed a deep appreciation among the faithful: It seems to identify the Church so closely with its divine head that it doesn't make enough allowance for sin and infidelity on the part of its members, corporately as well as individually.

The third image of Vatican Council II is that the Church is *Temple of the Holy Spirit*. Paul says the Spirit keeps the Church alive. And the Vatican Council's fourth image is the Church as the *Sacrament of Salvation*. As Christ is the Sacrament of God, so the Church is seen as the Sacrament of Christ. She makes him present and tangible in this world until he comes again. There are, of course, other descriptions of the Church today (in, for example, Avery Dulles, *Models of the Church*).

Through the ministry of the Church, whenever we receive the gift of the Holy Spirit's action in our lives we experience a little pentecost. Little pentecosts happen whenever we use the special gifts gently given us by the Spirit to serve all the other members of the community of humankind. They happen whenever we cooperate with God's inspiration to bring peace, to unify our parish, to do a good deed, to help a needy neighbor, to think kindly thoughts of others, or to allow God to forgive our sins.

Only when we cooperate with our little pentecosts can we have the wonderful experiences of the first Christian Pentecost. Then we may look to enabling better communication between those with wrinkled skin on their bent frames, on the one hand, and bearded youth with ragged shorts, on the other, and between staunch conservatives and radical liberals. Then we will dynamically share our faith and our joy. And, if some say we're drunk, as they did of the Apostles on the first Christian Pentecost (in the next few verses of the Acts of the Apostles), we can with St. Peter remind them that it's still early in the morning of our new life in the Spirit.

TRINITY SUNDAY
Ex 34:4-6, 8f.   2 Cor 13:11-13   Jn 3:16-18

The Triune God as Our Model
Stiff-Necked Humankind; Mysteries of God
and People; Keep the Faith; Images of God

Some preachers and other critics constantly deplore modern times for being different from the past, and usually worse. A close examination of history, however, might reveal the truth of the adage that "the more things change, the more they remain the same."

Take, for example, our belief in and conduct towards God. At the time today's first reading was written, the Jews could have remembered all kinds of God's wonders: Genesis's account of creation, God's call of Moses, the ten plagues on Egypt, God's sentence of death upon the Egyptians which brought deliverance and freedom to the Jews, the crossing of the Reed Sea and the destruction of the Egyptian army there, manna from heaven as their food, water from the rock, God's appearance on Mt. Sinai, their covenant with God, and more. Most of all, they could have remembered that their Lord wants to be "with" His people.

Yet the same Book of Exodus recorded the Jews' building the golden calf to worship instead of the true God. In today's passage Moses awesomely besought the "merciful and gracious God" to pardon this "stiff-necked people" for their "wickedness and sins." This is part of the mystery of both humankind and God. How is it possible for people to wander off from God when they realize that all the highest achievements of the human race have been made in God's name, and for God to respond to ingratitude and rejection by retaining His compassionate interest in people?

St. Paul faced the same mystery. Today's second reading contains the very last words of his Second Letter to the Corinthians. The Corinthians, too, were a stiff-necked people wallowing in all kinds of sins that we can imagine of any city of any time. Nevertheless, at the end of his chiding letter Paul wished everybody what we wish each other at the beginning of Mass: "the grace of the Lord Jesus Christ, and the love of God, and the fellowship of the Holy Spirit."

What beautiful words! The grace of the Lord Jesus Christ is God's creative, transforming love — in other words, God Himself freely seeking to give Himself to us. It's called the grace "of Jesus Christ" because, of all human beings, in Jesus infinite love is embraced, embodied, and carried out. When Paul wishes us "the love of God," he means the same reality under a different aspect: not Jesus who makes love known, but Jesus who is love's source.

The "fellowship of the Holy Spirit" is unique. There are thousands of different kinds of fellowship. Here we have *koinonia* in St. Paul's Greek, which can be translated also as "communion," "sharing," or "participation." It can reach from young married couples establishing a home to the human race setting up a United Nations. But the highest, deepest, and broadest fellowship is that with our God. If we have fellowship with our God, we will have fellowship with one another, and we will accomplish Paul's injunctions to encourage one another, live in harmony and peace, and greet one another with a holy kiss. These much-desired results for the human race can be accomplished in no other way.

Paul's words reflect a further revelation of God, made through Jesus: there are three persons in the one God. The Father loves the Son into existence, and their mutual love is so strong, personal, and personalizing that their love is the Holy Spirit. In our human way of thinking, we tend to attribute the external works of God to different persons of the Trinity: creation to the Father, redemption to the Son, and grace to the Holy Spirit. In reality, while we appropriate specific works outside God to one or the other of the three Persons, *all* the Persons of the one God are involved in all His external works. All three Persons created the universe, all three redeem, and all three sanctify.

What's more to the point here, though, is the *internal* relations among the persons of God. These are most intimate, most intense, and bonded by love. For human beings, who are created in God's image, these relationships are a model of the peace, harmony, and love which should characterize our community life with each other. Disharmony, discord, and wars among people arise when humanity wanders away from God.

In today's Gospel, Nicodemus was sufficiently troubled about Jesus' claim to have come from God that he came to Jesus to look into it for himself. He came at night, because as a member of the Jews' select ruling body he had a lot to lose if he were caught with Jesus.

Jesus' words to Nicodemus show that it was God — all three persons — who started the whole process of redemption, and the mainspring was love: "God so loved the world that he gave his only Son" (v. 16). Jesus tells us through Nicodemus that God's love for people is not only deep but universal. He loves not only one nation, or the good people, or those who love Him. Even the pagans do that, as Jesus reminds us elsewhere. No — as St. Augustine put it, "God loves each one of us as if there were only one of us to love." And if we let Him, He will love us into a quality of life beyond our dreams.

All who face Jesus reveal themselves. Condemnation, if it happens, will come not from God, but from ourselves. It happens in a way that we can describe only analogously. Suppose you want to share with a friend your enthusiasm about great music, or eminent paintings, or majestic scenery, or profound poetry. During the entire exposure, your friend looks bored or falls asleep. He thereby condemns himself, at least to the extent of showing a great blind spot in his soul. People who exhibit the same kinds of reaction when exposed to the ultimate greatness, God, also condemn themselves.

In this respect, we wonder about Nicodemus. John the evangelist tantalizingly doesn't tell us whether Nicodemus was converted to Jesus or not. We don't know whether his hesitation came from his lack of docility because he was a leader, or his fear of consequences to his career ambitions, or his lack of decisiveness as an intellectual. Nicodemus seems to be a symbol of those who have only a partial faith in Jesus. The Evangelist, in his comparisons between those who believe in Jesus as coming into the light and those who don't believe as remaining in darkness, might be said to speak of Nicodemus as only coming *near* the light. Our natural curiosity prompts us to ask, "Did he ever step into the light by coming into faith?"

The more important question is, "Have we?" Faith in the Trinity, for example, seems to have nothing to do with painting our room, tapping away at a computer, or doing the wash. Or does it? The Trinity touches our human life at every point. If we're made in the image of God, as the Bible tells us, we're made in the image of the Trinity, and the life of the Trinity must in some way be reflected in the pattern of our life. Perhaps one such mirroring is between the activities identified with each person of the Trinity and the categories of activity in which we engage.

Thus to the Father is attributed all that we understand by generation, creation, and maintenance. Everything we do to awaken and cherish new life, to fashion, mold, and develop our physical environment, shares in that work of the heavenly Father; fathering and mothering, designing and building, growing crops, shaping and tending the landscape, fashioning all kinds of things for our use and pleasure, all arts and crafts — in short, every kind of making — fall under this head.

Likewise, all human works of compassion, healing, reconciling, service, forgiveness, and making amends reflect the work of redemption and reconciliation and are identified most closely with the Son: all, that is, that falls under the head of caring.

Lastly, the special role of the Holy Spirit is reflected in every positive idea and inspiration, however slight and humble, in every advance in knowledge and wisdom, in every flash of imagination, in every movement of the heart.

To divide these categories of activity into neat compartments would clearly make no better sense than attempting to saw the Triune God into three pieces. In common experience they're functions of the same identity, and they intertwine, influence, and complement each other.

In these times, when so many people feel fragmented and divided within themselves and find it difficult to recognize or work to any clear pattern of life, there are here suggestive hints and glimpses of the contact between the Trinity's life and our own: hints of the unity in the Triune God that should characterize us who are made in His image, glimpses of His love that overflows and touches the whole of creation but especially human beings, hints of the ways we should illustrate the lovely qualities of our God, glimpses of the Gospel values that should permeate our lives, and a shape and sense of direction to all our human activities.

SOLEMNITY OF THE BODY AND BLOOD OF CHRIST
Dt 8:2f., 14-16   1 Cor 10:16f.   Jn 6:51-58

Devotion to the Eucharist
One-ness: with God and One Another; Memory and Religion;
Unity, Community, and Togetherness; Jesus the Sign of God's Care

One of the most useful of modern inventions is the computer. To list but a few of its accomplishments, it can dispense payrolls, discover future trends, get us into space, form conclusions from complex data, and pay our bills. But still more wonderful than the computer is the human brain which conceived it. One medical expert said, "If all of the equipment of all the telegraphs, telephones, radios, and television sets of the North American continent could be squeezed into a half-gallon vase, it would be far less intricate than the three pints of brain that fill your head." One of the many unappreciated capabilities of the human brain is its ability to remember.

When Moses on the way to the Promised Land told his people to "remember," he was dealing with some of the most important events of his people, especially the Passover, the most sacred feast in the Jewish calendar. In today's reading from Deuteronomy, Moses tells his people to remember especially the manna, a food that had been unknown to their ancestors (v. 16), by which God fed them. Manna was a sticky sweet resin exuded by trees like the tamarisk which, on hardening, could be eaten. The word comes possibly from the Aramaic *man hu*, "what is this?," which expresses the wonder of the discovery that God's love and providential care kept His chosen people alive on this substance.

The manna was not only material food giving physical life, but was also a symbol of God's word, which was the means of a superior spiritual life: the life of communion with God through the covenant. By the time of Jesus, the manna of the Exodus had come to represent the miraculous bread which God would give His people at the end-time.

Reminiscent of the manna, the sixth chapter of St. John's Gospel begins with the only miracle recounted by all four evangelists, the miracle of the multiplication of the loaves to feed five thousand people. The night of the miracle, when Jesus had escaped from the crowd that was eager to make him king and the Apostles had rowed across the lake ahead of him, he walked to them on the water.

When the crowd, curious miracle-seekers, followed on foot around the lake and found him, Jesus tried to raise their hearts from self-preoccupation to the meaning of the Eucharist. He asked the people to remember the manna, and claimed that he is this "bread" in person. The people were puzzled, and asked how this man could give them his flesh to eat (v. 52). Jesus replied by a solemn insistence on the literal interpretation of his words. People's spiritual life requires this eating and drinking of his flesh and blood, and like a good teacher with students blinded by too great a light of truth, he repeated the thought.

Who, indeed, could be expected to believe that Jesus was giving people his flesh to eat and his blood to drink? Literally, this would mean that by becoming one of us he became bone of our bone and flesh of our flesh. His listeners knew their longing for union with their God. They knew also that such a union would bring a closeness that's more intimate and more real than any union with other human beings.

It would be nice to be able to say that the story ended well, but it ended then as complex as it has ended throughout history. Our mental faculties, wonderful though they are and far superior to computers, aren't infinite in capacity. Only faith can find the truth and the nourishment in some of the hard sayings of the Messiah. Many in this audience, commenting on the hardness of this saying, asked who can believe it (v. 60). One's response to Jesus lies in the secret of each individual heart and no one can usurp that personal responsibility.

It's not as though we don't have reason to guide us. Some time ago, a street-corner preacher who knew how to make religious truth come to life was faced by a hostile crowd. "How," one of them demanded, "is it possible for bread and wine to become the body and blood of Christ?" The preacher looked calmly at the stout questioner for a moment and answered, "You've grown somewhat since you were a child and have more flesh and blood than you had then. Surely, if the human body can change food and drink into flesh and blood, God can do it, too."

"But how," countered the heckler, "is it possible for Christ to be present in his entirety in a small host?" The preacher glanced up at the sky and down the city street before them and answered, "This city scene and the sky above it is something immense, while your eye is very small. Yet your eye contains in itself the whole picture. When you consider this, it won't seem impossible for Christ to be present in his entirety in a little piece of bread."

Once more the heckler attacked. "How, then, is it possible for the same body of Christ to be present in all your churches at the same time?" The preacher's answer was, "In a large mirror you see your image reflected but once. When you break the mirror into a hundred pieces, you see the same image of yourself in each of the hundred fragments. If such things occur in everyday life, why should it be impossible for the body of Christ to be present in many places at once? And tell me, just what *isn't* possible for God, anyhow?"

Today's words of St. Paul to the Corinthians are a wonderful confirmation of the early celebration of the Eucharist and of the early mature understanding of Christ's presence in the Eucharist. Paul reminds us that our religion isn't a matter of just saving my own soul, but something greater and deeper through which we all share in the salvation of all. He also reminds us that at the Eucharistic meal we faithful actually participate in Christ's life.

Today, the Solemnity of the Body and Blood of Christ, let's use our mental ability to remember. Let's remember all of the associations of the Eucharist: the manna in the desert, the multiplication of the loaves, the Last Supper, the re-enactment today. Let's remember that the Eucharist is God's idea and not ours; we wouldn't have thought of it any more than we would have thought of making the dew. Let's remember that the presence of Jesus in the Eucharist isn't physical but a unique presence called sacramental, and deserves our reverence and respect in attitude, dress, and demeanor. Let's remember, in the few minutes we have when we return to our places after communion, to allow the Eucharist to speak to us in all its fullness.

Let's remember that in the Eucharist we commune with Jesus' life, death, and resurrection. Let's remember also that eating and drinking are meant to be symbolic of our wanting to live by the Word of God. As St. Augustine said: "It is no use feeding on Christ with our teeth if we are not feeding on him with our minds," that is, by faith. Union with Jesus and with one another takes place through the Eucharist, but that's only the beginning.

TENTH SUNDAY IN ORDINARY TIME
Ho 6:3-6   Rm 4:18-25   Mt 9:9-13

Who Are the Chosen?
God's Love for His People — All of Them; With Whom Should We Sit at Table?; To Whom Does the Saving Power of God Go?; Can Sinners Be Among "The Upright"?; Is Phariseeism Dead?

A newly-promoted military officer received a brand-new office commensurate with his new title. On his first morning behind his desk, there was a knock on his door and a young enlisted man asked to speak to him. The official, feeling the urge to impress the young man, picked up his phone and said, "Yes, general, thank you, yes. I'll pass that along to the President this afternoon. Good-bye." Then he turned to the young man and barked, "And what do *you* want?" "Nothing, sir. I just came to hook up your phone."

That officer represents the most difficult people in all the world to deal with or improve — proud people, "respectable" people, people who think they have everything. They build an impenetrable shell around themselves. Their resistance to the words of others may spring from their subtle forms of pride that won't accept anything from any source but themselves. Most people — not all — who have suffered rejection, misunderstanding, ill health, or other misfortune have no illusions about their ability to have the world spin their way. Their suffering has given them an open heart and a listening ear, so that they can more easily respond to the truth of another.

Today's liturgy affords a good contrast between the proud and the unaccepted. The Gospel opens with a "controversy story" about a man named Matthew, who was sitting at a customs post (v. 9). His tax-collecting post, a good one, was at Capernaum, on the border between the domains of Herod Antipas and Philip, where the Jordan River entered the Lake of Galilee and the great road from Egypt to Damascus passed through. His "take" was large. Sts. Mark and Luke in telling this story use St. Matthew's other name, Levi, to hide his identity, but Matthew humbly uses the name by which he was better known.

In the Roman system, there were all kinds of taxes: income tax, poll tax, tax on produce, import tax, export tax, road-use tax, sales tax, wheel tax on carts, and pack-animal tax. Tax collectors bid for their positions, promised to pay a certain amount to Rome, and were allowed to line their pockets with the remainder. Not satisfied with this, many tax collectors took bribes from the rich in return for decreasing their taxes, and leaned heavily on the poor.

The people's hatred of tax collectors was more than a matter of financial loss. The Jews were nationalists, and they believed that their God, not Rome or any other power, was their only legitimate king. The Jews considered tax collectors as a class to be moral reprobates. They barred them from the synagogue, declared them unclean, and forbade them to act as witnesses in court. Matthew loved money enough to have defied all that.

Matthew must have heard of Jesus, who by this time was a focus of attention. What's surprising, in view of who Matthew was, is the speed with which he got up and followed Jesus. When Matthew weighed everything in the balance — his material losses over and against his potential spiritual gains — he decisively opted for Jesus. Perhaps that was part of the good that Jesus saw in him. Grace had been freely and generously given him and Matthew freely and generously responded. Jesus saw in Matthew not only who he then was, but who he could become. Fortunately, Jesus does this with all of us.

Matthew threw a farewell dinner party for his friends — many fellow tax collectors and others considered to be sinners (v. 10): Damon Runyon characters and jailbirds all rolled into one. Oriental banquets like this were semi-public functions, so it was natural that the Pharisees saw this one (v. 11). The Pharisees were aghast at eating with *foreigners*, much less with *sinners*. To be sympathetic to people on the lower rungs of the social ladder just wasn't done. It made one unclean. Therefore they didn't enter the dining room but took Jesus' disciples aside and questioned them about what reason Jesus could have for acting like this.

Jesus, reacting strongly to their snobbishness, leveled them with three terse reasons. First, the Pharisees prescribe from afar for fear of contagion, but Jesus goes where sickness causes the greatest need. His second reason was from the nature of religion, especially as taught by the prophet Hosea in today's second reading, part of which Jesus quoted to say that what God wants are demonstrations of mercy (v. 13; Ho 6:6).

Even as Jesus spoke, Israel hadn't learned its lesson on the nature of religion any more than it had eight centuries before, when Hosea wrote. Overall, Hosea stressed God's marriage-like love for His people. In today's reading, he shows the fertility of a repentant heart in terms of dawn, light, rain, and spring (v. 3). It's evidently hard to learn that it's love of neighbor that gives value to the sacrifices which people offer to show their love of God.

True religion places human relations above cultic worship and above the observance of a merely external way of life. It expresses compassion for sinners. Jesus' association with tax collectors and violators of the law is consistent with his definition of religion, as well as with his teaching on the need of repentance. This reasoning led naturally into Jesus' third argument to the Pharisees — that he didn't come to call the righteous but sinners (v. 13). That, praise the Lord, involves us all.

If we want to belong to Jesus, we must look to his definition of true religion and to our faith in God. Our model of faith is Abraham, as cited by St. Paul in his letter to the Romans. Both Abraham and his wife Sarah were very old when God promised to make Abraham the father of many (Gn 17:17). But hoping against hope (v. 18), he believed God. This wasn't without obvious difficulty. Paul omits repeating another part of what Genesis tells us — namely, that Abraham fell on his face and laughed when he heard the impossible news that at his age he would have a son.

In the final analysis, Abraham believed in a God who can make the impossible possible, and who encourages people with proper faith to *dare* — to dare *anything*. Abraham's faith is the pattern for Christian faith, because its object is the same: belief in God who does all this. Abraham's belief foreshadowed the Christian's belief in the risen Jesus — whom, with Paul, we hail as Lord (v. 24). Jesus was handed over for our transgressions (v. 25), suffering for *all* of us, saint and sinner alike.

Some people, today as well as in the days of Hosea, Jesus, and Paul are more interested in preserving status than in helping sinners. They invite to their table and give their time and attention to those who can help their careers rather than those in need. They engage more easily in criticizing than in encouraging, in pointing out faults rather than in praising good points. They find condemnation easier than forgiveness. They prefer outward shows of orthodox form to pious inner substance. They don't recognize their illness of pride, self-righteousness, and self-sufficiency, and so will never invite the presence of Jesus the physician.

Only those who humbly confess that they're sinners will approach Jesus. And, no matter what their sin, Jesus will receive and welcome them gladly, since he is in truth the friend of sinners. He hates sin but loves sinners and wishes to set them free. There are two kinds of sinners. The first despise others and arrogantly consider themselves righteous. The second humbly acknowledge that they're sinners, know they need Jesus, trust him, and beg him to come and heal them. The first kind in their pride rule out Jesus. Hopefully we belong to the second kind.

ELEVENTH SUNDAY IN ORDINARY TIME
Ex 19:2-6   Rm 5:6-11   Mt 9:36 - 10:8

God Needs People
Vocation; Having a Mission; Joy in Being God's People; Leadership Theory;
We Walk with God; A Communitarian vs. A Do-It-Yourself Religion

If you work for someone else, you've probably often tried to fathom your boss's principles of administration. If you're a boss, you've undoubtedly tried to figure out the most efficient ways to conduct your job, impress your superiors, and get the best work from your employees. Today's liturgy shows how God needs people in His work.

The Gospel — verses that St. Matthew put together from Jesus' sayings — shows that the ideal of Christian administrative leadership isn't the wielding of power *over* others, as it is with some business people and politicians, but the use of power *for* others. It's not a political "might is right," but "might for right." It's a power to care, to share, and to heal. It's illustrated at the Round Table in *Camelot* by King Arthur, who dreamed of the possibility of a communion of people for the world, and who wondered about the pain and torment that even King Arthur's enemies were going through.

Jesus' heart was moved with pity (v. 36) for the crowds, a pity that went to the depths of his being. Jesus had been moved like this before: for the sick, for the blind, for those in the power of demons, for lepers whose life was a living death of isolation, for the widow mourning the death of her only son.

Now he's moved by the sight of the crowds, who were exhausted from poor people's thousand petty persecutions. Jesus sees in these people all the marginalized: the tired, the abused, the sad, and the abandoned. They're "like sheep without a shepherd." They're what the Pharisees called "the people of the land" — nice words, but a term of derision they used for the poor who didn't know the law very well.

The Pharisees' idea of leadership was to deal only with those who are profitable. Jesus saw the poor in a completely different way: These people are persons, and they're worthwhile. No matter how one views Christian administrative theory, the first necessity is prayer: "Ask the master of the harvest" (v. 38). Without prayer, the leaders risk preaching themselves rather than Christ, making the work their own rather than his, engaging in the process more to build their own kingdom rather than God's.

The first petition of Jesus' prayer is to send out laborers: Jesus realizes that God needs people. The amount of work seems way out of proportion to the resources. When he summoned his twelve disciples (10:1), it might have been glorious for some of them to think that they were numbered "The Twelve" after the twelve tribes of Israel. But they're just ordinary men without wealth, academic achievement, or social position: a few fishermen, a tax collector, a freedom fighter, a traitor-to-be, and other more shadowy people.

The list (vv. 2-4) singles out Peter as being first. It puts the twelve in pairs, mentioning the two sets of brothers first. It ranges from Matthew the tax collector to Simon who belonged to the radical anti-Roman revolutionary party. Were it not for the presence of Jesus, Simon might have killed the likes of Matthew. The only source of their unity is Jesus.

Out of this motley group, Jesus forms "Apostles" — people who are "sent out." Like a teacher with students, or a president dispatching ambassadors, or a general with his officers, Jesus gives his new

Apostles instructions. Though his instructions still constitute norms for all Christian missionaries, some of them were temporary. He says, for instance, that they aren't to go into pagan territory or enter a Samaritan town. In effect, this limits them to Galilee. He had nothing against pagans or Samaritans. As for pagans, he healed the daughter of a Syro-Phoenician woman, and would later give the command to go out into the whole world. As for Samaritans, he had told a story in which the hero was a Samaritan, and had acted kindly with a woman of Samaria. But for the time being practical administrative wisdom dictated that he limit his objectives.

The Jews have the first call (v. 6). The rest of the mission can come later. And they're commanded to *do* as well as to *teach*: for example, to cure the sick, raise the dead, seek the lost, and show compassion for the flock, especially the abandoned. They're to forget no one. Those who, like the leprous, are considered unclean, are to be cleansed, and people who are enslaved by demons, of no matter whose making, are to be set free.

Moses, too, had conveyed a mission to God's people: to be witnesses to the divine holiness. Today's reading from Exodus, the second book of the Bible, tells of the Jews' departure from Egypt and their journey to the Holy Land. Three months after leaving Egypt they came to Mount Sinai, where today's scene took place.

Amid clouds and thunder and lightning, Moses went up the mountain, where with solemnity and power God reminded His people that in Egypt He had borne them up "on eagle wings" (v. 3). In the intimacy of their relationship, He promised them that if they hearken to His voice and keep His covenant, they shall be His special possession (v. 5). It was an offer the Jews couldn't refuse. Salvation history thereafter, however, shows them, like all of us, often less than zealous in living up to their part of the covenant.

Inasmuch as the whole Israelite nation was consecrated to God in a special way, God made them "a kingdom of priests" (v. 6). Everyone participated in the liturgical sacrifices, even though the actual offering of the sacrifices was the exclusive prerogative of the priesthood of the family of Aaron. God's wise administration of humankind shows a similar situation in the New Dispensation: the whole Christian people shares in the Christian priesthood, being always on mission for God.

In today's reading from his Letter to the Romans (which is so important a letter that we shall be reading it for the next thirteen

Sundays), St. Paul tells us the tremendous extent and final proof of God's love: Christ died for the ungodly (v. 6). In life, it's possible to find heroes who have given their lives for great and good principles like democracy, or for their friends (v. 7). Society recognizes such sacrifice by awarding statues and medals to the families of such heroes. But Jesus died while we were still sinners — enemies. No one's love can go further than that.

The picture is not of Christ coming to assuage a vengeful God, but of the great way that God the Father loves us. That love is so monumental that it was that which sent His Son. God is hurt by our absence from the interplay of love — the spirit of love is diminished when we turn away from it — but God chooses to be willing to let us go and to suffer the diminishment. Erich Fromm, I think, was first to publish that most helpful distinction between "I love you because I need you" and "I need you because I love you."

There is no *quid pro quo* expected in the love between God and us: God loves us unconditionally. Even if we don't love enough in return, His love still surrounds us. The effect of the cross is that, whereas before that event people stood in fear of God's wrath, now we boast of Jesus making us right with God (v. 11).

In managing our salvation, Jesus never intended an individualistic approach. Our first reading recalls the chosen people's relationship with God to be communitarian. That relationship continues between Jesus and us. This means finding joy in being God's people. Should that carry us into a life of commitment like the priesthood, brotherhood, or sisterhood, Jesus is Lord. Should it be to the commitment of lay singleness or marriage, Jesus is the same Lord. St. John Chrysostom wrote: "Nothing is colder than a Christian who does not care for the salvation of others." Today we're called to break out of our little ice cubes.

The home, the parish, and the workplace offer opportunities for us to accept God's mission as ours. We should take seriously the lessons of an event that took place at the end of World War II, when United States soldiers in a bombed German village helped the villagers clear away the rubble and repair shattered homes. The big job was the ruined church. Slowly they patched the broken walls and the fallen roof. One day they began to put together the fragments of a statue of Christ that had tumbled from the high altar. When they lifted it back to its pedestal it was almost like new, except that they couldn't find the marble hands.

So at the foot of the handless Savior they wrote this poignant line: "I have no other hands than yours."

TWELFTH SUNDAY IN ORDINARY TIME
Jr 20:10-13   Rm 5:12-15   Mt 10:26-33

Fear, Confidence, and Love
What Real Death Means; Fear of Death; Awe and Reverence in the
Twentieth Century; The Indestructibility of the Human Spirit;
Courage in the Face of Intimidation

When the United States was in the midst of a great depression and there was misery and want everywhere, President Franklin D. Roosevelt coined a phrase that has rung through time. He said, "The only thing we have to fear is fear itself." But fear haunts everyone: fear for one's job, fear for the welfare of one's children, fear about sickness, fear about providing for one's old age — and fear of fear. For the Christian, the worst fear is that we would be seduced from our relationship with Jesus, through whom we are united with the heavenly Father.

The Apostles certainly had room for legitimate fear as they had to face the scary consequences of witnessing to Christ. In today's Gospel (part of Jesus' "Mission Discourse" or "Apostolic Discourse" in St. Matthew) Jesus, having shown up the sly methods of the scribes and Pharisees, tells his disciples what he hopes for from them. They're to engage in the confession that Jesus is the Messiah, and this commitment is to be a confession without fear.

What we're to fear isn't what hurts superficially, but what could damage the spirit — like letting others intimidate us to be careless about truth. There can be much self-interest in the propagation of what appears as truth. Map makers, for example, may create a map that best makes their case or supports their unconscious bias. Publishers may include nonexistent streets in their maps in the hope of trapping a careless competitor who has copied their map without paying for research. Government security people may camouflage map terrain to misinform military rivals.

Self-serving tourist operators and chambers of commerce may make highway interchanges look simple when in reality they could cause a screaming nervous breakdown. Housing developers may use maps to make their projects appear arboreally abundant when any trees that actually grace their site will be scrawny saplings until well into the next millennium.

As Diogenes's search discovered a long time before Christ, a truthful person is hard to find. Many people don't like the truth and like even less the consequences that may result from telling it. But truth will triumph (v. 26) and will be revealed either in our lifetime or later. We must listen to and learn the message of Christ, and speak up boldly and fearlessly despite the consequences (v. 27).

In the matter of proclaiming the whole truth about Jesus, as with all moral options there is still place in the Christian life for holy fear of the transcendent and immanent God. That kind of fear, involving both awe of God's holiness and trust in Him, should be reverential and not servile and intimidating. On balance, though, we realize that there are things that are worse than death — having to live with yourself, for example, when you've been unfaithful (v. 28).

Counterbalancing fear is confidence in God — a confidence that has underlying motives in all three persons of God. The heavenly Father's care extends not only to big things like armies in battle, but also to intimate little details like the life of sparrows (v. 29), an entire flock of which are nowhere near the worth of a human being (v. 31). We're confident also because Jesus the Son will take care of his own (v. 32). Matthew elsewhere reports Jesus as saying (10:19f.) that when you have to witness to him you're not to worry, because the Holy Spirit will speak through you.

Nevertheless, it's still possible for the so-called "Christian" to deny Jesus: by words, by cowardly silence (the most prevalent way of denial), and by actions. The actions can be in things like petty dishonesties with oneself and others, preferring one's ease and comfort to the rigor of the full Christian life, and living in bitter resentment of others.

In the face of it all, what Jesus advised elsewhere (Mt 10:16) is that we be wise as serpents and innocent as doves. The guile of the serpent and the innocence of the dove are to be present at the same time in the same person. No one is easier to fool than a good person. The one who never lies believes others easily, and the one who never deceives trusts others. Don't be so stupidly innocent that you give others the chance to be bad. Being part serpent and part dove shouldn't create a monster, but a virtuoso.

The sensitive Jeremiah, who had never wanted to be a prophet, knew these conflicts when he preached and suffered in Jerusalem before the Jews' sixth-century captivity. Then as now in the face of idolatry and social injustice, many people didn't want religion to go out of the sanctuary. What, they ask, does religion have to do with daily life? Though we have the motto "In God we Trust" on our money and national symbols, many don't trust in God in any way. We have God's name in our pledge to the flag but, sad to say, many interpret the separation of Church and State to mean separation of morals from the country.

For Jeremiah's speaking out in God's behalf, he was denounced and put in prison. Faithfulness to his mission brought him nothing but heartbreak. His former friends sided with his enemies. He knew the whispers of many. They had made several attempts on his life. They were watching for any misstep so that they could take revenge. Feeling alone, betrayed, discouraged, and even abandoned by God, he sensed anger against his prosecutors mixed in with his trust in God.

Nevertheless, he had a most sensitive understanding of God's love for His people and the bonds of love and loyalty that should exist between the Israelites and their God. In the heart-rending words of today's first reading, Jeremiah expresses confidence in God when on trial. In the midst of all the strong contradictions, he kept faith in Yahweh's promises and knew that the Lord was with him (v. 11). His feelings about being an outcast, a stranger to his brothers, and the insults against him, and at the same time his desire to praise God at the end of the passage finds perfect expression in today's Responsorial Psalm, asking God, in His great love, to answer prayers in times of terror. We're not to be afraid, but to speak out for Jesus. It's the central message of today's Mass.

St. Paul's message in his letter to the Romans is similar. Paul hadn't visited Rome yet, and there were no specific problems to discuss, so he became theological. Writing about how people become right with God, Paul says it's through faith in Christ. Because of the solidarity of the human race, by Adam's sin all human beings were alienated from God. By Christ's righteousness, however, all human beings again become right with God. The redemption of Jesus is more powerful than the sin of Adam; in Jesus and by his grace, we can conquer all sin.

Paul's frequent contrast between "one person" and "all" or "many" brings out the fact that the malevolent influence of Adam and the benevolent influence of Christ apply to all people. Through one person, Adam, sin entered the world. Though Paul doesn't use the term "Original Sin," he does affirm what's basic to that dogma. Paul isn't necessarily affirming the existence of hereditary sin. The sin that entered the world is a personified malevolent power, hostile to God and to His people. It's Sin with a capital "S." Humankind's guilt before God began with Adam, and in some way it infected the entire human race.

With sin came death. This typification of what the Greeks called *Thanatos* — everything opposed to life — towers over all humankind. It's a cosmic force, an enemy to be conquered. It doesn't mean primarily physical death, which is a biological essential that would have been a normal part of living even if sin had never happened. Paul means spiritual death, the eternal death which is the consequence of grave sin which can separate a person from God, who is the unique source of life. Paul observes that death comes to all. Though he doesn't say exactly *how*, it's "inasmuch as all sinned." Paul is referring not only to Original Sin, but to our personal, actual sins. Every time we commit sin, we cause some degree of spiritual death, which is separation from God.

Some people wish they'd never heard of sin or responsibility or fear of the Lord; they think their lives would be a lot more fun without them. In the long run, though, people are happier when they've done the right thing and have had the courage of their convictions. Humble meditation on today's truths will hopefully bring together reverence and awe before the Lord such that, like responsive children, we place all our confidence in God.

THIRTEENTH SUNDAY IN ORDINARY TIME
2 K 4:8-11, 14-16   Rm 6:3f., 8-11   Mt 10:37-42

Being Really Alive
Discovering Who You Are (through Jesus); Welcoming the Word and the
Bearer of the Word; Conversion; Hospitality; Commitment; Generosity

A certain parish badly needed money, and the pastor knew that some of
his parishioners weren't known for generosity. So he came up with an
interesting idea. He had an electrician wire some of the seats so that, at
the press of a button from the pulpit, people would receive a mild shock
— enough to make them rise from their seats. The next Sunday, he got
in the pulpit and asked for donations. He asked, "Who will give $100,"
pressed a button, and three people stood up. He asked, "Who will give
$500," pressed another button, and six people got to their feet. And so
it went through the $1,000 donations, the $2,000 donations, and up. The
drive was a tremendous success but for one adverse factor: ten people
were nearly electrocuted.

Such reluctant people share a false idea that to be alive means
having a lot of this world's goods. Jesus' idea of being alive is different.
In today's Gospel, for example, Jesus, with complete honesty, speaks
paradoxically of being alive as involving such a degree of generous
commitment to him as to be willing to let go of even those things we hold
dearest in life: our reputation, our physical wellbeing, and even our
family ties if necessary. Sometimes one has to choose between one's
closest ties on this earth and loyalty to Jesus. Those who would try
compromise as a way of "keeping peace" soon discover that "*keeping*
peace" isn't the same as "*having* peace."

Continuing his naked honesty, Jesus then tells us that whoever
doesn't take up his cross and follow after him is not worthy of him (v.
38). The people of Galilee to whom Jesus was speaking knew well what
a cross was. When the Roman general Varus had crushed a revolt in
Galilee, he had had two thousand Jews crucified there, and had the
crosses placed by the roadsides as a lesson to others. The people had
often witnessed the common practice of other condemned men carrying
through the streets the crossbeams of the crosses upon which they
would die, a practice which would later be applied to Jesus.

You might well ask, "Is this what you mean by being alive? What kind of life is carrying a cross?" It's the only kind of life worth living. People who seek only themselves bring themselves to ruin, whereas people who bring themselves to nothing for Jesus and give themselves to others discover who they are. And that's what life is all about: discovering the truth of who we are. This is no small value.

You can't *hoard* life, or you'll lose what makes life valuable and make yourself and others unhappy. Only when you *spend* life gloriously for God and for others will you find life, here and hereafter. Some religions speak of creation as a cosmic dance and of life as a dance with God as the Lord of the Dance. Pagans, on the other hand, agree with the stoic Roman Emperor Marcus Aurelius, who said that "the art of living is more like wrestling than dancing." Many martyrs in our tradition could have easily escaped death if they had recanted: escaped in the sense that they would have continued to breathe. But they wouldn't in reality have saved their lives. To live as Jesus wants is to bring to life self-discovery, fruitfulness, and spiritedness. Without that kind of living we're merely existing — a fate worse than death.

In living such a life, you may not be able to speak or write many fine words in God's behalf, because you have to work, cook, wash the clothes, clean the house, care for the children, do the marketing, or go to the office. But everyone can help in the work of witnessing for God — even if only in some small way like giving a cup of cold water. In the heat of the long, dry summer of the Holy Land, a cup of cold water is a welcome, if inexpensive, gift. In places that have plentiful water, Jesus' cup of cold water may be translated into a much-wanted letter, a smile of appreciation, an encouraging word — all as inexpensive as a cup of water in a dry country and all equally needed and appreciated everywhere. Even those small efforts in his name, says Jesus, will receive a prophet's reward.

The last part of the Gospel, the giving of a "prophet's reward," is perhaps the reason for the selection of the first reading, which is from the Second Book of Kings. The book, as its name implies, tells the story of the kings of Israel: their failures as well as their faithfulness. In today's section, the wealthy woman of Shunem kindly extended hospitality to the prophet Elisha, whom she perceived to be a holy man of God.

In biblical times, hospitality was considered an important virtue. This was especially true when extended to someone doing God's work;

the reverence in that case was extended to the office and not necessarily to the person. The woman's kindness in making special arrangements for Elisha was in reality a kindness to God. Even though she saw Elisha as God's representative, she didn't ask whether he was a good preacher, or had the right ideology, or was a "good Joe." Elisha, in fact, had a thorny personality. She acted generously and courageously in a land where wars raged, strangers were suspect, and the people were poor.

Just as the childless woman's hospitality went beyond what was expected of her, her reward went beyond her wildest hopes: the gift of a long-desired baby boy. Today's Responsorial Psalm, "Forever I will sing the goodness of the Lord," might be thought of as a song of praise on the lips of the woman of Shunem (and all of us) who was blessed. God appears to all of us in various guises — a child needing an education, a neighbor in pain, a cause that deserves our support — and we show hospitality to God by responding. This is the height of being alive.

The foundation of Jesus' requested commitment is recalled in today's section of St. Paul's letter to the Romans. Christians, in a world of sin, must live out their baptism. In Paul's time, baptism was by total immersion. This symbolized dying to sin so as to rise and live the new life that Christ intended: a life of liberation from the power of sin and death. This involves incorporation into Christ and into his body, the Church. Thus a new creation takes place whereby we begin the life-long process of dying to sin and becoming alive for God with the new life of the Gospel.

All of today's readings remind us that we become fully alive through the generous giving of ourselves. That doesn't mean only pulling out a checkbook and writing some figures for charity, important as that is to many worthy causes. It's more important to give of *ourself* to people: in the way we speak about them, in the way we forgive their failings, in the way we encourage them, in the way we show them hospitality, and even in the way we think about them. These types of generosity reflect a warmth radiating from the very love of God.

The generosity expected of us should be here and now, and not only something left to our Last Will and Testament. In a fable of the pig and the cow, the pig was lamenting to the cow one day how unpopular he was. "People are always talking about your gentleness and your kind eyes," said the pig. "Sure, you give milk and cream, but I give more. I give bacon, ham, bristles. They even pickle my feet! Still, nobody likes me. Why?" The cow thought a minute and then replied, "Well, maybe it's because I give while I'm still living."

When we can give generously of ourselves, let's not be electro-cuted by sticking too steadfastly to our seats. And let's extend our generosity first and foremost to God's work on earth: His Church, especially His representatives, no matter how unworthy, who labor in His behalf.

FOURTEENTH SUNDAY IN ORDINARY TIME
Zc 9:9f.   Rm 8:9, 11-13   Mt 11:25-30

Openness to the Spirit
Living According to the Spirit Rather Than the Flesh; Humility Rather Than Intellectual Pride; In God We Find Refreshment; True Normalcy

A variety of tests are taken every year, to determine many things. There are intelligence tests, even though there isn't general agreement on what intelligence is. There are tests of poverty, even though the meaning of poverty varies from culture to culture, country to country, time to time, and person to person.

And there are tests of personal normalcy, even though its meaning varies from psychologist to psychologist. What, for example, is normal for males in our Western tradition? Darwin's theory on the survival of the fittest finds expression, some might say, in the masculine need to compete. This in turn has led to guarded endorsement of controlled anger for males: boys must learn to fight. By the late nineteenth century the idea of a muscular Christianity seems to have been in vogue. The boy scout movement encouraged chivalry, thoughtfulness and consid-eration for others as ideals of manly virtue. The concept of "manliness" today therefore includes qualities which embrace physical strength, chivalric ideals, and virtuous fortitude, with military and patriotic elements thrown in. Which is normal?

Jesus didn't need tests to show that the intellectuals, those who were at the top socio-economic level, and the leaders of the people were rejecting him and the humble people accepting him. Nor did he need supernatural knowledge for it.

St. Matthew begins today's collection of Jesus' sayings with Our Lord's observation that the humble folk were God's kind of people; Jesus the carpenter was one of them. The message, of a piece with Older Covenant tradition, doesn't condemn intellectual pursuit or achievement. No, intellectual pursuit is praiseworthy, and our Church community needs more of it. What Jesus is condemning is intellectual *pride*. He's not connecting faith and *ignorance*, but faith and *lowliness*: this consisting of simplicity, openness, and trust — the kinds of virtues we observe in a child (and in mature adults). Jesus is saying that it's not by understanding alone that one accepts his message, but by divine revelation. That revelation isn't denied to so-called "wise and learned" people — provided they're at the same time humble, open, and trusting.

Jesus then comes to the greatest claim he ever made. It's a statement that's so lofty that one would expect it in the Gospel of St. John, whose symbol is the eagle. He says that no one knows the Son except the Father, and no one knows the Father except the Son (v. 27). This principle, that only God the Father fully comprehends Jesus' mission, and only Jesus fully understands God's saving plan, is at the heart of Christianity. It's a principle that Jesus gradually reveals to the intellectually humble, open, and trusting. His audience, now as well as then, is made up of those who are sincerely trying to encounter God, trying to be good, and finding it so difficult that they're being driven at times to exhaustion and despair (v. 28).

In Jesus' time and place, sincere seekers were hog-tied by the burdensome legal and moral prescriptions of rabbinic Judaism. This needed to be balanced by a prophetic vision in order to give joy to the Mosaic tradition. The good people were conscious of the burden of sin, which the Mosaic Law couldn't relieve. Many in our own time likewise find life burdensome. They, too, are confused by all the messages that come to them from so many sources. And Jesus still offers them refreshment. Our word "restaurant" is a French word that comes from the Latin *restaurare*, to restore to or to put back into an original state. It's said to originate with the beautiful direction of Jesus in today's Gospel that all of us who are weary and find life burdensome should come to him, and he will refresh us (v. 28).

The heart of Jesus' message is "Come to me" — a call to a personal relationship. The shift from "Keep the law" to "Come to me" is a significant one. A religion which is experienced only as adherence to legalistic impersonal norms and not as a joyful life-giving relationship with the Author of life is false. In coming to the person of Jesus, we discover that, far from being burdened, we're liberated.

Jesus invites us all to take his yoke upon our shoulders (v. 29). The yoke was the fitted wood collar placed on the back of an ox pulling a plow. It was custom-fitted so it wouldn't chafe or bruise the neck of the much-needed and very precious ox. This metaphor came from the carpenter shop, where Jesus the carpenter had undoubtedly made some yokes. God's yoke is custom-made to fit well the needs and abilities of each of us whom He invites to wear it. Love makes every burden light (v. 30). You remember the story of the small boy appearing out of a snowstorm with a still smaller boy on his back. When a compassionate adult observed, "That's a heavy load for you to be carrying," his answer was, "He ain't heavy, mister, he's my brother."

The portion of the Book of Zechariah in today's first reading is in this same tradition. Zechariah was a contemporary of Alexander the Great, who conquered the known world when he was 21 years of age and was, despite his having been educated under Aristotle, brash and arrogant. To the contrary, Zechariah saw a just savior (v. 9) as king, one who would be mindful of the poor and lowly. He would come riding on a donkey, as cited by all four evangelists on Palm Sunday. This is in contrast to Alexander and the last kings of Judah, who rode, proud and war-like, on chariots and horses, aggressively using bows and arrows (v. 10). The Messiah will ride on the mount of the humble. This doesn't signify humiliation, but humility, serenity, and peaceful intentions. Unlike other conquerors, the Messiah will establish peace by first establishing justice.

This entire tradition gives us a choice between two possible principles by which we can live life, as St. Paul reminds us in his Letter to the Romans. One is to live by the flesh. At the center of the "flesh" principle are such things as pride, arrogance, and ambition. Those who live according to the flesh (v. 13) give themselves to human logic and power alone. That's ultimately soul-destroying spiritual suicide.

The other choice is the Spirit. In this chapter, Paul uses the word "spirit" twenty times, to express the many-faced reality of the experience of participation in divine life. Those who live according to the Spirit give themselves over to Jesus. They're full of promise, life, and growth. Having been baptized is no guarantee that one won't still be interested in the pursuits of the flesh.

It's a question of seeking the best in our human development. And that doesn't mean adjusting ourselves to the ways of the world. A well-known modern psychiatrist states: "Of all the things I dislike about psychiatry, I most abhor the notion of 'adjustment.' What divine power ever said we should adjust ourselves to the ways of our world? Is our society so perfect, so just, so loving that it is worth adapting ourselves to? Think of the great spiritual leaders of history, and think of the most loving people you have known; were they 'well adjusted'? Were their hearts determined by what was 'practical' and 'proper'?" (Gerald G. May, *The Awakened Heart* [San Francisco: Harper, 1991], p.46).

For us, the best of what's normal is Christ. He, the son of God, became one with the best of what's truly human. He invites us to come to him. To see if we're capable of living the life of the spirit with him, we can test ourselves on the degree to which we have overcome intellectual pride, and on whether we have acquired the humility, openness, and childlike trust that Jesus practiced and loved.

FIFTEENTH SUNDAY IN ORDINARY TIME
Is 55:10f.   Rm 8:18-23   Mt 13:1-23 [or 1-9]

Moral Growth
The Lord's Seed; God's Perspective on the Good Earth;
The Destiny of Humanity and of the Universe; Hope

Humankind has always been fascinated by people's growth, especially moral growth. Some scholars have categorized the stages of moral growth. They've theorized that, for children, the first stage in what determines the goodness or badness of an action is the physical consequences, with no regard to any underlying moral order: "Might makes right." They say that the next stage decides matters in terms of satisfying one's own needs. This is followed by the conformist "good boy-nice girl" orientation, which is designed to please others. Next is a "law and order" orientation, in which there is a new awareness of the larger community. Some say this is the "official" morality of the United States constitution and government.

Next comes the autonomous or principled stage, which tries to define an individual's own moral values apart from the authority of any groups. The next stage is the universal-ethical-principle, which defines the "right" to be the decision of conscience in accord with such aspects of ethical principles as what applies to everybody: like principles of justice and respect for the dignity of human beings. This stage reveres people like Mahatma Gandhi and Martin Luther King. The highest level of moral development, though, is a faith orientation, which involves a person's resolution of such questions as" "What's the ultimate meaning of life?" and "Why be moral?" Relatively few people reach that stage.

Moral development is not, however, correlated with chronological age. Sometimes older people remain at the early stages, and sometimes, especially through pain and suffering, young people ascend to the heights. Nor is moral law related to intelligence.

Spiritual categories of people are what Jesus is talking about in today's Gospel. The sloping shore of the lake of Galilee (v. 1) provided a natural auditorium, and the water kept the crowd from pressing in too closely around Jesus. His audience knew that farmers sowed before they plowed: Because of the nature of the soil, time was too precious to waste in preparation; it was better to cast the seed everywhere. From God's casting the seed of His word everywhere, rather than confining it to rows, comes our word "broadcast."

Jesus compared people to four kinds of soil. Some people are like the hardened soil on the footpaths (vv. 4, 19) where people have walked, making the seed, which lies exposed, more easily spotted by those who approach, notably Satan (v. 19). Unreceptive, they hold on to where people have gone before, unwilling to accept anything new.

Other people are like "rocky ground" (vv. 5, 20): enthusiastic but unstable. They're opportunists who are possessed of a type of light-heartedness that makes them shallow. A third type of person is like the seed that "fell among thorns" (vv. 7, 22), a familiar picture in the more arid parts of the Holy Land, where thorn seeds, blown onto the arable land, was a constant source of annoyance to the farmer. These are people distracted by secular interests. In themselves they possess the proper dispositions for spiritual growth, but they're prevented from producing fruit because of external circumstances: care for this world and the deceitfulness of riches.

The good people at the apex of growth and development are free from all three of these obstacles, and produce fruit (vv. 8, 23). Inasmuch as the normal Holy Land yield was about seven-and-a-half to one, Jesus' assertion of a hundredfold yield, which would mean 250 bushels to the acre, is, according to the laws of nature, impossible. Jesus' numbers therefore suggest a fruitfulness that is supernatural. This class of person hears, understands, and performs. God blesses them with supernaturally abundant blessings.

Although Jesus originally spoke his parable to discouraged disciples, he meant hope today for all who feel down when they examine their lives and see painfully how little progress they seem to have made over the years. Through Baptism, there is a divine power for good deep within us, which continues to work in us despite our many failures and setbacks.

Today's reading from Isaiah adds substance to Jesus' parable. Concluding his message of consolation to the Jewish people during their exile, he urges them to be hopeful. He makes rain a symbol for the powerful Word of God. Rain comes down and makes the earth fruitful; just so, God's word rains down and enriches the world. The world, like parched earth, is waiting for the rain of God's word.

Isaiah, like any good preacher or reality therapist who tells it as it is, has no illusions about human nature — its occasional blindness, foolishness, and stupidity. As with a homily, some people listen, but don't really take the pains to fully understand. But Isaiah also has a message of hope. After all, God is alive and well, and no matter what the difficulties of any time or place, the facts of God's plan for the world are in the final analysis friendly.

Like Jesus' deceptively simple parable and the message from Isaiah, St. Paul, too, reminds us today that there's a much wider vision of life and the world than comprehended at first sight. Paul sees all of creation as joined to humankind in being wounded by sin and in its present misery. We're God's representatives in His marvelous creation, and human destiny is intricately interwoven with the world we live in: its sufferings, corruption, and agony. That means that we carefully nurture not only our personal moral growth, but also all of nature.

One well-founded theory has it that *Homo sapiens* is in imminent danger of precipitating a biological disaster to rival anything in evolutionary history. Important pharmaceuticals may be lost when certain species disappear. Climatic side-effects will probably follow large-scale deforestation. Killing species isn't just economically unwise; it's morally wrong. The diversity of nature is as much part of our heritage as paintings and buildings. We quite rightly go to great lengths to preserve the Parthenon and the Mona Lisa. But our descendants won't thank us if at the same time we allow hundreds of thousands of species to perish. And yet, despite humankind's sins against creation, because of Jesus we await the final outcome in hope (v. 20).

At present, though, both humanity and nature suffer. This suffering is a sign of how much all creation is damaged by sin (v. 22). Even so, we have received help: redemption by Jesus, and the Holy Spirit as the principle of our new life. Those who parrot the humorous canard that "the future ain't what it used to be" are wrong.

Let's take home with us today the fact that the conditions of the soil encountered by the sower aren't necessarily in four different fields; agricultural conditions in the Holy Land show that all the conditions may be found in one field. It's the same with each of us. Sometimes we can't take the word of God because our hearts are just too hard. Sometimes we're enslaved by the attractiveness of the world. And sometimes, when conditions are just right, we permit the rain of God's word to bring forth the blossoms of our love. If the results have been less than satisfactory, it's because we haven't matured fully enough to produce the supernatural yield of which Jesus spoke.

If we're discouraged about our own personal growth, let's remember the true story of a piece of marble that was hewn from one gigantic block, unwanted, and discarded for 38 years after being poorly rough-cut. Then the authorities commissioned a young 26-year-old artist to work on it. When in two years' time his sculpture was finished, art critics were ecstatic.

They reached the conclusion that Michelangelo — for the artist was he — didn't really intend by his David, the subject of the piece, to represent only the young hero preparing himself for battle against the giant Goliath. No, they said, he merged all ideals into one — *fortezza* (strength); this was at a time when the Republic of Florence found itself dangerously threatened and needed to recall its citizens to justice, liberty, civic pride, and virtue. Michelangelo thus made his David a universal symbol of a new human consciousness. The statue is probably the best-known singular work of art in the world, and people still come from all over to Florence to see it.

So it is with our own person. No matter how discarded we may feel at a given moment, we're valuable. With effort, we can become something beautiful, desirable, and admirable. The words of Jesus, who wants each of us to grow to our fullest potential, ring through the ages — that whoever has ears ought to hear (Mt 13:9).

SIXTEENTH SUNDAY IN ORDINARY TIME
Ws 12:13, 16-19   Rm 8:26f.   Mt 13:24-43

Our Need for a Strong Interior Life
Our Metamorphosing Power; Reflecting the Holiness of God;
Virtues of the Strong; Good Ground for Hope; Prayer and God's
Power; Prayer and the Holy Spirit; Personal Growth

Humankind has had a constant but strange fascination with the exercise of power. From ancient times right up to the powerbrokers of our day, we watch it with the same fascination as that with which we watch an approaching snake.

Today's liturgy makes a vital point: Power at its best isn't external ostentation that makes people's eyes pop, but the *interior* reality — that which imitates the power of God and transforms the individual and the world. The early Christians called that transformation *metamorphosis*, which added a super quality to a change in the person which the Greeks had called *morphosis*. Christianity challenged pathfinders and creative people to face themselves, to reassess their values, and to discover whether they had the virtues of the strong, like forgiveness and kindness and forbearance.

Those virtues may be especially needed as we, like the farmer in Jesus' parable, look around at the world, which consists of people who are both good and bad. In the parable the weeds were probably darnel, a quite poisonous plant which is virtually indistinguishable from wheat until the ears form. To sow darnel among wheat as an act of revenge was punishable in Roman law. The only realistic possibility for the farmer was, despite the temptation to retaliation, patience and tolerance until the harvest. God acts the same with good and bad people until He will make His great gathering. We need the same virtues as we await the growth of the Church, which will take place as surely as tiny mustard seeds grow into large productive bushes and a small amount of yeast raises masses of flour.

Meanwhile the individual — as our reading from the Book of Wisdom suggests — must reflect the holiness of God and learn from the behavior of God. The book was written about a century before Christ to the Jews of Alexandria, who were experiencing a great deal of pain from the Egyptians who mocked them, ridiculed them, and persecuted them. The author reminded the Alexandrian Jews that God has the ultimate power. Unlike the weak who think they have to prove their power by bullying others and who live by the maxim that "Might Makes Right," for God "Right Makes Might." By the time the Book of Wisdom was written, Judaism had arrived at the notion of a God who shows His strength more by leniency than by punishment — by the virtues of the strong and courageous.

The reading is a beautiful pen-picture of the God in whom we believe. He's a God whose power is unlimited, and whose concern extends to all creatures. His justice is above suspicion and His judgment is understanding. And this reading doesn't present God as a remote figure whose sublime qualities we might contemplate at a distance, but as one whom we might imitate in our daily lives. Sharing in His mildness and leniency doesn't mean that we agree with those who say that all morality is relative and that there are no objective moral standards. It means walking the fine line between a censorious self-righteous judgmentalism and a permissiveness which says that anything goes.

Who doesn't agree with St. Paul in his letter to the Romans — which has important hidden depths — that we weak human beings don't know how to fulfill the most basic of Christian duties: to pray as we ought (v. 26)? Prayer is a surge of the heart; it's a simple look turned toward heaven; it's a cry of recognition and of love, embracing both trial and joy (St. Thérèse of Lisieux, *Catechism of the Catholic Church*, 2559).

Most people confine their idea of prayer to petition. As a takeoff on an ancient saying that "he whom the gods destroy they first make mad," one writer said that those whom God would destroy He answers their prayers. We really don't know what's best to ask for.

For Paul, the fact that we don't know how to pray as we ought causes no concern, provided we let the Spirit come to the aid of our weakness (v. 26). The Spirit is within us, so that one spiritual author could properly define prayer as "the divine within us appealing to the divine above us." And Paul had pointed out that the heart of prayer is to be able to call God "abba," or "daddy," the intimate term that Jesus himself used. Paul had few illusions about the weakness and sinfulness of human nature, and yet he is a messenger of hope who believed in the possibility of the reformation of the world.

But the reformation of the world must begin with the conversion of individual persons. Metamorphosis is a special kind of change. Literally speaking, it's a change in form, usually but not necessarily abrupt. We're fascinated by the idea of it. It permeates such fiction as Robert Louis Stevenson's *Dr. Jekyll and Mr. Hyde* and Franz Kafka's *Metamorphosis.*

But we needn't turn to imagination. In nature, metamorphosis is real. The world around us teems with animals that undergo drastic changes in form. Metamorphosis is strikingly represented by butterflies. Without foreknowledge, no one would ever guess that a caterpillar would come to be an aerial creature borne aloft on colorful gossamer wings. If butterflies could think, imagine their astonishment and dismay at viewing their firstborn — a caterpillar, of all things! But the caterpillar from the day of hatching carries within its body small pockets of cells destined to form a butterfly.

Everywhere beneath the placid surface of quiet ponds, other exciting mutations are taking place — among dragonflies, for example, and beetles, and mosquitoes. The ancient Greeks and Romans believed all these to be among the nymphs that lived in and gave life to lakes, rivers, and springs.

Perhaps the most famous metamorphosis is that of the scarab beetle. It encases its larva in a dung brood ball and emerges as new life. Tourists to Egypt are offered for sale all sorts of images of the scarab, considered sacred to the ancients; some have also suggested that the pyramids may have been intended as brood balls for mummies.

Metamorphosis is by no means restricted to invertebrates. Many of our common species of toads and frogs change completely. From the moment in the spring when the tadpole emerges from the gelatinous egg, it is a creature of the water. As spring gives way to summer, strange things begin to happen. Little hind legs grow longer and longer, like Pinocchio's nose. The tail begins to shrink. Soon front legs appear. Inside, even more drastic changes are in progress. Lungs are getting ready to replace gills; the long coiled vegetarian digestive system is rebuilt to the shorter system of carnivores; the sense of smell which was most efficient for detecting watery chemicals is reorganized to detect scents in the air. There is now an urge to catch flies, sit on lily pads in the sun, and sing on still nights. The frog has been transformed — but, contrary to some fiction, he will never become a prince.

But something like the possibility of metamorphosing into princes and princesses is open to us — not all at once or overnight, but gradually. Within each of us the Spirit is sown. It may be difficult for us to grasp the extent of the change of which we're capable. We're born in the image of our parents and grow and mature with some predictability. We pass through infancy, childhood, puberty, adolescence, maturity, and old age with few visible changes other than those inevitably wrought by time.

Our metamorphosis needn't be spectacular or powerful as the world measures those things; it can be as silent and real as the germination of a seed, the formation of a butterfly, or under-water wonders. To be real, it must happen through the Holy Spirit and prayer. And the transformation of the world, if it ever takes place, must begin with the metamorphosis of you and me.

SEVENTEENTH SUNDAY IN ORDINARY TIME
1 K 3:5, 7-12   Rm 8:28-30   Mt 13:44-52

The Most Precious Things in the World
The Meaning of Life; Detachment and Attachment; An Understanding Heart;
Smell the Flowers as You Pass By; Be a Clown!; Be an Oxymoron:
A Wise Fool!; Total Commitment; Discernment of Priorities; Wisdom

Christian values appear to be topsy-turvy when compared to the world's. Many of Jesus' sayings could never have been spoken by a worldling: "The last shall be first and the first shall be last," for example, and "Whoever exalts himself shall be humbled, but whoever humbles himself shall be exalted," and "Anyone among you who aspires to greatness must serve the rest." Some say they're the ideas of a clown.

Indeed, Bozo the Clown originates in the Christian tradition — with a man named Boso, abbot of the Norman abbey at Bec, during the time of St. Anselm, who became Archbishop of Canterbury, England, in 1093. Boso is Anselm's foil in Anselm's perhaps most famous work, *Why God Became Man* (*Cur Deus Homo*). Like many works of the time, it's in dialogue form; Boso asks the questions and Anselm provides the answers. The progress of the argument demands that Boso be continually mistaken and corrected.

Jesus wasn't a circus clown, an entertainer, a trickster. But there are analogies between the clown and Jesus: joy in living, delight in simple things like the lilies of the field, simplicity, the ability through love to transform the ordinary into the sacred, average people sharing a spark of the divine, the vulnerability of a lover, and the humility of a servant.

And Jesus' actions and teaching style were a striking humorous contrast to the serious conventional piety of his time, and he wanted to show that religion should be a wedding feast for everybody, with a happy bridegroom leading the festivities. Although Jesus both fasted and attended parties, it was his feasting that caused trouble. The "religious" people saw in it proof that he was "irreligious."

If comedy consists in surprises and the unusual, Jesus was also comic. If a comedian says, for example, "Take my wife — please!" the comic element is the surprise of the last word. With Jesus, the surprise was, for example, that the "included" become the excluded and the "excluded" the included, the "unclean" the clean and the "clean" the unclean.

Today's liturgy calls all of us to be clowns in pursuit of the most precious thing in the world — the reign or dominion of God — and we should be struggling for those principles which alone can give our lives meaning and direction.

Two of Jesus' parables today make that point: the parables of the treasure and of the pearl. They differ from the other parables of the reign of God. Other parables of the reign of God — of the city on a mountain, the wheat and the weeds, the mustard seed, the net, the great supper, the marriage feast — speak of the members of the reign as a group; today's parables are addressed to the individual. In both sets of parables, the person sells all he has. Both demand renunciation, risk, and commitment. The emphasis isn't so much on the pain of the renunciation as on the supreme value of the reward: the reign. Jesus advocates total reversal of the past ("selling all") in order to gain a future.

In the ancient world, where the danger of foreign invasion or brigandage was often present, many householders and royal personages buried their gold, jewels, and other treasures in the ground, one of their substitutes for our modern "bank." They hoped to be able to recover their treasure at a later, more propitious, time. Because frequently the owner never returned, their treasures are sometimes still found.

According to the Palestinian laws of that time, the mere finding of buried treasure didn't entitle the finder to it unless he also owned the property. In Jesus' short parable, the finder doesn't tell the owner of the field about the treasure: he purchases it from him first, in order to be covered legally. Jesus passes no judgment on his ethics, and — as usual with parables — makes only one main point: *the* chance of a lifetime is to discover the reign of God, which one should pursue at any price. In modern terminology, you should take the risk of a speculator and sell all you have to buy what holds the promise of much greater wealth. In your personal regard, ask yourself this question: If you were sure that there is no reign of God, is there anything in your life you would change? If your answer is "no," you've been risking nothing.

Whereas the treasure was found accidentally, the pearl was found after a lifetime of diligent search. But the point is the same: the object is worth anything to have, the reign of God being one of the loveliest things in the world. In the ancient world pearls were special, not only for their value, but for their beauty; they could command fantastic prices. The main sources of pearls were the shores of the Red Sea and Britain, but merchants would scour the whole world for them, as we do for oil.

To help us understand the Church, Jesus tells one more story: the parable of the net. On the shores of the lake, he appropriately compares the Church to a fishing net which, when thrown into the lake, collected all sorts of things (v. 47). The net couldn't discriminate. When the fishermen brought it in, they had to separate the worthwhile from the useless (v. 48). Similar to last Sunday's parable of the weeds and the wheat, the theme is the presence of both good and bad in the Church. In both, the final solution is the same: tolerance of both good and bad until the end, when all will receive their just rewards. James Joyce said of the Church, "Well, here comes everybody!"

As the First Book of Kings tells us, one learned person who initially made the right choices for the reign of God was Solomon, who succeeded his father David as king of Israel about 961 B.C. In a dream the Lord told Solomon that he could have whatever gift he wanted. Probably at least once in our lifetime, the majority of us dream about what we would do if we had the same opportunity. Not a few of us might wish for limitless amounts of money. Some of our uses for it might be rather selfish: buying another house, a better car or cars, elaborate vacations. Other dreams might be expansively Christian: giving huge donations to relieve poverty, prevent the closing of hospitals or schools, fund projects for the mentally and physically ill.

Solomon prayed for a listening heart (v. 9) — in other words, wisdom, the ability to judge well when cases were appealed to him in his position of "Supreme Court" in the kingdom. Just as the greatest quality for which Abraham Lincoln became famous was compassion, Solomon's special gift for ruling God's people was wisdom.

Unfortunately, the exploits of Solomon have been exaggerated; he ultimately came to oppress the people with taxes to support his building campaigns, and even imposed forced labor on them. The final judgment was that Solomon was unfaithful to his gift. There's no such thing as final salvation in this world. There was never from the Garden of Eden onwards a perfect time, a perfect place, a perfect happiness, a perfect solution. As Cardinal Newman said: "In this world to live is to change and to be perfect is to change often." Our effort must be to see things for what they really are: on one level we call things junk, on another level we call them second-hand furniture, and on the highest level we call them antiques. One person's junk may be another person's treasure. For all who continuously try to order their priorities correctly, things work out for good.

If we reflect on our lives, we discover that seemingly unmitigated disasters have turned out for our benefit, whereas things that we strove hard for, without regard for how they affected God's reign or will, often spelled disaster for us.

The basis for our faith and trust is that all that comes from God is good and, as St. Paul puts it in today's second reading, all things work for good for those who love God (v. 28). God's plan is that we be conformed to the image of His Son (v. 29) — that Christians reproduce in themselves an image of Christ by progressively sharing more and more in Christ's risen life. In speaking of the final destiny of glory for all who put their faith in Christ (v. 30), Paul's use of a word that's translated into English as "predestined" shouldn't be equated with any later theological system of predestination, and doesn't take away human freedom.

Those who follow Christ must, like the people who discovered the buried treasure and found the valuable pearl, be clowns enough to sell all they have for it. Detachment from things is a necessary consequence of attachment to Jesus, in whom are all the treasures of wisdom and knowledge. This gives the joy of discovering the meaning of life and of finding ourselves involved in the adventure of holiness. People who risk wholeheartedly are ultimately peaceful. Like the early Solomon, such people have the wisdom to recognize dependence on God. Like Paul and like Jesus, such people handle firmly the troubles thrown their way and freely live by the spirit of God. Of such people did the poet (Douglas Mallock, *He Who Has Dared*) write:

> He who has dared, has done,
> Whether he lost, or won.
> No one has failed, who tried,
> Whether he lived or died.
> This is the truest truth
> Age would impart to youth,
> Only a few prevail,
> But only the quitters fail.
> Christ, on a bloody Cross —
> Yet who shall call it loss?
> One He had thought His friend
> Whispered, "It is the end."
> But where is the cruel crowd,
> Where are the princes proud?
> Dead like the mists of dawn.
> Only the Christ lives on.
> Honor is not alone
> Laurel, or wealth, or throne.
> Many a heart as brave
> Sleeps in a loser's grave.
> Whether he won or not,
> Heaven has not forgot.

He who has dared has done,
Whether he lost or won.

So, if God put the question to us that He put to the young Solomon
— "What would you like me to give you?" — what would our answer
be? Hopefully it won't be like the aged and jaded Solomon. Hopefully
also, may we not discover that at times we ask and we don't want, seek
and don't wish to find. We're often like somebody waiting at a bus stop
yet hoping the bus will never arrive.

EIGHTEENTH SUNDAY IN ORDINARY TIME
Is 55:1-3   Rm 8:35, 37-39   Mt 14:13-21

Invitations and Banquets: Earthly and Heavenly
Our Hungers and God's Generosity; Place of Disciples in the
Work of Christ; Satisfying Our Deepest Needs; The Nearness
of God; The Conquering Power of God's Love

Most people like to go to parties. United States politicians are said to
favor the two-party system: one every Friday and one every Saturday.
The character of parties differs. In the cold weather, it's formal dinner
parties and dress-up affairs, while warm weather favors the more
informal cook-out. There are vast contrasts between the parties of
children and youth over and against those of adults.

There was likewise a contrast between Herod's banquet of murder and Jesus' banquet of love. Herod's was a birthday party for himself.
At parties like Herod's, there are always social climbers who want to get
as much out of it for themselves as they can. And at parties like that,
people can lose their lives — either metaphorically through backbiting,
calumny, and deceit, or physically, through lust for power, lascivious-
ness, and drunkenness, as was the case with the sodden Herod and St.
John the Baptist.

Compare Jesus' banquet of the loaves. It's the only important
event before his triumphal entry into Jerusalem narrated by all four
evangelists. It's of great importance for two reasons. First, its extraor-

dinary character aroused the people to enthusiasm more than any other miracle. The concern about the assuaging of hunger may be hard for us to imagine in a country like ours, where food is plentiful, supermarkets bulge, fast food establishments are commonplace, and many people are overfed. But most of the world then and now has to work at backbreaking labor for long hours just to get enough food to keep body and soul together. Unless we can get a picture of real hunger, we can scarcely appreciate the image of heaven as a banquet. And that leads us to the second reason for the importance of this event, which is that Jesus' taking bread, looking up to heaven, blessing the bread, breaking it, and giving it to the disciples to distribute to the people had a very obvious relation to the Eucharist.

The scene began with Jesus' emotion on hearing of the murder of his cousin, John the Baptist. That and the constant press of the crowds brought it about that he just had to get away. Galilee was a small area (about 50 miles north to south and about 25 miles east to west); at that time it contained about 204 villages and towns, none with a population of less than 15,000 people. It was therefore not easy to get away from people for any length of time. Southeast of the town of Bethsaida, however, was a large plain that stretched away to the hills, which might be described as a deserted place (v. 13) — not in the sense of a sandy waste, but in the sense that there were no people living there. Jesus therefore had some fishermen friends take him there across the lake by boat.

But the crowds heard of it and followed him on foot from the towns. The public is merciless on a busy leader, and the Apostles, though by now used to handling crowds, were aware of their need for rest and of further instructions. In the midst of all this was the wonderfully human Jesus, whose heart was moved to pity for the people (v. 14). He was curing their sick and caring for their needs to such an extent that one has the impression that he was forgetting the time — because it was already evening when the disciples approached him (v. 15) with the suggestion that he dismiss the crowds so that the people might go to the villages and buy some food.

The Apostles were also not unmindful of their own need to get away from the crowds and to eat — enough is enough! Jesus, with a twinkle in his heart if not in his eye, told them to give the people something to eat themselves. This failing, he had the Apostles seat the people on the grass and, in words remarkably similar to those he would use a year later in instituting the Eucharist, multiplied the loaves and fish so that all had their fill.

Matthew shows his own delight by the whimsical touch that the men who had wanted Jesus to deny hospitality to the crowds ended up as the banquet's waiters. They gathered up twelve baskets of fragments, and the five thousand people who had eaten didn't even count women and children. Some scholars say there were about a half million people in the Holy Land at the time of Jesus; if so, Matthew intends to show that Jesus was feeding a substantial percentage of the population. The whole idea was to characterize abundance — the abundance of the messianic age.

This banquet has been understood mainly in three ways. Some look upon it as being something very precious indeed, but belonging to the natural order. They would say that the crowd had had the foresight to bring their own food with them, but were — like the anonymous members of most crowds — selfish and unwilling to share. Jesus, in blessing and dividing the few loaves and fish he and his disciples could uncover, shamed all into sharing, and there was more than enough to go around. The miracle consisted in changing selfish people into generous people. Others look at it literally as a simple multiplication of loaves and fishes, limited to its facts and never to repeat itself.

But a third way of understanding what happened is to see the miracle as Matthew, the author of the Gospel, saw it: as full of symbolism about Jesus the Messiah. This understanding especially looks upon the incident as a foreshadowing of the sacrament of the Eucharist. This wasn't a meal where people merely satisfied their physical appetite, but one where they received something more. This "something more" made them happy and strengthened them for wherever they were going and whatever hardships they had to face. It wasn't something that happened only once, but would be re-enacted at every table of the Lord; and it wouldn't be only that crowd in Galilee whose deepest hungers were satisfied, but all people of all time. Today's Responsorial Psalm puts the idea well in saying that the hand of the Lord feeds us: He answers all our needs.

Isaiah the prophet reminds us of that. Today's passage imitates a literary genre running through all major world religions. First the god invites humans to a banquet, then offers a life of fellowship with the godhead, and lastly advises the invitees to leave aside a life of folly in order to gain spiritual insight at God's table. At a difficult time when all kinds of bickerings, avarice, and disagreements were breaking out among the people, Isaiah used the imagery of a feast, a banquet of divine joy (a frequent scriptural symbol of God's love), for what should characterize God's people. Through good things to eat and drink that are scarce in the Holy Land (water, corn, wine, milk, bread) Isaiah speaks of satisfying the deepest longings of the human heart: longings for human presence and loving relationships. God will provide in sufficient abundance that you may have life (v. 3).

Isaiah's poetry has been compared to music. If it were a symphony, today's passage would be its coda, summarizing under full orchestration all the major themes that had gone before. In this "Book of Consolation," as it's been called, Isaiah makes God's invitation universal, extending not only to those who had accommodated and done well in Babylon, but to the poor, God's beloved *anawim*, as well. How wonderful! The only condition is a thirst for God. For neither the independent wealthy nor the dependent poor would it be completely easy, but God's word is a banquet for those who listen to it.

In today's magnificent climax of St. Paul's Letter to the Romans, he has essentially the same message. One of the most magnificent statements in all the Bible, this too may be compared to the coda of a symphony at full volume. Paul outlines everything he had sought under the Jewish law: freedom, knowing how to please God, God's presence, new life, becoming a true child of God, the hope of glory, and the knowledge that everything would work out for the good. Here Paul, a true Jew who found conversion to Jesus difficult, enumerates seven different troubles to which human flesh is heir and which may come thick and fast. His initial list of hardships (v. 35) says that the disasters of the world won't separate a person from Jesus. Indeed, if properly used, they bring one closer. Thus we conquer overwhelmingly through him who loved us (v. 37).

Then Paul lists (vv. 38f.) a series of ten terrible extremes that will never break our love relationship with Jesus. Death, which is neither the end nor a separation, is really a step closer to the presence of Jesus. Angelic powers, some of them evil, won't separate us from him, nor will any age in time. At a period when astrology tyrannically ruled many people's minds, giving rise to superstition, Paul defied it all by declaring that stars at both their zenith and their nadir would be powerless to destroy this relationship. And, looking into the future, he declared that not even another world can take away our being enveloped in the love of God if we don't let it.

To be in need of love and friendship is to be human. God extends us a standing invitation to His party. Our invitation to the world's party is also always open. Both are R.S.V.P. and urgent. To which are we responding affirmatively right now?

NINETEENTH SUNDAY IN ORDINARY TIME
1 K 19:9, 11-13   Rm 9:1-15   Mt 14:22-33

Preconceived Ideas vs. Faith
Are We "Of Little Faith?"; A Calm and Saving
Island in a Turbulent Ocean; Where We Find God

Even the best of people have preconceived ideas about God. A man named Smith was sitting on his roof during a flood, and the water was up to his feet. Before long a fellow in a canoe paddled past and shouted, "Can I give you a lift to higher ground?" "No, thanks," said Smith. "I have faith in the Lord, and he will save me."

Soon the water rose to Smith's waist. At this point a motorboat pulled up and someone called out, "Can I give you a lift to higher ground?" "No, thanks. I have faith in the Lord and he will save me."

Later a helicopter flew by, and Smith was now standing on the roof with water up to his neck. "Grab the rope," yelled the pilot. "I'll pull you up." "No, thanks," said Smith. "I have faith in the Lord and he will save me." But after hours of treading water, poor, exhausted Smith drowned. As he arrived at the Pearly Gates, Smith met his maker and complained about this turn of events. "Tell me, Lord," he said, "I had such faith in you to save me and you let me down. What happened?"

The Lord replied, "What do you want from me? I sent you two boats and a helicopter!"

To judge our own preconceived notions, let's look at our attitudes toward very tiny parts of creation: bugs or, as most of them are technically called, invertebrates — animals that lack backbones. Aside from pretty ones like butterflies, useful ones like shrimp and bees, and those with recreational value like mollusks whose shells are collected at the seashore, they're unappealing to most of us. Their overwhelming numbers and rapid reproduction rates challenge us; their ability to invade human space so ingeniously threatens our feelings of control and security; they seem devoid of feelings. And they remain largely alien and unfathomable.

The truth is that bugs keep this planet livable. Humans may think we're evolution's finest product, but the creepies, crawlies, and squishies rule the world. Remove people from the face of the earth and the biosphere would perk along just fine, ecologists say. Remove the invertebrates and the global ecosystem would collapse, humans and other vertebrates would probably last only a few months, and the planet would belong mostly to algae and fungi.

Invertebrates account for 90 to 95 percent of animal species and total animal weight on earth. In the United States, for instance, the combined biomass, or dry weight, of earthworms, insects, and spiders, is 55 times greater than that of humans.

Partly because of their sheer numbers, invertebrates are the biological foundations of every ecosystem. They maintain the soil structure and fertility on which plant growth and thus all higher organisms depend. They cycle nutrients by consuming decaying matter, pollinate crops and other plants, disperse seeds, keep populations of potentially harmful organisms under control, and eliminate wastes. In the United States, humans produce some 130 million tons of excreta annually, livestock an additional 12 billion tons. Of this waste, 99 percent is thought to be decomposed by invertebrates, leaving one to wonder, if not for our "little friends," what humans would be up to their eyeballs in.

Today's Gospel tells us indirectly that the Apostles shared the preconceived ideas of their people as to how God should act. As a result of Jesus' miracle of the multiplication of the loaves and fish that we heard about last Sunday, the Apostles seemed to like the peoples' idea of making Jesus their king. At least, St. Matthew tells us that Jesus *made* the disciples get into the boat (v. 22) and that he actively had to *dismiss* the crowds.

Admittedly, it's difficult to conform to God's way of thinking in the face of the earthly thoughts all around us. Yet Jesus, who always sought his heavenly Father's will, did precisely that. Jesus in this moment of triumph went up on the mountain by himself to pray (v. 23).

The Gospels make special mention of Jesus praying alone at night before important stages of his life. This time, it was because the next day he would talk about the Eucharist.

Another example of how the Apostles let their own preconceived ideas blind them was the incident of Jesus and the Apostles on the Lake of Galilee. The Apostles, hard-pressed by having to row against strong head winds in their little boat, at about three o'clock in the morning saw something coming toward them on the water. It seemed to have a human shape, so the only thing they could think of was a ghost. They were more afraid of that than of the winds, to which they were accustomed. Their shouts were not merely out of fear, but — in accord with the superstition of the time — they thought that this was the way to get rid of ghosts.

When Jesus reassured them that it was he, St. Peter, in vintage impetuosity, asked Jesus to let him walk towards him across the water. At Jesus' bidding, Peter began to walk on the water. But then his preconceived notions took over. When he realized that walking on water just didn't happen, he had enough faith to believe that Jesus could do the miracle, but not enough faith to believe that Jesus would do it for *him*.

Then he made the mistake that many of us make in the face of difficulty: he took his eyes off Jesus. As his faith lost its buoyancy, he began to sink into despair. Jesus, coming to his rescue, chided Peter — not for having no faith at all, but for having *little* faith (v. 31). Matthew records for the first time in the synoptic Gospels that anyone — here everyone in the boat — called Jesus "the Son of God."

Even holy prophets like Elijah had preconceived ideas. When Elijah's contact with God took place, he was on the run from Queen Jezebel, after he had slaughtered her pagan priests of Baal. Although the people were for the moment impressed enough to have returned to the Lord, they were — like people of all time — fickle and could at any moment fall back into idolatry. Elijah was so discouraged that he just wanted to die. He retreated to a cave on Mt. Carmel.

God began his encounter with Elijah in his sheltering cave by telling him that he should be on the lookout, for the Lord would be passing by. When a wind came, so strong and heavy that it was tearing at the mountains and crushing rocks, the fiery prophet thought (as would most of us) that all this power was a sign of the Lord. Not so. Surely, then, God would be in the next shattering phenomenon, the earthquake? Again Elijah was wrong — confusing the *manifestations* of God with

His *presence*, as would many of us. Then came fire, a frequent symbol of God because of its brightness and intensity, but this time God wasn't in the fire, either.

Then came the most ordinary of events, a tiny whispering sound. There, lo and behold, in this much more subtle way, the way most people might hear the Word of God, was the presence of the God of gentleness. Before Him Elijah reverently covered his face with his cloak, realizing like the disciples in the Gospel his nothingness in the presence of the divine.

God is less frequently found in spectacular phenomena than in the gentle things of life and in quiet and peaceful reflection. Quiet prayer doesn't mean escape from reality. To the contrary, it means involvement with God and the world. Nor does it necessarily mean comfort. That depends on the Lord. With Elijah, after the still small voice God sent him back to overthrow two kings.

St. Paul in his letter to the Romans seems to have learned something of these lessons. Like other Jews, he had been fascinated by manifestations of God's power in behalf of his people. Water in a river had drowned the Egyptians and water from a rock had provided drink for his people in the desert; a plague of insects bothered the Egyptians, while quail fed the Jews; God sent a rain of manna for the Jews, storms for the Egyptians; He sent darkness upon Egypt, a guiding pillar of fire for the Jews; He had Egypt's first-born killed, but preserved the lives of the offspring of the Jews.

Now Paul gave vent to an outburst — most dramatic, even for him — about his discouragement over the Jews' rejection of Jesus, always a great mystery to him. He spoke of the privileges of the Jewish people. The first of these privileges is *adoption*, by which the Israelites are in a special sense the children of God. The whole Bible is full of this idea. Next Paul mentions the *glory* of God. Again and again in the history of Israel the Scriptures mention the *shekinah*, God's splendor of light which appeared when God was with His people in a special way.

Paul reminds us that Israel had the *covenants*, the special pacts which sealed the relationship of mutual friendship between God and His people. God's first covenant with humankind was with Noah after the flood, the sign of which was a rainbow in the sky. God's covenants after that were with Abraham, the sign of which was circumcision; with the people through Moses on Mount Sinai, whose basis was the Commandments.

The Israelites also have the *Mosaic Law*, through which God told them what He wanted them to do. They have the *worship in the Temple*, a special way of bringing the people closer to God and one another. They have the *promises*, whereby they knew from God that they could, if faithful, be destined for greatness. They have the *patriarchs*, or fathers, who gave them a tradition, a history, and a heritage. The culmination of all the privileges is that from the Israelites came the *Messiah*, the Anointed One of God, for whose coming everything else had been a preparation.

Why did the Jews reject Jesus as Messiah? In part, at least, because they had their own preconceived ideas of how God should act; they especially couldn't accept the scandal of the cross. Paul's reaction, like God's most likely, wasn't one of anger, but of heart-broken sorrow over the people's rejection.

There is no sign in the Scriptures or anywhere else that God has ever withdrawn the privileges He extended to the Jews. And there is no justification in history for human beings taking upon themselves any judgmentalism that results in racial prejudice or anything like a Holocaust. Places like Auschwitz are a Christian moral problem.

Let's learn from the holy people we've been thinking about today. Elijah had to venture out of his cave — out of himself, really — and live with the courage that his faith demanded. Peter was called to leave the protection of the boat and walk upon the surging, chaotic waters. Paul came out of his relative security to proclaim with courage and conviction the insights of his conscience.

Often, like them, we're afraid to step out of our secure positions. Preconceived ideas take over, fear overcomes our faith, and we remain safely inside ourselves. Let's leave ourselves open — truly and completely open, without preconceived ideas — to God's way of being and doing in our lives and in our world. Then let's not look for God in the spectacular, but try to see Him in the quiet, simple things of life, and make our lives conform to the *true* image of God.

FEAST OF THE ASSUMPTION
Rv 11:19; 12:1-6, 10   1 Cor 15:20-25   Lk 1:39-56

The Results of Christ's Work: God's View
Humankind's Potential; Results of Christ's Work:
Realization of Humankind's Potential; Ease vs. Greatness;
The Timeless Gigantic Struggle between Good and Evil

Modern popular art forms, especially the movies, often depict the struggle between good and evil. They incessantly depict the fight, from the "bad guys" in the black hats and the "good guys" in the white hats of the Western, through the cops and robbers of the urban setting, to the futuristic star wars and intergalactic battles for supremacy over the universe. But in comparison with real life, movie offerings have at least two important limitations. First, they're always confined to a time: past, present, or future. Secondly, despite tremendous imagination, a frequent cast of thousands, vast sets, and painstaking technical details, they're not big enough to depict the ongoing warfare between the culture of life and the culture of death!

St. John's view in his Book of Revelation, the last book of the Bible, depicts the immensity of the struggle between good and evil without any confines of time or space. If motion-picture promoters were to advertise John's portrayal, they would have to use adjectives like colossal, gigantic, mammoth, and massive. To depict the vastness of the struggle, John adapted his ideas from the world in which he lived. From India to Rome of that time, especially in Babylonia, Egypt, and Greece, there was a widely-believed myth that a savior-king was to appear.

In writings of this kind, the goddess who was to bring forth the savior was pursued by a horrible monster. Protected in an extraordinary way, she would give birth in safety, and her child would soon slay the evil monster, thereby bringing happiness to the world. John's version differs in some important respects from the pagan versions. John, who abhorred the pagan world, adapted this story mostly to illustrate the immensity of the struggle.

John focuses our attention not upon the savior-king but rather upon the woman, who remains present even after her son has been

---

Note: For other approaches to the Assumption, see Cycles B and C.

enthroned in heaven. Who is this woman? Most commentators identify her as the Church. That's appropriate, because the woman is presented throughout the book as oppressed by the forces of evil, yet protected by God; furthermore, the image of a woman as a symbol for a people, a nation, or a city is common in ancient secular Oriental literature as well as in the Bible. It's fitting, then, for the woman to represent the true People of God, the Church. It's not, however, the earthly Church with all its faults and failings, but the ideal, the heavenly Church.

A number of commentators see the woman as Mary, the mother of Jesus. Though this interpretation is especially desirable on this feast of Mary's assumption into heaven, it provides difficulties: for example, the mother enduring the worst of the pains of childbirth (v. 2). It's entirely possible, however, that John had in mind both the People of God in general and Mary in particular, a member of the Chosen People of God, who gave birth to the Messiah. And it's fitting. In a sense, the people of God gave birth to Jesus and the Christian Church; Mary, in a completely different sense, gave birth to Jesus.

John speaks of the ark of the covenant (v. 19), the place where the tablets of Moses and other sacred artifacts were kept, because he wants to indicate that God is no longer hidden, but present in the midst of His people, and accessible. The celestial woman is adorned in splendor (12:1), clothed with the sun, and crowned with twelve stars to symbolize the twelve tribes of Israel and the twelve Apostles. She wailed aloud in pain as she labored to give birth (v. 2) because the arrival of the new age was compared to childbirth, which is ordinarily accompanied by great pain. The last era on earth begins with the birth of the Messiah.

The huge red dragon (v. 3) was considered to be the epitome of the forces of evil in opposition to God. Popular tradition had it that God had defeated this monster at the moment of creation, but its final repudiation was deferred to the end of time. Its seven diadems were symbolic of the fullness of its sovereignty over the kingdoms of this world. Then John (v. 4) suggests the colossal size and power of the monster, whose tail swept away a third of the stars in the sky and hurled them down to the earth (v. 4). Her son was a boy who was destined to rule all the nations (v. 5), to break the sway of the dragon over the world. The reading concludes with a hymn of praise to the triumph of God and His Messiah.

In this mammoth struggle in front of the gigantic backdrop of good and evil, the one who defeated sin, overcame death, and freed humankind was Jesus Christ. In imagery that would have been familiar to every Jew, St. Paul in his First Letter to the Corinthians tells us that the first fruits of Jesus' victory are the resurrection of everyone from the dead (v. 21) and being brought to life again (v. 22) — up to the very end, when Jesus hands over the kingdom to his God and Father (v. 24).

After Jesus himself, Mary is the first of those who belong to Jesus (v. 23). It's because of this that she was assumed into heaven. She's a special example of the efficacy of God's grace when combined with a person's cooperation. She shows the paradox of Christianity that's revealed in all the saints: a tremulous joy at her great privilege and, at the same time, a sword which pierces her heart.

Today's Gospel tells of an incident in her life that illustrates this. In language that St. Luke deliberately took from the scene in the Jewish Scriptures of the coming of the Ark of the Covenant to Jerusalem, he speaks of Mary as the new Ark of the Covenant, the bearer of that which is holy. Luke tells how Mary visited her cousin Elizabeth who was pregnant in her old age. It was in haste (v. 39) that she walked the 90 miles from her home in Nazareth to the little hill town of Ain Karim, to share her joy at her own annunciation and to be of help to her cousin. This was despite the dangers of the journey in that season: landslides, rocks, cloudbursts, seasonal swift brooks, pits and holes, snakes, scorpions, and robbers.

When she arrived, Mary humbly greeted Elizabeth, paying that deference to an older woman which is becoming for a girl. The charm of her smile showed Elizabeth that she was aware of what was happening to both of them. Elizabeth, under the inspiration of the Holy Spirit, uttered those immortal words that resound to our own day as the first part of the prayer we call the "Hail Mary." Mary, for her part, sang the beautiful prayer that has come down to us from its first word in Latin as the "Magnificat." Her song showed that she had pondered much. We ponder too little.

With an intimate knowledge of the Jewish Scriptures, especially the hymn of Anna (1 Kings 2:1-10) and the Psalms, Mary's prayer first praises the mercy of God in the work of the incarnation; then extols God for His power, displayed through the history of the chosen people; and ends acclaiming God's fidelity to His promises concerning the Messiah. Her response makes her the spokesperson for the great themes of Luke's entire Gospel: joy in God's saving mercy, the reversal of values whereby the lowly are exalted and the proud sent away empty, and an anticipation of the Beatitudes and the life of the early Christian community.

The titanic struggle between good and evil, the forces of light and the power of darkness, the life offered by Jesus and the death offered by Satan, goes on. We're all in it. To learn how to perform our role, we have the example of the best of our race, Mary. Her life showed a great sanity, in centering outside of herself. She showed that Jesus and his religion make one joyful. Her son's victory over the dragon's death, a victory in which she was the first to share, changes the whole meaning of human life and death: "Sergeant death," a mystery that inspired fear, has become "sister death," a way to life.

Mary's Assumption is a passing over of her whole person into the glory of the Lord. It's an image which speaks to us of the final success of tenderness, of gentleness, and of mutual loving. It's an underground movement of new life which is fighting moral decay, pollution, and evil. Its victory means that nothing true, good, or lovely in human life will be lost.

TWENTIETH SUNDAY IN ORDINARY TIME
Is 56:1, 6-7   Rm 11:13-15, 29-32   Mt 15:21-28

Ecumenism
Jews and Gentiles, or Jews vs. Gentiles?; A House of Prayer for
All Peoples; Walls Come Tumbling Down; Is the Church for Everybody?;
How Decide Who Belongs to God's People?; Expand Your Horizons;
Avoid Prejudice, Narrow-Mindedness

One of the tragedies of life is the walls people build around themselves. It's bad enough when this is done to hem people in, as happened with the Berlin wall, but even worse when it's to keep the world out, as with some psychotics.

Today's Gospel is one good example of Jesus bringing down walls. He had withdrawn from Galilee to the area around the commercial cities of Tyre and Sidon (v. 21); the frequent invectives of the prophets against these two pagan cities made them for the Jews proverbial examples of corruption and wickedness. But Jesus wanted to avoid the harassment of the Pharisees and Herod, and to gain the advantage of closer contact with his Apostles in peaceful solitude. He could be sure that no Jew would follow him into this enemy territory.

But he was recognized as soon as he entered the area. A woman who was desperate because her beloved daughter was seriously ill, and who had undoubtedly tried all other remedies, took the chance of coming to this stranger for help. She was like good mothers all over the world. In at least one respect they're all the same — they stand loyal to their children. Rob a bank, commit murder, blow up the government, and nothing will shake a mother's conviction that in the first place you didn't do it, and in the second place somebody made you.

Even before she began, this mother had three strikes against her: women weren't supposed to speak to men in the street, she was asking for the cure of a *girl* and not the more favored *male* child, and she wasn't only a Gentile but from a hostile tribe. So she had to face the enmity of the Apostles, for whom the avoidance of contact with Gentiles — the "goyim," "goys," or non-Jews — was a mark of one's inclusion among God's chosen. The Apostles wanted coldly to get rid of the woman (v. 23).

But God perceived in her something that the Apostles missed — not unusual. She was a good woman, or she wouldn't have been so concerned about her daughter. She had come with love, and there's nothing nearer to God than that. But she presented Jesus with a dilemma. If he granted her request, he would seem to be indifferent to those who considered themselves God's chosen people. If he didn't grant her request, he would be going against his innate compassion.

He brought her near. If his initial not saying a word in answer to her (v. 23) and his dialogue after that seem harsh, it was only to test her. When she knelt and called him "Lord" (v. 25), Jesus gave her the space to articulate her need. You can't treat harshly someone who is kneeling before you. More importantly, she showed that her faith had been growing even as she was having contact with Jesus. She changed from the superstition that had brought her here: her request to a man changed into a prayer to the living God, and her prayer was persistent and in deadly earnest.

The dialogue was a test of faith for her and a match of wits between her and Jesus which he intended to be humorous. In what must have been a disarmingly wry tone of voice, Jesus mentioned the Jews' name for themselves — God's children — and contrasted it with the term "house dogs" (v. 26). The term "Gentile dog" was about as customary an expression for Gentiles among the Jews as the term "damn Yankee" in the United States' South.

Why did Jesus use the term? Was he trying to shock her, put her off, test her faith? We shall never know, but there's a theory that great teachers have great personalities, and the greatest teachers *outrageous* personalities. The theory says that decorum and rectitude have little place in a classroom, and prefers a climate of feverish melodrama. A great teacher, says this theory, is the student's adversary and conqueror. He leaves the student grateful. Bad teachers don't touch the student; the great ones never leave him.

In this case, the woman's conduct showed that she wasn't insulted, and her repartee showed extraordinary ingenuity. In her reply, she changed his word "house dogs" to a diminutive meaning "pet dogs," "little dogs," or "puppy dogs."

To her persistence and her language of faith, Jesus' final reply was as enthusiastic and warm as his initial approach had appeared to be aloof and cold. He granted her request: her daughter was healed from that hour (v. 28). He was tearing down the walls that separated Jew and Gentile and showing God's wish to have an end to barriers based on religion.

Six centuries before Christ, the disciples of Isaiah, who wrote today's first reading, were saying essentially the same thing. Some of the Jews' original enthusiasm over their return from Exile had begun to wane. In addition to the literal walls of their Temple, they were putting up metaphorical walls to keep some people out. Isaiah contradicted all that and extended a welcome. He called God's house "a house of prayer for all peoples" (v. 7), an expression that Jesus quoted when he cleansed the temple of moneychangers. Today's Responsorial Psalm's "O God, let all the nations praise you!" repeats Isaiah, and that emphasis is consonant with the best of both Judaism and Christianity.

When St. Paul wrote to the Romans, he was writing to a community that was a cultural crossroads of Jews and Gentiles, with Gentiles in the majority. Paul reminded both sides that *all* people are saved only by the free grace of God, and not because they belong to the "right group." Paul's first few lines present his *hope*. This "apostle to the Gentiles" (v. 13) hopes that his ministry and the conduct of the Gentile Christians will rouse at least some of his fellow Jews to jealousy (v. 14). One of the surest ways of making people want Christianity is to have them see how well practicing Christians live.

The second part of Paul's message (vv. 29-32) presents a *warning*. He tells the Gentiles that God's gifts and call to the Jews won't be taken back (v. 29). The Jews were now rejecting God's gifts and call, and the Gentiles were now accepting them. Paul warns both Jews and Gentiles to be faithful, and sees the ultimate solution in God's mercy. That warning still holds.

In today's world, in which the tables have turned and anti-Judaism rears its head, it's good to remind ourselves of some things. Jesus was a Jew. He was born under the Law (Torah), presented in the Temple, circumcised, made a pilgrimage to the Temple at the age of 12, and was expert in the teachings of the Law. His Apostles often called him "rabbi." He based his commandment of love on the teaching of the Jewish Scriptures. As his Apostles he chose twelve Jews, symbolizing the twelve tribes of Israel, upon whom he set up his Church. In his last days on earth he observed the Passover supper, and on the cross he recited a Psalm of David. He was buried according to Jewish custom. After his death and resurrection and the coming of the Holy Spirit, the Apostles continued to worship in the Synagogue and observe Jewish law.

Uprooted from its native soil, the Church became de-Judaized, and anti-Jewish sentiments developed early on. Some Christians saw Jews as rejected by God, unworthy, faithless, Christ-killers, and enemies of Christianity. From these views emerged Christian anti-Judaism. In the Christian Middle Ages, Jews were often humiliated, ghettoized, harassed, and even murdered.

Since the Nazi atrocities against both Jews and Christians, most mainline churches have issued documents which have in one way or another condemned anti-Judaism as un-Christian, called for a cessation of teaching that depicts Jews as rejects of God or Christ-killers, emphasized the rich Jewish roots of Christianity, affirmed the validity and permanence of God's covenant with the Jewish people, and called for fraternal dialogue between Christians and Jews to promote cooperation in pursuit of social justice, peace, and other common goals. Both sides are urged to what the Jews call *teshuva* and Christians call repentance.

Realizing that all of us set up walls which separate us from God and from one another, let's try to develop three attitudes. The first is gratitude for all the blessings we have. Second is humility and the avoidance of smugness that can turn other people away from what we stand for. Last but not least is compassion, by which we can truly "feel with" the sufferings of others to the point of breaking the vicious cycle of evil by repaying evil with good. These attitudes in turn might inspire others to further positive attitudes which might help make the walls that separate the human family come tumbling down.

The foolishness of prejudice is put well by a poem ("The Cold Within" [Subtitle: "200 Years of Prejudice"], by James Patrick Kenny):

> Six humans trapped by happenstance, in bleak and bitter cold,
> Each one possessed a stick of wood, or so the story's told.
> Their dying fire in need of logs, the first man held his back
> For of the faces round the fire, he noticed one was black.
> The next man looking cross the way saw one not of his church
> And couldn't bring himself to give the fire his stick of birch.
> The third one sat in tattered clothes; he gave his coat a hitch.
> Why should his log be put to use to warm the idle rich?
> The rich man just sat back and thought of the wealth he had in store,
> And how to keep what he had earned from the lazy, shiftless poor.
> The black man's face bespoke revenge as the fire passed from his sight;
> For all he saw in his stick of wood was a chance to spite the white.
> The last man of this forlorn group did naught except for gain,
> Giving only to those who gave was how he played the game.
> Their logs held tight in death's still hand was proof of human sin.
> They did not die from the cold without —
> They died from the cold within.

Twenty-First Sunday in Ordinary Time
Is 22:15, 19-23   Rm 11:33-36   Mt 16:13-20

Peter, the Pope, the Church, and You
Who Is the "Son of Man"?; Peter, the Papacy, and the Church;
Personal Commitment to Jesus; Christian Decision-Making;
Authority in the Church and Personal Freedom

As you go up the chain of being from stones to God, life becomes more and more complex. It's much more difficult to figure out the ways of people than of, say, monkeys. St. Paul recognized the limits of the human mind and, as for God, in today's prayerful portion of his Letter to the Romans he touches the awe of humanity before God. He acknowledges the inscrutability of God's judgments and the unsearchability of His ways, at the same time honoring the riches of God's wisdom and knowledge (v.33).

Mindful of all that, we approach today's profoundly important Gospel reading, a central moment in the life of Jesus Christ and his Apostles. He and his Apostles were in the region of Caesarea Philippi, about 25 miles northeast of the Sea of Galilee and outside the domain of Herod Antipas. The name "Caesarea" was given the city in order to curry the favor of the Roman emperor, or Caesar. The name "Philippi" (of Philip) was added because it had been built by Philip the Tetrarch, a son of Herod whose territory this was; it had to be distinguished from the other Caesareas, principally the big one on the Mediterranean coast where the Roman procurator lived.

This was a place where many religions met. There was, for example, a great temple of white marble built to the godhead of Caesar that reminded you, even from a distance, of the power and splendor of Rome. And in a large cave beneath a great hill a deep lake, allegedly one of the sources of the Jordan River, was said to be the birthplace of Pan, the great Greek god of nature. In fact, the original name of the town was Panias, and even today its name is Banias. There were, besides, no fewer than fourteen temples dedicated to the worship of the ancient Syrian god Baal. It seems that, for whatever it was that he was about to do, Jesus deliberately chose the backdrop of the splendors of the world's religions of the time and would invite comparisons.

Jesus realized that his days were numbered and he wanted to do something to continue his work. He was now some time on the roads of the earth, and there were all kinds of differing opinions about him. He had to know if there was anyone who recognized him for who he was and would be able to carry on after he was gone. He led up to that by first asking what *people* thought of him. The answers were highly complimentary. "John the Baptist," said some, mindful that the superstitiously fearful Herod Antipas at times thought Jesus was John come back to life to haunt him. Those who thought of Jesus as Elijah the prophet come back to life (v. 14) were saying that Jesus was as great as the one whom they considered to be the greatest of the prophets. Those who said that Jesus was "Jeremiah or one of the prophets" were asserting him to be God's helper and near to the kingdom of God.

Then came the fatal question: "But who do you say that I am?" (v. 15). At that, there may very well have been a long silence, as with anyone fearfully on the spot in the face of a probing and delicate question. The disciples may have begun following Jesus for a variety of reasons. Some thought he was a good teacher. Perhaps others (like Simon the Zealot) thought that he might lead a desired revolution against Rome. Others followed him because they thought he was a prophet. Perhaps some knew him as a peasant social reformer.

But the Apostles were for the most part unlettered fishermen answering a vagrant, indigent woodworker, who — amazingly — expected the answer that he was the Son of God. If they understood that he was the Messiah foretold by the Scriptures, he could tell them what God expected of the Messiah, what sort of death was decreed for him, what glory was reserved for him, and — not least — what would be expected of *them*.

Jesus hung on what their answer might be. Into the silence, finally, Simon Peter spoke. He knew that the human categories of the tributes just given to Jesus were simply inadequate to describe him. So he blurted, "You are the Messiah, the son of the living God" (v. 16). Jesus' response began with a comparison of Simon with a rock (v. 18). This was, in view of Peter's record to this point, hard to see.

And Jesus was giving Simon a name which had never appeared before as a proper name in the history of the world: "Peter," a name which means "rock" in Jesus' language of Aramaic, and in the major languages of the time, Greek and Latin. The metaphor, however, wasn't strange to Jesus' hearers. The Rabbis had applied the word "rock" to

Abraham, and the Scriptures had applied the word "rock" to God. Jesus applied it to Peter because Peter was the first person on earth to make the leap of faith —how appropriate for Peter to leap! — a leap which saw Jesus as "the Son of the Living God."

That Jesus was giving Peter a very special office in the Church was reflected in many other places in the New Testament. Peter is always first in any list of Apostles. Peter gives the first sermon in the Church. Peter receives into the Church the first Gentile, Cornelius. In John's Gospel, Peter is told to feed the lambs and the sheep of Christ's flock. In the Letter to the Galatians, Paul pays a left-handed tribute to the position of Peter when he says that in an argument he withstood Peter to his face — implying that to withstand the visible head of the Church was a great thing.

At this instant came a wonderful new prospect, also never present before: the human race organized for the pursuit of an altogether new ideal. Jesus would build a Church — a word used only in the Gospel of St. Matthew. This Church would be an *organization* with Peter as its first head, as well as an *organism* working quietly for optimal personal fulfillment and for good within society like leaven or seed.

To show Peter's authority, Jesus said he would give Peter the keys to the kingdom (v. 19). To have the keys to a place designates a special kind of power. If you've ever bought a house or leased a car or rented an apartment, at the moment you were handed the keys you had authority. The tradition is also an ageless ceremony that turns up whenever a visiting dignitary — politician, astronaut, Olympic hero — is presented with a huge beribboned key to the city: in spite of the fact that the town is no longer, and never was, protected by walls with lockable gates.

In Latin, key is *clavis*. Thus, the clavicle (*clavicula*, little key) is the collarbone, from the fact that this slightly key-shaped bone helps to hold the upper body together. The musical clef is also derived from *clavis*: as a key opens a door, the musical key opens the song. And the keystone is the wedge-shaped block that confines the other stones or bricks in an arch. Keys are also an important symbol of domestic authority, a foremost model of which is St. Martha, who was devoted to home and hearth.

The Church selected today's first reading from Isaiah because it gives further meaning to the word "key." Isaiah tells of Shebna, who was removed from his position of controlling access both to the city and the king. Shebna had violated the presuppositions upon which people give authority: that the power won't be abused, that advantage won't be taken of others, that power will not corrupt but be for service. Isaiah presents (v. 22) a picture of Eliakim, Shebna's successor. Though he would have the "robe" and the "sash" to show that he was Master of the Palace and second in command to the king, a pale reflection of which might be the modern "official limousine," it was the "key" more than anything else that designated his position and authority.

Jesus further promised Peter that whatever he bound on earth would remain bound, and whatever he loosed would remain loosed, in heaven. Did Jesus' promises extend to those who claim to be Peter's successors —the popes? Well, early on the bishop of Rome had a certain preëminence and exercised authority outside his own territory. Given the resentment to civil Rome as a hostile persecuting power, this must have required some action by the Holy Spirit.

Yet there's a paradox here. One doesn't enjoy true power until one uses it for others. The grand irony of the life of George Washington, for example, was that, whereas in the beginning his life had been based on ambitious acquisition, he didn't secure his desired reputation of patriot and become the father of his country until he gave up the power he sought. At the height of his popularity, he became the man who would not be king. In the process, George Washington assured the success of the world's first modern democracy.

Among Peter's moments of darkness was when the cock crowed and the tears fell. The occupants of the Chair of Peter haven't always been what we would have hoped, any more than Peter was. He and all his successors were human beings. They've at times claimed more authority than Jesus granted them. They've claimed the power to depose earthly monarchs and to rule over secular matters as well as spiritual. They've at times condemned everything that seemed good for society, like freedom of religion and freedom of conscience. They've at times appeared to support tyranny against the forces of democracy. And at times their moral lives left much to be desired.

But Peter's successors have in the main remained faithful to their privilege and their responsibility as a force for good in the world. This is awesomely symbolized by St. Peter's basilica in Rome, with its church and piazza built in the form of a huge key over the tomb of Peter. And every man elected Pope from Peter's day to this has dropped his old name and taken a new one, as Simon was designated Peter by Jesus.

All who believe that this passage provides the promise for the foundation of the Church, a promise that was fulfilled after Jesus' resurrection, owe allegiance to the Church and to Peter's successors. We should pray for the successors of Peter, that God will guide them: in holiness so they're images of Christ, in wisdom so as to be God's humble servants, and in truth so as to be conscious of their weaknesses.

We should likewise pray for those who suffer from crises in recognizing the authority of God in his Church and have difficulty accepting the Church as a sure guide in matters of faith and morals. Beyond that, each of us must make our own personal discovery of Jesus, and each must answer the living question, "Who do you say that I am?"

TWENTY-SECOND SUNDAY IN ORDINARY TIME
Jr 20:7-9   Rm 12:1-2   Mt 16:21-27

The Great Challenge: Practical Christian Living
Faith and Doubt Appearing Together; Think Like God;
Go God's Way; Self-Giving; Taking Up Your Cross;
The Conditions of Discipleship; The Value of Suffering

In all the universe there's no dignity comparable to even the humblest of people. You can give them gray hair and fallen arches, fling them on a park bench without a penny in their pocket, stand them on a street corner with a tin cup, cover them with loathsome disease, rob them of every outward charm, and they will still remain at the center of the universe. Every wind of boundless joy and endless woe that blows will react on the quivering human soul, as that delicate instrument loves and suffers, thrills and fears, struggles and dares.

Most of the arts, sciences, and professions center around human beings. Physicians study the body; lawyers try to secure justice; psychologists and psychiatrists try to interpret people's innermost drives; sociologists derive understanding from group conduct; historians arrive at conclusions from humankind's record. But not too many people put it all together to come up with overall suggestions for the best way to live. As good a way as any to do that is to understand the Scriptures.

Today's Gospel is an example. After St. Peter's sublime insight into Jesus' identity as the Son of the living God, which we saw last week, Jesus began to show that he must suffer greatly and be killed (v. 21). But that the Messiah suffer was far from the minds of the Apostles; they expected that he would always be a winner. There had been moments in the life of Jesus when he had indeed been a winner: the Sermon on the Mount had been welcomed by the multitude; his miracles and parables were the gossip of the countryside; in the youth of his ministry the people had been eager to crown him king. So the very same Peter who had enjoyed this great insight into our Lord's identity now remonstrated with Jesus that no such thing as suffering would ever happen to him (v. 22).

Peter was being logical enough. He'd been brought up on the idea of a Messiah of power and glory. As the Messiah's very name and all the teachings about him pointed out, he would save his people from their sins; he would impart life, not receive death. How, therefore, could Jesus suffer at the hands of those he had come to save?

Logical or not, the one Jesus had dubbed "Rock" had now become a stumbling-stone. Peter's suggestion of avoiding suffering wasn't unlike Jesus' earlier temptations when Satan had urged him to take the road of power, draw crowds, and share in the magnificence of all the kingdoms of the world; so Jesus now called Peter not a rock but a tempter, informed him he was thinking not as God does but as human beings do (v. 23), and told him to go away. The confrontation was serious, and Jesus addressed Peter with a tone of disappointment and heartfelt sadness at his sincere but mistaken love.

As for the crowds whom Jesus had won over by his words and his kindness, were there many who were ready to follow him under any conditions? To them, he said that whether anyone wants to come after him (v. 24) is voluntary, but once people accept, they must know that God then expects an ascent of one's soul into higher realms, an ascent that begins with denying one's very self. Because now our life has a new meaning and a higher purpose, we must say "no" to self and "yes" to God. The highest point of our ascent arrives when we take up our crosses, whatever they may be, out of the joy that follows upon love. Remember that, at the time Jesus spoke these words, the cross was the symbol of ultimate degradation.

Then Jesus spoke words which have rung through the ages as not simply good Christianity, but — as we come to know more about human beings through some of the newer sciences — good psychology as well: Whoever wishes to save his life will lose it, but whoever loses his life for Jesus' sake will find it (v. 25). There's a difference between *existing* and *living*. The path to worldliness, and to spiritual destruction — which means just existing — begins with small steps: I'm too busy, too tired, not ready for anything serious.

Someone once bitterly wrote on the tombstone of another, "He was born a man and died a merchant." If we substitute "merchant" for our own position — manager, clerk, lawyer, housewife, laborer — we might ask ourselves whether we've spent so much time on unimportant things that we've become less a person; in other words whether somewhere along the line we've lost ourselves. The mentally healthiest are those who have never stopped finding ways to lose themselves in other people for Jesus' sake. At the same time, we must balance this out with other parts of the Scriptures, where Jesus advises us to exercise our responsibilities: to pay off our debts, for example, and to take care of our family and help better world conditions.

It's a question of balance, as Jesus illustrates in his next momentous questions: What profit would there be for you to gain the whole world and forfeit your life? Or what can you give in exchange for your life? (v. 26). The selling or giving away of self happens every day — with flatterers and "yes-men" who curry favor with their bosses, with the weak who surrender themselves to stronger personalities, with those who have never developed any lasting principles to guide their lives. Once we've sold ourselves or given ourselves away, our most precious possession — our "self" — is gone, and it becomes extremely difficult to get it back.

All this advice is very practical. Equally practical is the advice St. Paul gives in the beginning of the conclusion to his letter to the Romans in today's second reading. To worship God properly involves one's whole self and one's whole life, which includes the body. In church, that means speaking a body language that's an indication of one's inner self: keeping silence when that's called for, being respectful, taking part in the prayers and hymns, and doing everything else that indicates a living sacrifice, holy and pleasing to God (v. 1).

Among Paul's further practical advice is not to conform ourselves to "this age" — the world still under the domination of sin, which can bribe us away from the ideal. We see in Paul, as we saw in Peter, the fact that something in all of us wants to be recognized by the world, praised by the powers that be. The Christian in every age and culture has to face the temptation to be popular. Although Christians aren't to be as chameleon-like as worldlings, who constantly take their color from their surroundings, we are to be always changing — by growing (v. 2). We're to live a life that's not only pragmatic, satisfying material needs, but a life dominated by the Holy Spirit of God and by God's way of thinking.

A good example is Jeremiah the prophet. His words in today's first reading constitute what we might call his "true confessions," a genre of literature which has degenerated into titillation in our day but which once enjoyed a reputation as being a revelation of one's innermost thoughts, as with St. Augustine's "Confessions." Jeremiah was called to be a prophet as a very young man, probably even a teenager — unwelcome in most societies, but especially in a society that valued the wisdom only of old men. Besides, he was called even though he seems to have had a speech impediment. And he was called to be a prophet of doom: Judah had become so evil that it needed to be called to repentance. Jeremiah's reward for his message was to be accused of treason. Now he was tired of the pain. He was daring enough to tell God that God had seduced him —and furthermore that he had allowed himself to be seduced.

In Jeremiah, faith and doubt existed together, along with disordered desires, resistance to God, and temptations to bitterness — as they do with many of us. But at the same time the urge of prophecy — to speak in behalf of God — was irresistible, a primer in the formation of conscience, becoming, as Jeremiah put it, "like fire burning in my heart" (v. 9). It's the same struggle that's reflected in Jesus' admonition to show our love by bearing our crosses.

If we seek Jesus or Church or faith *only* because we're seeking self-satisfaction, or because we need an emotional crutch, or because we want a solution to all our problems, we're going to be sadly disappointed. It's true that for a time that kind of faith will provide fulfillment. But the time comes when we must shoulder the cross and give ourselves. Such times come when we wonder where God is, when prayer is difficult, and when God seems not to care. It's at such times that we may find helpful the words of the anonymous poet who wrote:

> Let others cheer the winning man,
> There's one I hold worthwhile;
> 'Tis he who does the best he can,
> Then loses with a smile.
> Beaten he is, but not to stay
> Down with the rank and file;
> That man will win some other day,
> Who loses with a smile.

Like Jeremiah we can decry our age: an age in which the romance has been taken out of love, the commitment out of marriage, the responsibility out of parenthood, togetherness out of family, learning out of education, civility out of behavior, patience and tolerance from relationships.

We can in addition suffer the crosses of ridicule and condescension if we're loyal to the values of Jesus in areas like abortion, the value of suffering, euthanasia, and standards of morality other than the principle that "I'm number one." Those who study human nature deeply find that the cross which stands atop our churches is a symbol of what our Scriptures teach us to be the finest symbol of love and of life.

TWENTY-THIRD SUNDAY IN ORDINARY TIME
Ezk 33:7-9   Rm 13:8-10   Mt 18:15-20

Being Present to Others
Correcting Others; Love's Most Painful Duty; Personal Responsibility;
How to Correct Another; Be There When Others Need You; Our Responsibility
for the Lives of Others; I Am my Brother's and Sister's Keeper

Some things we take for granted, as though they were always the way they are now — like the existence of police. Surprisingly, police forces as we know them have existed for only a couple of hundred years. England didn't have professional police until the "bobbies" of the nineteenth century, named after Sir Robert Peel. The British were afraid of the oppression of police states — a justified fear which found its way into the United States Constitution. Before that there was mostly only a not very effective night-watch, which called out the weather, the hour, and the fact that "all's well."

Today's reading from Ezekiel refers to a primitive kind of police: the watchman. He stood on the Palestinian hills and blew his trumpet to warn of invaders. To protect fields and vineyards, especially at harvest time, owners built towers to house watchmen. Cities had towers built into their surrounding walls for the same purpose. Prophets like Ezekiel saw themselves as watchmen over the spiritual dangers that threatened God's people. The prime qualities of such lookouts, then and now, are meaningful presence to others and personal responsibility. At a time when Israel had a great sense of *corporate* responsibility, Ezekiel is often called the prophet of *individual* responsibility. In his view, individual responsibility includes our responsibility for each other.

That's the lesson of today's liturgy. In a time when it's fashionable to say that we mustn't impose our own moral beliefs on others, we must be meaningfully present to and take personal responsibility for other people. If a sentry fails to warn he bears a grave responsibility. Regardless of how well or ill others receive our message, we, like Ezekiel, keep our integrity by speaking out. In our role as lookouts, we shouldn't only be as in a state of siege wary of enemies in war, but acting in the moral threats of everyday life. That means helping people discover the unique talents with which the Lord has blessed them, encouraging their gifts, and putting all at the service of the whole body of Christ that is the Church.

Meaningful presence to others and personal responsibility for them are also what today's Gospel is about. It's from St. Matthew's "Sermon on the Church," which deals with the relationships of members of the Church.

The most painful obligation of watchful love is fraternal correction. Because that's so difficult, we use many escape hatches. One is the languid tendency to live and let live. Another is a preponderance of fear over hope. We're afraid of anger, or rejection, or another blow from the wrongdoer, and we can't arouse enough hope of improvement to approach the offender.

Still another escape hatch is constant questioning. Does correcting the faults of others to their face require us to express everything that's on our minds? Are we expected to be "Reality Talkers," people who always tell the complete and unvarnished truth, no matter what the consequences? Do you say to your host, "Wow, this food tastes awful. Mind if I just spit it out on the table?" Wouldn't most people rather prefer to be treated courteously than to be told the truth? Our answers to such questions can lead us to gunny-sack our feelings until we explode or nag too much.

To approach this painful duty of fraternal correction entails many qualities: courage, compassion, patience, gentleness, humility, sincerity, reverence, a desire to preserve the other's good name, prudence, delicacy, tact, mutual dialogue, true listening, and mercy. It's a minefield that can also involve unwarranted meddling, condescension, busybody interference, and thoughtless gossip.

Those undesirable qualities are reminders of the story of four old cronies, all pillars of the same community, at a businessmen's convention. They got together in a hotel room and before long they were discussing their shortcomings. "Well," said one, a leading businessman known as a teetotaler, "I confess I have a little weakness. I like to drink. But I never let it interfere with my work. Every now and then I go off to another town, take a room in a hotel, have a little binge and come back home again, none the worse for wear."

"I have to confess my weakness is women," said another. "Now and then — a lonesome widow — very discreet, you know, and nobody's the wiser. . . ." "Mine is betting," said the leading banker. "When I get a chance, I put a little on the horses. Not much — but I just have to give in to my weakness now and then."

They all looked expectantly at the fourth member of the group, but he didn't seem inclined to volunteer anything. "Come on, now," they said, "How about you?" "I — I — just don't want to tell. . ." he stalled. They all looked askance. What sinister vice was he covering up? They coaxed and coaxed and finally told him he was very unfair, since they had all been so frank.

"All right," he said reluctantly. "If you must know — it's gossip. And I just can't wait to get out of this room!"

With gossip, even its name hisses. It has no respect for justice, ruins lives, is cunning and malicious, gathers strength with age, makes victims helpless before its facelessness, irreparably tarnishes reputations, ruins careers, wrecks marriages, causes heartaches, and makes innocent people cry in their pillows.

On the level of grace — that is to say, of bringing a person to a true conversion based on love — even more is required for fraternal correction. Two aspects of Jesus' teaching here are striking: He has standards, and he uses a wise progression. The *first* step of the progression is forthrightly to go to the offender and point out his or her fault one-on-one between just the two of you. This should be done in a way that won't humiliate the offending person — indeed, it should make him realize that, as St. John Chrysostom wrote, the wounds of friends are more to be relied upon than the voluntary kisses of enemies. Always remember, though, that advice is sometimes transmitted more successfully through a joke than through grave teaching.

If the first step doesn't work, the *second* step is to bring one or two others along with you (v. 16) — not for the purpose of proving the other person wrong, but to help in the process of reconciliation. If that doesn't work, you proceed to the *third* step, which is to refer it to the local community of faith, the Church (v. 17). This is far better than going to the civil courts, because courts settle nothing concerning personal relationships and can, instead, cause further complications. The whole process should be motivated by a spirit of forgiveness.

If none of these steps works, Jesus advises his Jewish audience to treat the offender as they would a Gentile or a Roman tax collector. Surprisingly, for him that means continuing friendship. The Gospels call Jesus a friend of sinners and tax collectors, and Jesus reconciled many sinners with the heavenly Father: Mary Magdalene, Matthew, Zacchaeus, the woman taken in adultery, and others. He was often criticized for that. With him, though, reconciliation depends on the sinner's willingness to reform. And, if after you've tried your best a sinner is not properly disposed, you must treat him differently. Otherwise, as Ezekiel warned, you share the blame.

All else failing, there is always common prayer. United prayer is more powerful, sensible, and effective than resentment in our responsibility toward one another. Such prayer must never be selfish, but must be primarily for the good of the fellowship, remembering that where two or three are gathered together in Jesus' name (v. 20), he's in their midst. Jesus' two or three is as small a number as one can have to make a community.

The very first sentence of today's portion of St. Paul's letter to the Romans supplements the over-riding motivation of our responsibility for the members of our community: love (v. 8). Obligation ceases to be an issue when there's a fullness of love. It's easy for us to think of love as "doing good things," like feeding, clothing, visiting, and the like, but the most important aspect of love is to see to another's eternal welfare. At times, though, this means "tough love"; among the "toughest love" must be to offer fraternal correction. Paul contends that people who honestly try to discharge their debt of love will find all else falling into place — including possible temporary embarrassment over fraternal correction.

To love in the context of being present to others conveys an awareness that we're not here primarily to see through one another, but to see one another through. It also conveys expecting goodness from people, no matter how serious their transgressions. To expect nothing from another person is to condemn that person to death. To continue to hope in the other, even in the face of bad odds, is to gift that person with life. Let's begin our positive duty of responsible presence to other people by growing in love for one another. Then may we by our presence to others lift those who have fallen, calm those who are frightened, forgive those who have done wrong, give mercy without judgment — and welcome corrections of our own faults from others.

TWENTY-FOURTH SUNDAY IN ORDINARY TIME
Si 27:30-28:7   Rm 14:7-9   Mt 18:21-35

Forgiveness
Sin: Awareness of It, and Conduct (Both God's and Man's) Toward It

Mercury, if held tightly in the hand, will run away; it's only the open palm that can hold it. Another item that can be lost if not held in an open palm is what today's liturgy considers: forgiveness. And if we lose that, we can lose that of which forgiveness of sin is a part: the ability to give and receive love. There's a difference, of course, between crime and sin. You forgive sin; you punish crime. Pope John Paul II forgave his would-be assassin; he didn't ask the Italian government to release him from jail.

It's ironic that in today's Gospel it's St. Peter who asked about forgiving another; after the resurrection he would be one of the first to need the Lord's forgiveness. But right now he understood that if God forgives, as Jesus taught and showed, then God's disciple must be ready to forgive, too. So Peter wants to know *how often* he should forgive (v. 21). He suggests seven times, meaning by that number *perfection*, completeness — as in seven days for the creation of the world. He thought he was being generous and expected warm commendation for it. Jesus' answer, that we should forgive seventy-seven times (v. 22), is also symbolic, meaning without limit, *infinite*. No matter what number we put on it, it won't be enough, because forgiveness is a matter of love, not of how many times.

Then Jesus likens the kingdom of heaven to a king (v. 23), and goes on to present one of the sternest passages in the Gospels. The details of the parable shouldn't be allegorized. The conduct of the king, an Oriental despot, isn't a model for the mercy of God (which is better illustrated in the merciful father in the parable of the Prodigal Son). The significant item is the comparative amounts owed to and by the king's high official: millions versus practically nothing.

The king had the power to order his official to be sold, along with his wife, his children, and all his property, in payment of the debt (v. 25) because a man's wife and children were regarded as his property. To take a man's family in lieu of his debt was common practice, especially among the pagans; among the Israelites the Mosaic Law tried to mitigate its evils. The guilty official threw himself on the mercy of the king. Not trusting the king's goodness completely, however, he asked only for a moratorium on the debt (vv. 26f.).

What the servant owed the official was a much smaller amount (v. 28) than the official owed the king. Despite the servant's pleas for mercy (v. 29), the official put him in a debtor's prison (v. 30) until his relatives and friends would get the money. Before we condemn the official, let's remember the times when we've self-centeredly elbowed our way through life by being hard, cold, and unforgiving. The master, hearing of his official's hardness (v. 31), sent for him (v. 32) and addressed to him the point of the parable: "Shouldn't you have had pity, as I had pity on you?" (v. 33). No one, of course, is recommending that the man who embezzled the huge amount be made treasurer of the United States or that the man who owed less be allowed to borrow any more.

Another part of the story that grates harshly on our ears is that the master handed him over to the torturers (v. 34). Tyrants, especially in the Orient, made use of torture in order to wring from their victims the confession of a hidden source of wealth or to have the victim's loved ones pay the required money. (Despots, Oriental and Western, still use torture to wring confessions.) In this case the debt was so large that it couldn't be paid back. Jesus' conclusion is that his heavenly Father will do the same to anyone who won't forgive his brother or sister — from the heart (v. 35). We can lose God's forgiveness by hoarding ours in a tight fist and not sharing it from an open hand.

The holy teacher Ben Sira, or Sirach, who wrote in Jerusalem about 180 years before Christ, is probably the closest the Old Testament comes to Jesus' standard of forgiveness. Much of what Sirach said is common sense, and in considering forgiveness we can't eliminate common sense.

Common sense tells us much more. It tells us, for example, that there's often not much external reward for forgiving. And forgiveness is not just a feeling, or condescension, or righteousness. Or conditional: "I'll forgive you if you'll apologize (or change, or make amends)." Forgiveness is a *decision*. That decision is a first step. What happens then depends upon the individual. Forgiveness is showing mercy not only when there's an excuse for what was done, but *even when the injury has been deliberate*. If we hang onto hurts, they'll eventually destroy us. We can only let go of them by forgiving others as God forgives us. Forgiveness is *from the heart*, not an offering that's grudging.

Forgiveness is *accepting people as they are*: the child for being awkward, the spouse for being a klutz, the relative for being noisy, the friend for always being late. Forgiveness is *taking a risk* — making yourself vulnerable. That may be easy once or twice, but after we get burned several times, we can become skeptical and cautious. Overcoming the fear of being hurt again is the price of love. Some would call it foolishness, but to renew my commitment even to the friend who has betrayed my trust is to trust *myself* to handle being hurt again. Forgiveness is *accepting an apology* — graciously. Forgiveness is *a way of living*: developing a habit by pardoning others for the little everyday hurts and annoyances — and pardoning ourselves for small things, too. In short, forgiveness is *choosing to love*. It takes the hurt, acknowledges the problem, accepts the person, and goes forward from there.

Consider the alternative. Without forgiveness, you're condemned to live with resentment — or guilt. Without forgiveness, these feelings will deepen and harden. Instead of human fellowship, there will be separate individual prisons. When someone injures us and we hold onto the hurt, we can't love. We wall off that person from ourselves and, to some extent, we wall off others, too. Forgiveness *frees* the forgiver — and the person who accepts forgiveness — to love and to grow. It *heals* relationships and heals the spirit. It takes the sting out of what memory may remain.

On *how to forgive*, common sense provides no easy answers. Try looking squarely at the injury that's been done. Acknowledge your feeling of resentment. Take some action as soon as possible: a letter, a word, a kindness, a hug, an apology, a prayer. Your apology may be the key that will free you from guilt and bring peace. If the other doesn't want your forgiveness, give it silently, in your heart. For your own transgressions, if you can't say "I'm sorry," pray for the strength to say it.

But both Sirach and common sense fall short of what Jesus said. Sirach's first reason for forgiving injuries, apart from the fact that vengeance belongs to the Lord alone, is that we all share a common fate, death, so life is too short for grudges and we stand together in our need for forgiveness (v. 6). His second reason is the high esteem in which the children of the Covenant should hold one another (v. 7) —that is, their fellow countrymen only.

As St. Paul shows in today's second reading — the last portion from his Letter to the Romans for this year — Christians go deeper and broader than the common sense of which Sirach spoke. Paul presents as one of our motivations for forgiveness, as for all other Christian values, that there's no such thing as a completely isolated life (v. 7): No one is an island. We can't isolate ourselves from the *past* — our history, our family, our heredity. No one is isolated in the *present*, where our increasingly smaller world brings other places and other peoples closer. And no one is isolated from the *future*, into which we hand on whatever we've become. More importantly, still less can we isolate ourselves from Jesus (v. 8). Both in life and in death, he's our living Lord. That's the whole reason for Christ's death and resurrection: that he might be Lord of both the dead and the living (v. 9).

To err is human, to forgive divine. We must imitate divine forgiveness. It's a fearful thought that others may only see God as they see Him in us! Yet forgiveness can be a difficult business. It's often easy for me to love the whole world, but hard to forgive the person who lives or works next to me. But what's impossible to nature is possible to grace. And if we try tight-fistedly to hoard this final form of love called forgiveness, we shall find love itself slipping through our fingers.

TWENTY-FIFTH SUNDAY IN ORDINARY TIME
Is 55:6-9   Ph 1:20-24, 27   Mt 20:1-16

Avoiding Envy
God's Ways Are Not Our Ways; A God of Surprises;
Let God Be God; The Gratuitousness of God's Gifts; Divine
Generosity; Conforming Our Thoughts to God's

If Jesus were telling the parable in today's Gospel for the first time in
today's media, there would most likely be demonstrations in the streets,
the phones would ring off the hooks to and from every union hall in the
country, and workers would be carrying picket signs outside Jesus'
hotel. Jesus' parable is not, however, intended to give moral guidance
on labor-management negotiations or any justification for unbridled
capitalism. It's to give food for thought on avoiding that green-eyed
monster, envy.

Jesus' parable says that the vineyard owner went out the first time
at dawn (v. 1). We don't know why the owner had to hire the workers
with such urgency, or why he went out so often. Perhaps it was because
the rains were on the way, and if the grapes weren't taken in before the
rains they would be ruined. The workmen were generally to be found
gathered early about the gates of the town or in the market-place,
prepared for any kind of work. They were in a buyers' market, having
to agree upon whatever conditions of work they could get.

The usual daily wage (v. 2) was, pitifully, barely a subsistence
amount. If a worker missed one day's work, he and his family went
hungry. Though five groups were hired, only the first group contracted
for the usual daily wage. The midmorning group received a less definite
promise of whatever was fair (v. 4), and the last groups no promise at
all (v. 7). Naturally, when all hirees received the same pay the early-
comers complained (v. 11).

From the beginning of Christianity, that phenomenon hasn't been
unfamiliar to us. In the crowd around Jesus, the Pharisees resented
Jesus' idea that the common people, and tax collectors and prostitutes,
had a chance of being on a par with them. Then, after him, early Jewish
Christians complained about equal treatment accorded the Gentiles
coming into the Church. Today's established parishioners often think

they have rights over newcomers. Many lifelong Christians resent "deathbed conversions." The attitude is understandable.

But there are other ways of thinking. One is the answer of the vineyard owner. In essence, what he's saying (vv. 14f.) is that the laborers are dissatisfied not for what *they* receive, but that *others* receive as much. Although the complainers would call their cause fairness, they had a classic case of *envy*. All sins have contrary virtues for which they're sometimes mistaken: love and lust, prudence and avarice, self-respect and pride, righteous indignation and anger, caution and sloth, good fellowship and greed. The contrary virtue of envy is justice.

In the Judeo-Christian tradition, Satan's envy of God brought the first temptation into the world, and envy was the cause of the first sibling rivalry, the first murder, and the first death. Envy can fester in individuals, hierarchies, families, and in structured societies of all kinds.

Envy says not, "I want what you have *too*," but "I want what you have, and I want you *not* to have it." Unlike jealousy, its close relative which simply focuses on possessing a coveted object, envy says "I want to take it away from you, and if I can't do that, I'll spoil or destroy it for you." So whereas jealousy can be based on attraction (of an object), envy originates in hatred (for people). But envy goes beyond hatred. When we hate, we want to demolish what we see as bad; but with envy, we want to destroy what's good in people's lives. Envious people live in a perpetual state of focusing on what others around them have and what they themselves lack — mostly material things: big houses, fancy cars, stylish clothes, the best brands. We can be tempted to envy also when we see former sinners attain positions of eminence and when we observe people who are less talented than we advance in their careers.

The envious focus not on what's distant, like a billionaire's fortune, but on what's close to them, like the neighbor next door who makes $20 more a week than they. Envy can have a dehumanizing effect on those who are guilty of it, as with Cinderella's cruel stepmother and ugly stepsisters.

Envy is a social sin as well as a personal one. In the seventeenth century, the Dutch had a Golden Age. But people became envious of their good fortune, as we're reminded by the numerous Hollandophobisms that entered the English language during that period: Dutch uncles doled out Dutch consolation, parsimonious hosts offered a Dutch treat, out of the bottle came Dutch courage, and naughty children didn't get in trouble, they got in Dutch. As a social sin, envy confuses self-worth with the glittery look-alike of social status.

Because envy leads to further sins, it's a capital sin as well, possibly coming to involve gossip for a start and slander next, with malice calling all the shots and with deep-seated hatred that leads at times even to murder. Envy works inwardly; concealment is part of its nature. While the noble person lives in trust and openness with himself, the person of envy is neither honest nor straightforward with himself. His soul squints; his spirit loves hiding places, secret paths, and back doors; he understands how to keep silent, how to wait, how to be provisionally humble.

Today's parable teaches, too, that nothing God gives us is due us; everything He gives is from His free bounty, and we can't possibly earn it or deserve it. What God gives isn't pay, but a gift, and God is generous to us all (v. 15). Are we envious that He's generous to others, too? His divine freedom sometimes sets aside our human expectations in a display that results in a God of surprises.

Today's parable also shows the tender compassion of God. A man out of work is a tragic figure, and all that the pitiful latecomers wanted was the chance to work. God our vineyard master pays all of us much more than we deserve, rescuing us from the streetcorners of unemployment. And the fact that the first will be last and the last will be first (v. 16) can give comfort to all. God's gifts to those who are last should bring not envy, but loving joy.

The logic of our contemporary industrial relations, which dictates that those who work a full day receive a full day's wage while those who work a shorter time receive less, is acceptable enough. But as Isaiah suggests in today's first reading, these laws if applied to God are too narrow to contain the great size of His loving generosity. Isaiah invites his people to a new way of life: to seek the Lord, to call upon Him, and to take today's golden opportunity to straighten up and go to God. Isaiah marvels at the distance between human stinginess and divine liberality, quoting God as saying: "For my thoughts are not your thoughts, nor are your ways my ways."

One who understood all of this well was St. Paul. We see his understanding reflected in today's passage from his Letter to the Philippians, the first in a series of readings on the next four Sundays from that lovely letter which has been variously called Paul's epistle of joy, his farewell discourse, his most human letter, and his most thankful letter. The Philippians were probably Paul's favorite converts. Living in a city that was a "little Rome" with law and order, they were now much better off than Paul.

Paul — the great apostle, the considerate pastor, the tireless preacher, the fearless debater, the great human being — is now (about 56 A.D.) in prison in Ephesus, awaiting sentence, which will very possibly be death. No one came to his aid except his beloved Philippians, who sent food and other things, for which he now writes to thank them. Though troubled, he's serene. Facing his sentence, and uncertain whether he will live or die, Paul reflects that for him both life and death take their meaning from Christ (v. 20). With a true sense of the nearness of God, to him life is Christ, and death is gain (v. 21). Though for himself he would prefer death so that he could be with Christ, he sees that on the other hand living can mean fruitful labor (v. 22), and he's torn. Either way, Paul sees it as important that the Philippians conduct themselves in a way worthy of the Gospel of Christ (v. 27). No envy there!

Left unresolved, envy can become crippling. If envy were tangible and had a shape, it would be the shape of a boomerang. The spiral of this capital sin can, in addition to what we've already mentioned, return depression, destroy relationships with friends and spouses, and even feed suicidal tendencies.

There are remedies for envy. One is to imitate the generosity of God and never to begrudge God's grace to others, whether they've been called early or late. Beyond that is self-bolstering: if we find ourselves measuring up as persons, we feel good whether we're a prince or a pauper; if we have low self-esteem, we're not happy no matter how much we have. Selective ignoring also helps. Understand that what we're lusting after isn't that important after all to the goals that are truly worth pursuing in our life. Finally, there's self-reliance. Self-reliant people don't allow themselves to feel envious about what they don't have.

Once owned up to, envy can be transformed from a detour into a direct route of new challenges and opportunities for growth, a recognition that fulfillment will come not from some *things*, but from Some*one* in whom we live and move and have our being. When we come to welcome whatever is good in those who came into the vineyard long after us and share its rewards, we will be replacing envy with its opposite: generosity of spirit.

TWENTY-SIXTH SUNDAY IN ORDINARY TIME
Ezk 18:25-28   Ph 2:1-11   Mt 21:28-32

Accepting Personal Responsibility
Jesus Is Lord; The Shame of Religious People;
Definitive Choice; Talking vs. Doing

In a road fog, a driver pulled over on the Santa Ana Freeway in California to change his flat tire. To avoid hitting him, the car behind slowed down so abruptly that a third car crashed into him. This was repeated by 200 cars in a 5-mile pileup that, in addition to the 200 collisions, wrecked 60 cars, injured 50 people, and killed one. Crumpled cars, like a cast-away bunch of dominoes, were pointed in every direction. The first driver fixed his flat tire and left during the ensuing confusion, oblivious to the massive chain-reaction he had touched off.

Many of us may never be aware until we stand before God of the far-reaching results of little things we do — or fail to do — during our lives. Among those who *are* aware of taking responsibility, there are two kinds of people: those whose mouthing of words is far better than their actions, and those whose actions are far better than their words. The latter frequently claim to be hard-boiled about other people, but somehow they're often found doing kind deeds, almost in secret.

That is, essentially, what today's Gospel is about. Jesus is entering Jerusalem for the last time on one of the early days of Holy Week, and the stage is set for the conflicts that will lead to his arrest and trial. Today's talk is aimed at the chief priests and the elders of the people, with the Temple as backdrop and the dark clouds of Jesus' Passion gathering quickly overhead. Jesus wants to show that, because of the way each group addresses personal responsibility, sinners are making their way to the Kingdom of God while many so-called "religious" people are not.

In Jesus' deceptively simple parable, almost all parents can recognize a real-life situation with some of their children. But Jesus meant much more. The story is another devastating condemnation of the religious leaders. The elder son, who cons his father by agreeing to work in the vineyard and doesn't, represents the Pharisees. The second son, who initially refuses to work and then, thinking it over, regrets his decision and does the work, represents the hated tax collectors and rejected prostitutes.

Both groups are imperfect. Those who regretted their refusal and then did the work spoiled their doing good by the awfully ungracious way they did it. But it's far more noble to change your mind and do good than to remain set in the direction of evil. We're not saved by belonging, but by becoming. The criterion of the healthy relationship is "actions speak louder than words."

The ideal way is both to promise and to do — and that with graciousness. The good Christian would accept the father's orders respectfully, and carry them out fully. With no mention of himself, Jesus points to John the Baptist as a model. He had lived an austerely holy life and died for one of the commandments of the Law of Moses. Yet it was only the tax collectors and prostitutes (v. 32), and not the Pharisees, who believed in John. Obviously, neither the tax collectors and prostitutes nor the Pharisees are our model.

We're to make our own personal choices. In those choices, we're free, and individually responsible. A long time ago, Thomas Hobson ran a rent-a-horse agency for the hard-riding scholars of Cambridge, England. His system was not customer-friendly. Renters could take only the next available horse, thereby saving wear and tear on the more popular steeds. This led the poet Thomas Ward to coin a phrase in 1630: "Where to elect there is but one / 'Tis Hobson's choice, — take that or none." "Hobson's choice" is not like ours.

In today's first reading, Ezekiel, a dramatic prophet of the Jews' Babylonian Captivity, teaches the same lesson: that every individual must decide what to do about the word of God, and all people must take the consequences of their choices. Ezekiel's generation felt that their troubles (the fall of their nation and the Exile) were a punishment for the sins of others, usually their ancestors. Ezekiel, on the other hand, is the prophet of individual responsibility.

In that, the people to whom Ezekiel spoke are no different from us. Students blame their teachers for bad grades, teachers their students for not working hard enough; wives blame their husbands for family problems, husbands their wives; parents blame their children, children their parents; Catholics blame "the Church" for all sorts of things. And like children who constantly complain that someone or something isn't "fair," we complain that life isn't fair, and that God isn't fair. And it's true: God isn't fair. And it's good that He isn't. If He were, we'd all be in trouble. Fortunately, though, as today's Responsorial Psalm reminds us, God is merciful.

Ezekiel rejects excuses as a cop-out. To support his position, he cites two cases. The first (v. 26) justifies the punishment of a wicked person. The second (v. 27f.) points out the rewards of a person who has turned from wickedness to being good. In Ezekiel, "to die" and "to live" refer not so much to physical realities as to the quality of life that stems from decisions made. His implication is that all of us have the responsibility to act with awareness of the consequences of our actions.

St. Paul, too, believes strongly in personal responsibility. Today, in one of the most beautiful passages of the entire Bible which ranks with the Prologue to St. John's Gospel and Colossians 1:15-20 for depth, he motivates the Philippians to exercise their responsibilities as Christians by eliminating the differences that harm the community (vv. 1-4). We're to become one and reflect the self-effacement of Jesus, the model of Christian service. Paul encourages us first in Christ (v. 1), because no one can be in unity with Christ and at the same time be in disunity with others. He pleads next in the name of the solace that love can give. Christian love is that benevolence which never knows bitterness and never seeks anything but the good of others.

Paul mentions participation in the Spirit as another motive for us to make the right choices. The Spirit binds a person with God and with other persons. People who live in disunity with others are proving that they don't use the gift of the Spirit. Paul mentions last the motive of compassion and mercy — which can change people from snarling wolves to fine human beings.

Paul's passage concludes (vv. 6-11) with a hymn which reflects both the divinity and the self-effacement of Jesus. Jesus is in his very essence God: unchangeably, inalienably. His being in the form of God (v. 6) wasn't just a superficial outward form which can change. The outward appearance of roses, tulips, and crocuses differs, but their essential form of being flowers remains the same.

The key is what is called Jesus' *kenosis* — the fact that he emptied himself (v. 7), pouring himself out until there was nothing left. He didn't empty himself of his divinity, but of the privileged status of divine glory. Unlike the Greek gods, whose myths said they became human beings but kept their divine privileges, Jesus' characteristic quality was self-renunciation. He didn't want to dominate people, but to serve them; not in his own way, but in the Father's; and not to exalt himself, but to humble himself.

His obedience went beyond that expected of an ordinary human being to that which was expected of a good slave: that is, obediently accepting even death — heroically, the degradation of even death on a cross! From that lowest point, Jesus' upward movement began: God exalted him and bestowed on him the name that is above every name (v. 9). Jesus' new name is *Lord*.

Paul's statement that "Jesus Christ is Lord!" (v.11) is Jesus' highest point. It means that Jesus is the master of all life, a cosmic influence over all creation. This statement was the early Church's first creed, and it's the essence of ours. We give Jesus an obedience, a love, and a loyalty we can give no one else. At his name, every knee must bend (v. 10) — not in broken submission to might and power, but to the influence of love. And all is, as was Jesus' life, to the glory of God the Father. That's our exalted motivation.

But many of us have been the irresponsible people of Ezekiel's time, as selfish and snobbish as some of the people of Philippi, and both the first son and the second in today's Gospel. We have to remember that we're all in this together. A cartoon shows passengers fleeing a sinking ship. As the survivors huddle together in a small lifeboat, their nightmare worsens as their boat springs a serious leak. One passenger irresponsibly remarks, "At least it's not our half that's leaking."

One of our problems is that we don't know how influential we are. Our actions are often, without our knowledge, like those of the driver on the Santa Ana Freeway. *Those* effects, though serious, were only *physical*. Much more important are the *spiritual* effects of our actions. And for those, ever since Adam blamed Eve and Eve blamed the serpent, it seems part of human nature to want to "pass the buck." But for the responsibility of the making of our lives, the buck stops with each of us.

TWENTY-SEVENTH SUNDAY IN ORDINARY TIME
Is 5:1-7   Ph 4:6-9   Mt 21:33-43

Life in Focus
Good Mental Hygiene; How to Handle Anxiety; Thankfulness;
Day-to-Day Dutifulness; Holiness Attained through Little Things

Perspective is important. In film, the same object can as easily be seen as a long shot of the surface of the moon, or a shriveled, pock-marked basketball photographed in close-up. Cockroaches at their own eye level are as big and menacing as jackals. An old-fashioned steam radiator with a slight adjustment in lighting looks on film like the facade of an opera house. A close-up of the striking of an ordinary kitchen match can erupt with the roar of a blast furnace.

Jesus had a proper perspective on life, and offers it to us. Consider, as one example, today's Gospel. Jesus had now been about his heavenly Father's business long enough to have acquired some of the smug Pharisees as his dire enemies. He now knew that his death was certain just as soon as they could pin something on him. Yet his focus on life was such that he had an inner peace that enabled him to control situations as they arose. How did he handle his reverses? Well, on this occasion he told a story.

His stories were often parables and allegories. In a parable, there's only one main point, and the details aren't to be stressed; in an allegory, every element has a meaning. Today's story is close to an allegory. It's a story about God and the human race, and uses a metaphor to describe that relationship. The Bible uses many metaphors to describe God's relationship with His people. One of these metaphors was "covenant" — that God has a contract or covenant with His people — and "marriage" was another.

Jesus' metaphor of the vineyard was obviously from the "Song of the Vineyard" in Isaiah: a "divine love-song" in which God sees His people as His own vineyard, into which God has put great effort. Every Jew would have been familiar with stories of vineyards. From the Book of Genesis at the beginning of the Bible to the Book of Revelation at its end the symbol of the vineyard is mentioned over a hundred times. The vineyard was depicted in the golden vines decorating the entrance to the

Temple. It was a sign of prosperity and a summary of future rewards for
the faithful. The prophet Micah's picture of happiness (4:4) was that
"every man shall sit under his own vine."

As today's Responsorial Psalm says, "The vineyard of the Lord
is the house of Israel." It was a sign of the proper perspective of Isaiah
and other prophets that, whereas much of the literature of their time —
as of ours — has spoken on behalf of kings, the aristocracy, and the
economically powerful, the prophets gave unique testimony to concern
for the poor, the victims of society's power structure who are forgotten
by all but God. And the choice fruit expected of us in that vineyard are
such virtues as love, justice, integrity, mercy, peace, and reconciliation.
Each of us has a significant role in making our local Church a living
community.

Whatever choice God made of the original Israel wasn't because
of merit or distinction. Israel's election to be a holy nation carried with
it a responsibility and an obligation toward all people and not just to a
privileged few. Israel was meant to mirror God to the nations of the
world. Too often, though, Israel was a vineyard that produced bitter,
rotten grapes. Unfortunately, the same may be said of the new vineyard
of the Lord: the Church.

It was a further sign of Isaiah's proper perspective that even in
serious times he could use what was originally a folksong of joy, one of
those sung at the harvest of the grapes (the end of August into
September). Though in the form of a ballad, it made a good story in that
it had a surprise ending. In the very last verse it becomes evident that
God's people were responsible for God's disappointment.

The elements of Jesus' story begin with his hearers' knowledge
of the facts. Around every vineyard there was a wall, made either of
hedge or piled stones, to protect against foxes, wild boars, and thieves.
Inside the wall, there was a vat to press out the grapes when they were
ripe and a watch tower in an advantageous place to house the guards as
the grapes were ripening. In Jesus' troubled times, the owner was
frequently an absentee landlord. He might receive his rent either in
money, or as a fixed amount of the grapes or other crop, or in an agreed-
upon percentage. The landlord sent his servants at the appropriate time
to collect his rent.

Jesus, like Isaiah, was no mere minstrel or story-teller, but a
prophet who urged his people to repentance. In the application of
today's story, the tenant farmers were the religious leaders charged by

God with the welfare of the nation. The slaves or messengers were His prophets, and comprised two groups: those coming before the Exile and those after. The final envoy, the heir, is God's own Son. Like Isaiah, Jesus' story had unexpected twists worthy of an Agatha Christie or an Alfred Hitchcock. Among them were the long-suffering patience of God, the vineyard owner, because of God's *hesed*, or loving kindness and mercy; the killing of those sent because of human treachery; and the loving owner sending his son even after all that.

Jesus' audience had no way of knowing the surprise climax, which was that Jesus would be dragged outside the city and put to death, and that *they*, the religious leaders and their followers, were the ones who would do it. Part of the story too are we, the new Israel, the Church, which is the reason the Gospels repeat this story. At least as surprising is that the Kingdom of God would be given over to the poor and the outcasts. The last is because of other qualities of God such as *zaddiqah*: His integrity, uprightness, justice, and steadfast loyalty.

Jesus' vineyard stories, because they were aimed at the smugness, vanity, and self-seeking of the leaders of Israel, must be labeled among his "parables of contention." Jesus, with his death drawing nearer, faced his current problems by drawing attention to himself more boldly at this point in his life — the beginning of Holy Week — than he had ever done before. He referred to himself as the keystone of the entire structure of man-God relations. In the words that Isaiah put in God's mouth, Jesus is saying, ultimately of all of us: "After all I did for them!" All of us who have felt let down by those we've helped, only to have them push our help back in our face, often say that: parents of their children, employers about their workers, employees about management.

St. Paul followed through on the same theme in his "Epistle of Joy," a tender encouragement to his close friends at Philippi. For the Christians living there, added to the ordinary worries of life was the fact that as Christians they were always subject to persecution. As an antidote, Paul could with justification have been full of gloom. Instead, in one of the finest passages among the rich treasure of spirituality in his Captivity Epistles, he recommends a proper perspective to the end that, as we pray after the Lord's Prayer at Mass, we obtain peace and are protected from all anxiety. Paul knew whereof he spoke: He was writing from jail, where he was awaiting death.

Paul presents advice on how to achieve the peace of God from the

God of peace. His essential advice is prayer — prayer which shouldn't be a negative flight from anxiety, but positive requests which, along with thanksgiving, apply to *everything*, tears as well as laughter, anxiety as well as calm. Prayer implies, in addition to gratitude, a perfect submission to the will of God. God is greater than all our troubles and can give us His peace, which is beyond anything we can come up with on our own. Of all Paul's titles for God, "God of peace" (v. 9) is the one he seems to like best.

For the God of peace to be with us, Paul lists qualities for us to cultivate. He says we're to set our minds on all things which are *true*, that is, not deceptive or illusory; on everything that's *honorable*, and not the world's tawdry, flippant, and cheap fly-by-nights; on all things *just*, in the sense of duty faced and done, not giving in to the merely pleasurable, the easy, or the slipshod; on the *pure*, not the soiled or smutty; on the *lovely*, in the sense of that which calls forth love —like kindness, sympathy, forbearance, and forgiveness; on everything *gracious*, or what has a good name; and on all that's *worthy of praise*, because praise from good people can be uplifting. For Paul, those virtues and others all form a single reality: life in Christ. All is not only proper perspective, but also good mental hygiene.

We all have anxieties: guilt about the past, lovelessness in the present, death in the future. Some of them come not as crosses from God, but from our own deficiencies. All of them can drag us down. But we have to get into the habit of seeing everything in life in perspective, from atomic explosions to cap pistols, from suffering to joy, from headaches to cancer. One of the reasons for youth problems may be that young people haven't endured a sufficient number of life's struggles to place poor achievement, rejection at school, or a breakup with a friend in their proper perspective. If we give some attention to putting perspective and focus in our lives, our problems can lift us up. Basketball or moonscape, cockroach or jackal, radiator or opera house, striking match or blast furnace, obstacle or instrument of growth, depends on us.

Twenty-Eighth Sunday in Ordinary Time
Is 25:6-10   Ph 4:12-14, 19f.   Mt 22:1-14

Serenity in a Sea of Trouble
Jesus the Party Boy; Joy Amidst Anguish; Caring;
Cooperation with Grace; Living Christian Paradoxes

How do you interpret the statement that "there are no exceptions to the rule that everybody likes to be an exception to the rule"? What's the truth of the proposition that "religion tries to satisfy people while its essential purpose is to make them dissatisfied"? These sentences are an interesting form of speech called the paradox, which is a seemingly contradictory statement contrary to expectation. Christianity, like the rest of life, is full of paradoxes. Today's liturgy contains at least one of them: namely, that it's possible to have serenity even in a sea of troubles. That calm and serenity comes only from many attempts at a life in God. It's as though we were like swans: all calm and serene on the surface, but paddling furiously underneath.

In today's Gospel, Jesus answers the hatred of the chief priests and Pharisees by repeating his prediction of God's rejection of Israel in strong terms under the form of a parable. Like last week's parable, this one also approaches allegory, in which each element, and not just the overall point, is important.

Today's Gospel is full of paradoxical questions, among them the following. Why would the king's servants be killed for no more than bringing an invitation? Why would the king, in retaliation, burn an entire city? Why would he take the time to do this while his painstakingly-prepared wedding banquet was getting cold on the table? And why throw out a guest for not wearing proper clothing, when the invitation had come with rather short notice?

In our time, dress seems to signify little. A staid-looking gentleman was upset at the dress of some young people on the street. "Just look at that one," he barked to a bystander. "Is it a boy or a girl?" "It's a girl," said the bystander, "She's my daughter." "Oh, forgive me," apologized the man. "I didn't know you were her mother." "I'm not," snapped the bystander. "I'm her father." The wedding garment expected of us is the personal commitment required in order to take our place at the feast. We're weaving our garment daily by the way we live.

The answers to the Gospel's paradoxical questions lie in the background and meanings of the two stories — for there are two: one for the then and there, and the other for all time. For the then and there, the customs related in the stories are accurate. People giving parties wouldn't mention a specific time on their initial invitation. As the detailed preparations made it clear to the host when things would be ready, he sent out the final invitation to let people know the more precise time he would expect their arrival. Under the circumstances, a first refusal wasn't surprising. But to refuse after having first accepted was considered an insult, even if there were weighty excuses.

The wider meaning for all time has to do with a short summary of the tragedy and the promise of salvation history. The king sending the invitations is God the Father. The reason for the party is the union of God with humankind in the person of Jesus. The Bible often describes salvation as a great banquet, a banquet long associated with God's final victory.

Atheist critics often mock the notion as "pie in the sky when you die bye'n'bye." What's important is to realize that there's more to live for than what we see in this present world, interesting and challenging though it is. That means more than sitting down to an eternal eating and drinking festival somewhere in the stratosphere.

The banquet represented, besides, an end to the constant worry of humankind concerning provisions for the future. With sufficient food life is assured, and a feast like this becomes a symbol of unending life, companionship, and joy. The joy results from the fulfillment that comes to human beings by reason of their share in the ineffable union between God and people. We think too little of joy in the Christian life. Because Jesus wants the party to be a tumultuously joyous one, he sends his invitations far and wide, even into the slums. And if we don't understand the metaphor of the banquet as eternal life, it's perhaps because our country has more plentiful food than anywhere else on earth, and spends less for it as a percentage of income than any other nation. What Jesus intends here is for us to imagine the happiest experience of our entire life, and then to tell us that that would be nothing when compared to the eternal joy of our heavenly banquet with the Lord.

The first invited guests are the Israelites. The people in the byroads who are invited last are the Gentiles, non-Jews like most of us, who are willing to accept God's word. The servants sent out with the invitations are, as in last week's story, the prophets. As for some of the Jews killing the servants, and the king in retaliation sending his army to destroy those murderers and burn their city, there is evidence to suggest that this may once have been a separate parable and these aren't the words of Jesus but of St. Matthew. Matthew was writing between 80 and 90 A.D., after the destruction of Jerusalem in the year 70. Jerusalem's fate at that time was something so horrendous he couldn't forget it. Yet Jesus' appeal is not to punishment, but to make us see what we miss if we refuse God's invitation to His party. This divine invitation of grace is, however, an offer we can refuse.

The main paradox is serenity in crisis. Here Jesus was, knowing that his death was to take place in a few days, yet possessing a tranquility that could only come from a life in God. The same composure allowed him, paradoxically, to speak, in the midst of the plotting hatred swirling around him, about the joy of a wedding feast. Times of peace are not a true test of real self-possession; times of trouble are.

But Jesus warns us with the separate story of the man without proper clothes, whom he has expelled even though he wants his party to be full of people. That man can be anyone who accepts the invitation but fails to live accordingly. We may be responding in a half-hearted way, donning our baptismal garment but never really wearing it, receiving Jesus in the Eucharist and going through other right motions while, all the time, the values by which we live speak of lack of integrity of life.

Today's reading from Isaiah contains the same paradox of serenity in the midst of problems. Again we see the beautiful, consoling, serene picture of the heavenly Zion, with God receiving all peoples (not just Israelites) on the mountain, the place of His presence. Again we have the image of an abundance of life and a heavenly party, the symbol of eternal happiness, anticipating the wedding party in today's Gospel. Isaiah's image of salvation is the fulfillment of our deepest longings: the absence of hunger, mourning, death, and shame. Sadly, the vision is to some extent unrealizable in this life.

God's party of juicy, rich food and pure, choice wines (v. 6) opens up to a deeper meaning. It's the "Day of the Lord," which was the messianic hope of God's people, about which Isaiah wrote those beautiful words. And again, the eighth century before Christ, when these words were written, was a time of great trouble: the military juggernaut of Assyria was terrifying both Israel in the north and Judah in the south. But the words, "This is the *Lord* for whom we looked" (v. 9), indicates that the people recognized God as being with them.

Today's extract from Paul's lovely letter of joy to the Philippians — the last for this year — continues the same paradox of serenity in the midst of trouble. Paul had experienced life as it is for many of us: a mixture of poverty and plenty, joy and sadness, the valley of darkness as well as green pastures. Now he was in jail, in the custody of the praetorian guard (1:13), knowing that any false move meant immediate death. The Philippians, hearing of Paul's problem, had sent Epaphroditus and financial help to sustain his needs. Paul here expressed his thanks but, paradoxically, communicated that he wasn't dependent upon their gift, and was serene. His serenity wasn't because of his own strength but, even in his current life-threatening situation, was because he had discovered the paradox that the Lord's power is made perfect in weakness.

Paul was proud to be *God*-sufficient, instead of *self*-sufficient as others preached. Right before this passage (v. 11), Paul had mentioned the Stoic ideal of *self*-sufficiency (*autarkeia*). That's the self-sufficiency of striving people of the world. The Stoics advised eliminating all emotion, feeling, and desire, until you came to the stage where you no longer cared.

Epictetus, one of the Stoics' most famous leaders, advised to begin with breaking a cup and to say disdainfully, "I don't care." Then you go on to break a chair, then a table, and then ever more precious household utensils, and do the same. Ultimately, you go to yourself, and if you're hurt you say the same thing. If you do this long enough, you'll come to the stage of being able to watch your closest loved ones suffer and die, and say, "I don't care." You were to do this, the Stoics said, deliberately, so that you could finally come to see everything that happened in this troubled world as the will of God. Their notion is very different from what Christians call serenity. As one writer said, "The Stoics made of the heart a desert, and called it peace."

There are still Stoics among us; some of them masquerade as Christians. But true Christians live their lives, paradoxically, in serenity while at the same time having deep compassion for suffering. The true Christian has joyfully accepted God's invitation to His party, at the same time realizing that, as with the Eucharist, to share a meal is to accept a commitment to the person whose guest we are. In whatever hardship happens to us, we pray the beautiful words of today's Responsorial Psalm: "The Lord is my shepherd." That can provide us with the paradox of true serenity even in a sea of trouble.

TWENTY-NINTH SUNDAY IN ORDINARY TIME
Is 45:1, 4-6   1 Th 1:1-5   Mt 22:15-21

The Church and Politics
Participation in Civic Affairs; Glory and Honor to the Lord, Taxes to the State; Jesus: a Revolutionary or a Collaborator?; The Gospel and Prevailing Ideologies; Sovereignty: God's, or Government's?; God and Caesar; Moral Courage; True Patriotism; Church-State Relationships; Commitment; Good Politics

In the arena of politics, there's one word that has the power to elect or defeat politicians to office, finance battleships, cause economic strain, and get people to pull their hair out. Wars have been fought over this word, nations established, and people sent to jail for not taking heed when this word was spoken. The word is taxes.

That word had similar power in our Lord's day. The Savior of the world was born where he was born because of a decree issued by Caesar Augustus that all the Roman Empire should be taxed (Lk 2:1). Religious Jews looked upon their nation as a country with God as its head, and so to pay taxes to any earthly king (especially the occupying power, Rome) was for them an admission of the validity of that power and an insult to God. They adhered to this principle even though people then paid far less taxes than in any modern democracy.

So when the Pharisees went off and plotted how they might entrap Jesus in speech (v. 15), the issue they decided to use was taxes. The Herodians whom the Pharisees enlisted were the party of the dynasty of Herod the Great, who was king by leave of the Romans, and so they were the toadies of the Romans. The Pharisees didn't have much in common with the Herodians, but they often joined forces to gang up against Jesus. In order to make their plot less obvious, they sent their disciples (v. 16). These piously posed as men resolved only to follow their conscience.

After beginning with unctuously flattering words, they proceeded
their loaded question: "Is it morally acceptable to pay the census tax
to the emperor or not?" (v. 17). Now, the Christian Scriptures generally
see Rome as a positive influence. Rome provided order and stability,
and was, in the early days, the protector of the Church against Jewish
zealots, those first-century ancestors of the Stern gang and the Irgun
Zvai Leumi of the 1940's. But should a person pay taxes to an empire
which worships pagan gods? to an emperor who considered himself a
god? In the highly-charged atmosphere of oppression, Roman taxation
posed a cruel dilemma to God-fearing Jews.

So the question to Jesus was like a parent asking, "How do you
like the twins?" If Jesus said the tax should not be paid, he would be open
to a report of sedition by the Herodians to Rome and arrested for it. But
to say the tax should be paid would be false to Israel's most cherished
hopes, would lose even good-willed Pharisees, and would constitute a
public renunciation of his messianic character which so excited the
enthusiasm of the people. What the Herodians and Pharisees wanted
was some rash statement, either in favor of Roman rule or in total
rejection of it.

Jesus, wanting to let them know that he was on to their trickery,
asked, "Why are you testing me?" (v. 18). He called them hypocrites,
because both groups were in fact publicly paying the tax, and their
embarrassment was fake. Then he shrewdly asked, "Show me the coin
that pays the census tax" (v. 19). Because using the coinage of Rome
acknowledged Rome's authority, religious Jews weren't supposed to
carry Roman coins. Besides, on the coin at that time was the image of
the currently-reigning Emperor, Tiberius, and around its edge the
inscription, "Tiberius Caesar, Son of the Divine Augustus," and images
were against Jewish law. Jesus didn't even have a coin. But the
Pharisees and Herodians did — showing their willingness to use
Caesar's money when it suited them.

Jesus answered their question by telling them to repay to Caesar
what belongs to Caesar, and to God what belongs to God (v. 21). It was
an invitation to work out for themselves the proper interplay of political
and religious loyalty. In one master stroke, he was saved from both
pious accusation and political self-incrimination. Yet the Man for
Others wasn't interested in a crafty escape from his enemies. His is not
a preoccupation with self but with the life of his listener. Jesus intended
his classic answer not as statutory law, but rather as a principle. It's a

balance. It doesn't equate the entire mission of Christianity with social justice, but at the same time doesn't endorse moral quietism either.

Jesus' answer leaves the individual to ponder and to decide: What is God's, what is the State's? The State has many obligations: public services, water supply, schooling, social welfare for the poor and aged. Religion's duties are to connect people with God, the ultimate answer to our questions and the basis of our life's decisions. But the dichotomy between the secular and the sacred isn't absolute. The motivation for public services, schooling, and social welfare, for instance, is often religious.

So the boundaries between the two can sometimes be difficult to set, and allow many vexing questions to remain. In the Church's early days, when refusing to worship the emperor (symbol of the Roman authority) became a punishable offense, many Christians endured persecution rather than obey. Today, should there be any connection between religion and government? Between Church and State? Should tax money be permitted for church-affiliated schools? Directly or indirectly in the pulpit, should a rabbi be permitted to solicit funds for Israel, a priest for the Vatican, a black minister for a civil-rights candidate?

Should the Church as a center of charity be replaced by funds administered by business people and social workers? Should the Church, which once restored tranquility of soul, be replaced by gland specialists, dietitians, psychiatrists, and psychologists? Should the Church make room for thoughtful criticism of itself as part of "rendering to God"?

Christian responses have run the gamut from seeking domination over the world, to accommodation with the world, to cooperation, to aloofness, to hostility and antipathy, to imagining a grand diabolical conspiracy, to hatred and withdrawal, and all parts in between.

Today's reading from Isaiah, like Matthew's Gospel, was written in a political climate and took political positions. It was the period from 587 to 539, the greatest catastrophe in Hebrew history, when the Babylonians had reduced the Temple and the city of Jerusalem to ruins, had carried the important people of Judah into captivity, and demolished Judah as a nation.

When in turn the Persians captured the Babylonians, their enlightened King Cyrus "the Great" acted in accord with his usual enlightened practice of not imposing Persian culture even on captured peoples. He released the Jews from captivity, sent them home, and subsidized the rebuilding of the Holy Temple and the city of Jerusalem. So, because Cyrus had been God's instrument for good, the very first line of this passage calls him God's "anointed," a title otherwise reserved for good kings like David, and some prophets, and some priests; the Hebrew word would pass into English as "Messiah," and into Greek as *Christos*, or "Christ." In other words, Cyrus was truly God's instrument of justice, though an unknowing one and a pagan who worshiped the god Marduk. God often works through people who may not even recognize His name.

There are political overtones also in today's reading from St. Paul's First Letter to the Thessalonians. Written twenty years after Jesus' crucifixion, it's the earliest document we have in the New Testament. Excerpts from it shall constitute our second reading in these final five weeks of this liturgical year. Thessalonica was on the Roman Via Egnatia, or Egnatian Way, in northern Greece. This road ran roughly in a straight line from the heel of Italy's boot to today's Istanbul, and Thessalonica was a seaport town about mid-way between them. The city was politically and in many other ways important to Christianity. If the Gospel message were to take hold there, Christianity would be more easily able to move both east and west. Paul had preached in the synagogue at Thessalonica, and had won a favorable hearing. This had stirred up jealousy and controversy among the Jewish leaders there, and Paul had had to leave secretly and in a hurry. He sent Timothy back to see how things were going. This letter is a reaction to Timothy's report to him.

The cheerful opening of the letter contains what we today would put on the outside of the envelope: the names of the sender and the addressee. It adds a wish for grace and peace, which we still use to open our liturgical assembly. The verses of this passage show Paul at his best, a politician in the best sense of the word. He's going to have to rebuke the Thessalonians, but he knows that if you want to overcome others' faults you first praise their virtues. So he begins with praise, thanking God (v. 2) that the Christian life is being lived in Thessalonica. Then (v. 3) Paul picks out the three essential responses of people to the Gospel: their "work of *faith*," their "labor of *love*" (*agapé*), and their patient endurance of suffering "in *hope*" — hope of the Lord's Second Coming. You can endure a lot if you have hope, because then you're walking toward the dawn.

The side of Jesus' principle that's liable to suffer most is giving to God what is God's. To make a just society, we must renew our moral courage to stand up against error and evil, withstand embarrassment and ridicule, and speak out about God's rights. Though we're advised not to be *of* this world, we must live *in* it. The true measure of our worth has to do with the likeness and inscription not on our coins, but on our person. As Caesar cast the denarius in his image, God has cast us in His. As Caesar sends out as wage and calls back in tax, God sends out the bearers of His likeness and calls us back, demanding of us the sum of our lives.

THIRTIETH SUNDAY IN ORDINARY TIME
Ex 22:20-26   1 Th 1:5-10   Mt 22:34-40

Three C's: Conviction, Courage, and Commitment
True Love of Neighbor; Humanitarianism True and False; Faith, Hope, and Charity = Conviction, Courage, and Commitment; The Theological Virtues

A missionary learned that one of his prospective native converts had five wives. "You're violating a law of God," he said, "so you must go and tell four of those women they can no longer live here or consider you their husband." The native thought a few moments, then said, "Me wait here. *You* tell 'em."

In a very minor way, that story illustrates several Christian values our society needs. Today many people are without the value of *conviction.* One belief is considered as valid as another, and consequently life hasn't much meaning. This is one of the reasons why there's so much youth disenchantment and suicide. Another value, *courage,* is often considered to be foolishly against enlightened self-interest. And the value of *commitment,* at least on religious grounds, is considered antiquated. Those three values of conviction, courage, and commitment are modern aspects of *faith, hope,* and *charity.*

Today's Gospel begins with the Pharisees approaching Jesus to ask which commandment in the Law is the greatest (v. 36). They believed not only in the Law of Moses, but also in 613 rabbinical traditions, the "fence around the Law" to protect a person from inadvertent transgressions. To teach the people, the Pharisees often looked for summaries that were clear and concise; but because of the many traditions they often found it difficult to get to the heart of what was essential. Phariseeism, from which modern Judaism comes, was lofty in its moral teaching. St. Paul was a Pharisaical rabbi, and some disciples of Jesus (such as Nicodemus and Joseph of Arimathea) were Pharisees.

Jesus' answer gives the two texts from the Jewish Scriptures that underlie all of New Testament morality. The first (Dt 6:4) is the Jewish morning and evening prayer, the prayer with which every Jewish service still opens today, the first sentence every Jewish child commits to memory, the prayer recited by Jews often, the prayer which is placed in the phylacteries on their arm and forehead and in the mezuzah at the doorposts of Jewish homes, the prayer which all religious Jews hope to have on their lips when they die. It says, "You shall love the Lord, your God, with all your heart, with all your soul, and with all your mind" (v. 37; from Dt 6:5). The heart was considered the center of knowing and feeling, the soul the principle of life and the source of all one's energies, and the mind the center of perception. The text means we're to love God with everything we have: a love which is whole-hearted, not laid back; dynamic, not phlegmatic; outgoing, not introverted; performed with conviction, courage, and commitment, not lackadaisical.

The second greatest commandment, Jesus says, is like the first: "You shall love your neighbor as yourself" (v. 39; from Lv 19:18). A mother, trying to translate that to her son, stressed that we're here to help others. He considered this, and then asked, "What are the others here for?"

Although the Jews divided their precepts into "heavy" and "light" and rabbinic tradition classified this precept as "lighter" than the first, Jesus put it right up with the other. The novelty of Jesus' answer doesn't consist in quoting these two texts: both were in the Jewish Scriptures. Jesus' novelty consisted in putting both texts side by side with *equal weight*, rescinding all the "heavy" and "light" regulations that suffused Jewish living. *This* was new, and has no parallel in all Jewish literature.

The second precept is the manifestation of the first. Love of God issues forth in proper love of ourselves and other people. Many warm people who don't believe in God love themselves and other people. But it's really only when we love God that human beings become *deeply lovable* — not with sentimentality, but with commitment. There's an intimate connection between our faith in God and our relationship with our neighbor. It's only in and through the proper love we bear for self and one another that we *actualize* our love for God.

One basis for people's being lovable is that we're made in the image of God (Gn 1:26f.). That was an explosively powerful idea when it first came to light — in ancient Egypt, in Mesopotamia, and especially in the Roman Empire, when three-quarters of the people were either slaves or descended from slaves, and only one man, the Emperor, was thought to be in God's image.

But it's not only Jews and Christians who honor these great commandments. The very name of Islam implies surrendering completely to God. The heart of the Hindu *Song of God*, the *Bhagavad-Gita* is God's request for complete, unconditional love. Buddhists seek the inherent compassion existing at the root of reality. In all these faith traditions, love calls for a dedication of one's whole life, a consecrated self-giving so complete that the human will can never accomplish it. Because it's beyond the will, it's beyond all moral codes of behavior. In every deep world religion, these commandments go to the very core of being, and there it depends radically upon grace.

Jesus concludes by saying that all of the law and the prophets depend on these two commandments (v. 40). That means the whole of the First Testament. Part of that Testament is the Book of Exodus, the second book of the Bible, which tells of the Sinai Covenant between God and the Israelites. Today's reading is drawn from that part which deals with "social laws." Some of the words are not those of dispassionate contemplation, and are graphic: interest on money loaned out is related to the Hebrew word for "bite"; God's anger will blaze out; He will murder His people!

Very few of these laws are found in other ancient Near Eastern codes of morality, leading us to realize that their development is closely related to the role of God in the lives of the Hebrews. Laws of compassion based on the need of charity rather than only justice usually are related to the presence of God.

These social laws prescribe that we're to be holy, like God our model. God is loving and compassionate, rich in mercy. He cares for those who can't help themselves. God reminds the Israelites to be compassionate also to *aliens*, because they were once aliens themselves in Egypt (v. 20). Good Israelites should be concerned about the *widow* and the *orphan* (vv. 21-23), too, because they have no one to defend

them. And the Israelites' love must embrace the *poor*. Even good people
have to remind themselves that they must *always* show love by caring
for the powerless. The ideas in these social laws give a strong basis for
Jesus' innovations on loving in today's Gospel reading.

In today's portion of his First Letter to the Thessalonians St. Paul,
in a mood of joy and encouragement, puts before us two major themes
to purify our love. The first is the imitation of Jesus (vv. 5-9), who is the
supreme revelation of the heavenly Father's love. The sign that we're
truly imitating him is our love for one another. As Paul imitated Jesus,
so his converts imitate Paul, holding on to their faith even in great
affliction (v. 6). The Thessalonians' love was something of which they
didn't have to be ashamed, and from them the word of the Lord has gone
forth (v. 8) everywhere. As humorist Will Rogers put it in secular terms,
"Live so that you wouldn't be ashamed to sell the family parrot to the
town gossip."

Paul's second theme (vv. 9f.) is a summary of the message of the
Gospel as preached to the pagans. That message is faith, hope, and love:
conviction, courage, and commitment. As for the first, faith or conviction, Paul's message began with a polemic against idols. For Jews, idols
were absolutely forbidden by the First Commandment. For Gentiles,
idols were images of some false god to which worship was offered with
the same seriousness, affection, and passion which some people give
modern idols like actors or money or sex.

The Thessalonians' faith, or conviction, was evident in their
converting to God from idols (v. 9). Their love, or commitment, was
evident in their coming "to serve the living and true God" (a traditional
biblical expression for worship and the total relationship of people to
God). And the Thessalonians' hope, or courage, was evident in their
patient waiting (v. 10).

While our theme in this homily has been the theological virtues
of faith, hope, and love — or conviction, courage, and commitment —
one has tended to become a rather neglected subject. We pay attention
to faith because much of religious education is concerned with the
content of faith, namely what we believe. We learn that love is the virtue
which sums up all of the other virtues, so we see the importance of love.

The relatively neglected subject is hope. Giving up hope may
reveal itself as simply the quiet absence of meaning and purpose. The
giving up of hope may even wear the face of smiling resignation on the
part of those who have found nothing in themselves or in the world that

gives them reason for optimism. The opposite of hope need not always be despair. More often it's boredom, a life with little interest in itself. The person who lacks hope isn't necessarily the person who declares that God doesn't exist. Rather it tends to be people who believe that God is no longer present and will no longer change them, as expressed in phrases like, "I'm too old," or "It's too late," or "I've tried too often." These phrases can be a part of one's attitude at any age in life.

If our crisis is a crisis of hope, we have a crisis indeed. One definition of hell is hopelessness. That's why it can be said that living without hope is no longer living. One of the world's masterpieces of literature is Dante's *Divine Comedy*. In it the poet takes a personal journey through hell, purgatory, and heaven. Since hell can be defined as life without hope, it's no accident that as the poet begins his journey through hell, he sees at the entrance these words: "Abandon all hope, you who enter here."

By way of contrast the good news of Jesus Christ has much to do with hope. The Gospel invites us to a realism which takes into account the harsh realities of life along with Christian hope. It's easy to emphasize one to the exclusion of the other. Realism without hope may easily lead to a kind of self-defeating cynicism, bitterness, and despair. On the other hand hope without realism may lead to a kind of ivory tower day-dreaming. To combine them both — this is the enormous task: to be an idealist without illusion, to keep our head in the stars but our feet firmly planted on the earth.

Let's pray not only for the three C's — conviction, courage, and commitment — but also for all those qualities of life that make them possible: social justice, for example, without which genuine love isn't possible; truth, which is another name for God and which means being faithful, trustworthy, and loyal; and freedom from internal as well as external constraints, that basic theme of the entire Bible that's necessary to even begin loving.

FEAST OF ALL SAINTS
Rv 7:2-4, 9-14   1 Jn 3:1-3   Mt 5:1-12

What To Be When We Grow Up
Blueprint for Happiness; The Christian Constitution; The Heartpiece of
Christianity; The Summary of Christian Doctrine; Christians at their Core;
Our Invitation to Sainthood; The Epitome of Our Faith

Ghosts don't enjoy a good reputation. They're unreliable, irregular, anti-social, uncommunicative, and inclined to be noisy — all habits they share, if stories are to be believed, with today's teenagers. Time was when they — ghosts, not teenagers — behaved otherwise. In ancient Homer, tribes of the dead arrived in tens of thousands, giving eerie cries. By the time of Periclean Athens, things changed considerably in the spirit world. The dead confronted the living; they demanded and threatened; even worse, they gave advice.

In early Christian times, St. Augustine complained about drunken parties and feasts held at gravesides. And Christians weren't supposed to pay for any ghostly ferrymen, as the Greeks had done, putting coins in the mouths of the dead. By the fourth century, those about to die partook of the Eucharist instead. By the Middle Ages, the holy dead were said to return to bestow benefits like healing sickness, more for two reasons which became an increasing priority for ghostly visitants over the centuries: to request proper burial for their bones, and to help sort out murder investigations. Later spirits became more vengeful.

When Christianity encountered Germanic and Celtic peoples north of the Mediterranean, the missionaries had to emphasize otherworld life to attract their uneducated converts. By the late fourteenth century ghosts appeared to testify to the need to atone for sin while still alive. With the Reformation, the Council of Trent reaffirmed the existence of Purgatory. Today, the *Catechism of the Catholic Church* removes some of the frightening aspects of Purgatory by calling it a place of final purification for those not yet perfectly purified, so as to achieve the holiness necessary to enter the joy of heaven (1030). This understanding of purgatory fits well with a notion of God who is never vindictive and whose love is unconditional.

For Protestants, though, there was no official Purgatory, so their ghosts were likelier to be demons, which made them more sinister. But not everyone took apparitions seriously. There is some evidence that "common folk" whiled away the long evenings scaring one another with spooky stories.

The birth of electricity probably spelt the death of the ghost. The ghost since Victorian times, despite lurid reports, is a mere shade of its former self, although — such is the progress of feminism — there are now more female ghosts, appearing to more female victims. When atheism and spiritualism crossed the threshold, ectoplasm came into being as an explanation of ghostly phenomena. But adults are easily sated with the "ghostly" pranks that accompany Halloween.

Halloween, like many other Christian feasts, became mixed with ancient superstitions. In ancient Britain and Ireland, from which some of our Halloween customs come, huge bonfires were set on hilltops to frighten away evil spirits, the souls of the dead were said to revisit their homes, and ghosts, witches, hobgoblins, black cats, and demons of all kinds were said to be roaming about. Gradually, the Christian festival of All Hallows' Eve, or Eve of the feast of All Saints, gave way to secular observance. Immigrants to the United States, particularly the Irish, in the late nineteenth century introduced secular Halloween customs that became popular.

Adults consider All Saints' Day to be more appropriate for celebration. In the early Church, as persecutions raged, Christians had a special reverence for those who had died for Christ. The remains of these martyrs were reverently gathered together, at first in catacombs, and later, when the Christians were free to build churches, in or near the altar. Also out of reverence, Christians kept holy the dates on which saints entered eternal glory. For some of the saints, however, no date could be verified. Besides, there came to be so many that their dates exceeded the number of days in the year. Therefore, today's Feast was created to cover all the saints.

In the great summary of Jesus' teaching that has been called the "Sermon on the Mount," Jesus announced the themes of invitation and promise for all people to become saints. St. Matthew added here many sayings of Jesus from other times and places, in order to present an ordered, developed, over-all-picture of Jesus' teaching, especially the moral note. The setting was comparable to the solemn moment when God revealed His Law on Mount Sinai to Moses.

The *crowds* under Moses were the afflicted Jews on their long and painful way from their captivity in Egypt to the Promised Land. Under

Jesus, the crowds were those who brought to him from all over people who were sick and racked with pain. The *leaders* were, in the one case, Moses who was called by God, and in the other case the disciples called by Jesus. The voice that was heard was in the case of Sinai the voice of the Father and here the voice of Jesus, in whom God is fully present.

The basis of Jesus' whole sermon was the beatitudes. The word Jesus used, which we translate as "blessed," is a very special word that contains elements of joy, happiness, serenity, and loveliness. They're not the "entrance requirements" for the Kingdom of God, but rather the qualities which with God's blessing will come to full flowering when the Kingdom of God is fully inaugurated. There's no tense to the beatitudes: their blessedness exists in the present and continues forever. For depth and breadth of thought, this passage is on a level with the Decalogue in the Older Covenant and the Lord's Prayer in the Newer Covenant, and this passage surpasses both in its poetical beauty.

And, even though Matthew uses the passive voice, all the beatitudes are to be understood as being *active*: the meaning is that God blesses all those who fit into the categories called the beatitudes. The categories aren't as concerned with states of privation such as poverty, affliction, or hunger, as with qualities that regulate relations with one's neighbor. So the promised rewards allude to a new relationship between God and people.

The first four beatitudes constitute an announcement of the Kingdom of heaven and an invitation into it. They begin with the poor in spirit, which speaks of absolute and abject poverty, the kind that brings people to their knees. The *anawim*, as they were called, are people who, because they're poor, have no influence or prestige; they're therefore walked on by others; and, because they have no earthly resources whatever to which they can be attached, they put their whole trust in God. In the second beatitude, those who mourn are those whose hearts are broken not only for their own losses, but who passionately lament for the suffering of the whole world. God promises that out of their sorrow such people will find joy.

The "meek" of the third beatitude refers to people who are self-controlled. They perform the difficult task of being always angry at the right time and never angry at the wrong time, always angry with the right person, to the right degree, for the right reason, and in the right way. They have every impulse and passion under control because they themselves are God-controlled, and have the humility to realize their own weakness.

As for the fourth beatitude, people "who hunger and thirst for righteousness," most of us don't know what it means to be truly hungry and thirsty. In the ancient world, and in some few places of the modern, most day-laborers were never far from starvation. The case was even worse with regard to thirst. It wasn't possible to turn on a tap for water, and a person on a journey facing the hot wind and sand might become parched with thirst. Anyone who wants holiness as much as such people wanted food and water will get it.

The next four beatitudes state the right norms of conduct for admission to Christ's Kingdom. They recognize that we're all born to die, and so we're also born to grieve. But we remind grieving people that we don't honor the dead by dying with them. There are many stages of grief, and men frequently find it more difficult to handle grief than women, because they're taught to suppress emotion. Time doesn't heal, but it's what we do with time that can heal. Friends can share grief by doing many things. They can, for example, just be present. The presence of a friend is worth more than words. Friends can recall happier times, acknowledge the right to grieve, comfort with a touch, be of service, and retain their contact.

Those who show mercy are those who forgive injuries, go with others through what they're going through, see with others' eyes, think with their thoughts, and feel with their feelings. The clean of heart of the sixth beatitude are those whose motives are absolutely pure and single as God is pure and single. Their eyes, thus pure, shall see God. The greatest degree of perfection begins with the seventh beatitude's beautiful word "peacemakers." The beatitude speaks not of peace*lovers*, but of peace*makers*: those who, because their God is the God of Peace and because Jesus came to bring peace, actively do all in their power to make this world a better place by establishing right relationships between people. They're truly children of God, because their work is Godlike.

Those who have really arrived at saintliness are capable of the final beatitude, persecution for the sake of holiness. The early Christians' religion could put every aspect of their life out of kilter: their work, their social life, and even their home life. The last was the worst, fulfilling Christ's prediction that one member of a family might become Christian while the others did not, and thus family members would be set against one another. Yet those who took Jesus seriously followed his advice in the last beatitude to rejoice and be glad, loving him so much that they were happy to be able to show their love by suffering for him.

Accompanied by our recollections of all those from whom we've learned what it is to be a child of God, let's remember that with every person who became a saint, the individual personality — quirky or rugged or suave or retiring, beggars or royalty or scholars or soldiers or religious — cooperated with the grace of God. A child, asked what a saint is, and remembering the figures in the stained glass windows at church, answered, "A saint is someone the light shines through." And that's quite true: saints are the light of Christ in the darkness. Let's begin our response to Jesus' invitation and the example of himself and all his saints by using our own limited endowments to cooperate with the grace God has given us to become saints.

THIRTY-FIRST SUNDAY IN ORDINARY TIME
Ml 1:14-2:2, 8-10   1 Th 2:7-9, 13   Mt 23:1-12

Selfless Service vs. Titles, Honors, and Power
Vanity in the Church; Elitism; Wearing Overalls Rather
than a Crown; Forgetfulness of Self; Practicing What You Preach;
The Corruption of the Best Is the Worst; Sincerity in Faith

In a cartoon, a prospective secretary sitting before a personnel officer's desk says to her interviewer, "I'm not obsessed by wealth, power, and prestige. Then again, I'm not obsessed by poverty, subservience, and anonymity either!" And there's a saying that it's futile to try to sell a jacket to a man with a phi-beta-kappa key. And people with a doctoral degree will often use it to get a reservation in a crowded restaurant. All show that tinges of Phariseeism are still with us.

In today's Gospel, St. Matthew collects into one place many of Jesus' strong criticisms of the scribes and Pharisees — mainly two. One is the general strictness of their interpretations of the Law, a strictness which wasn't humane, and which was at times criticized also by some rabbis. With their 613 rules and regulations, the Pharisees were making religion an intolerable burden. If any religion makes life depressing instead of joyful, a hindrance rather than a help, a weight to drag one down instead of wings to lift one up, it's a menace to people.

Jesus' second criticism is of the religious leaders' vanity and hypocrisy. One thing they did was to widen their phylacteries (v. 5). Phylacteries are little boxes containing Scripture texts which the Jews bind to their forehead and left wrist when saying their prayers. The Law had commanded to keep the Law as a sign on the hand and as a memorial between the eyes. They interpreted this literally instead of figuratively, the sense in which the regulation was probably meant. There was nothing wrong with that, except when they widened the phylacteries in order that everyone would see them. They were not unlike moderns who put all kinds of signs on their car: medallions of their memberships on their windshields, statues of saints on their dashboard, police connections on their rear windows.

They also lengthened their tassels. Originally these were to be worn on the four corners of the cloak as reminders of the Law. The Pharisees enlarged them out of ostentation. And they coveted places of honor at banquets (v. 6) and the front seats of honor in synagogues. The back seats were assigned to children and the unimportant; the further front the seat, the greater the honor. The most honored seats of all were those that *faced* the congregation. If you were seated there, people could see that you were present, and you could act piously to impress them.

They also loved greetings in marketplaces (v. 7). Though courtesy demands that marks of respect be given proportionate to the dignity of a person, to seek greetings was a self-serving status symbol. And they were fond of the salutation "Rabbi," which meant "My master," a teacher of the Law. A title coming into use at this time, this was often a term of address for Jesus in the Gospels, sometimes as a sly introduction to a nasty question.

Jesus rejects three honorary titles (vv. 8-12): master, father, and teacher. If this prohibition were taken literally, it would mean that we shouldn't call our physician "doctor," because that word means "learned one," or anyone "mister" because that means master and ultimately comes from "magister" or teacher, or our physical father "father" or our spiritual father, the priest, "father." What Jesus forbids is that Christians use titles for mere ostentation, arrogance, or pomposity. He also wants to nudge people not to use these terms in a childish way that refuses to question authority. Titles aren't to be given without recognizing that any "fatherhood" that one might have is in God, from whose heavenly Fatherhood the authority of earthly fatherhood derives.

Jesus then repeats what he had said elsewhere: "Whoever exalts himself will be humbled, but whoever humbles himself will be exalted" (v. 12). As St. Augustine said, there's something in humility that exalts the mind and something in exaltation that abases it. Humility makes the mind subject to what is superior — ultimately, God. Exaltation, on the other hand, spurns subjection to *anything*, even what is superior.

There's nothing wrong with ambition. Jesus simply turns ambition around: ambition to serve instead of for personal gain, to do things for others instead of having them do for us. But to have the ambition to be the last one of all doesn't mean being apathetic. With Christians, if they let people see their good deeds, it's for the purpose of glorifying our heavenly Father.

The attitude of leaders seeking titles, honors, and power didn't begin or end with the Pharisees. The last of the prophets, an anonymous writer who used the name Malachi, which means "God's messenger," in about 440 B.C. made observations on the sins of the priests similar to those in Matthew's Gospel. After the Exile, awareness that obedience to the Law had preserved the identity of the people now led to over-rigorous exaltation of the Law, which in turn led to the abuse of religious power.

Malachi shows the high estate from which priests as well as people had fallen. The priests, who were supposed to be leaders of their people, were offering sacrifices in the Jerusalem Temple of sick and worthless animals, seeking favor with the rich and powerful, and showing partiality in decisions. Worse, they were deficient in the very areas where they should have been specialists. The people were giving God only lip service. Malachi provides a reminder that all too often everyone can lapse into a thoughtless, rote religion void of heartfelt enthusiasm.

Equally timeless are questions like Malachi's: "Why. . . do we break faith with each other?" (2:9). Why do marriages fail and friendships grow cold? Why do we belittle each other, exploit each other, betray each other, kill each other? Why do we, who were born for loving God and each other, kill love? Our lives become a reaching for ways to fill or to hide our needs, ways that often lead away from God and people in a spiraling downward thrust into the dark corners where we sometimes keep ourselves imprisoned. Like children's little creature of fantasy who lies hidden in the conch shell, we hide away behind an exterior that's pharisaically built to be impressive and which we present as the real "us."

Coming forward in time to about 51 A.D. when St. Paul wrote his First Letter to the Thessalonians, we find no essential change. Out of envy of his leadership, many slanders and calumnies were being leveled against Paul: he was a dictator, he was deluded, his motives were impure, he was seeking to please people rather than God, he was looking for praise (v. 6). Some were saying that he was in the business of preaching the Gospel for what he could get out of it. (Unfortunately, free-loading did happen in the early Church as well as elsewhere.)

Knowing that his motive was selfless service, Paul charmingly compared himself to a nursing mother (v. 7). Just as nursing implies the giving of self, Paul shared with his dear Thessalonians his very self (v. 8). He mentions the toil and drudgery he underwent in order not to burden any of them (v. 9). The toil he worked at for a living was tentmaking (Ac 18:3). Paul's way of living was, in contrast to the Pharisees', consistent with his preaching.

There are lessons in today's liturgy for both the Church at large and for each member. As for the Church, wherever it becomes strong because of persecution as in Poland, or looked up to for having fought for human rights as in Central and South America, or respected because of history as in Ireland, there's a danger that the Church may use power incorrectly. Power tends to corrupt, absolute power to corrupt absolutely. After all, an antithesis of love is not necessarily hatred, as most people might say; nor indifference, as the more sophisticated might think; but unfettered human power. Some of the Pharisees used their power wrongly, going so far as to take upon themselves titles which belong only to God. Paul, despite the slander and calumnies against him, correctly put his power to the loving and humble service of Jesus.

Every Christian, despite the temptations to Phariseeism in all of us, is to seek to render selfless service rather than to obtain titles, recognition, or power. The best soil for the growth of Christian virtue is humble service and detachment: detachment from not only things, but from praise and prestige. In the humble Christ — poor, shunned, and oppressed — is where the growth of virtue always finds a home.

THIRTY-SECOND SUNDAY IN ORDINARY TIME
Ws 6:12-16   1 Th 4:13-17   Mt 25:1-13

Coming Events Cast their Shadows
Foresight; *Semper Paratus*; Wisdom and Foolishness; For Whom
the Bell Tolls; The *Leitmotif* of our Lives; Our Need to Reflect

One of Richard Wagner's greatest contributions to music is the *leitmotif*,
a recurring theme which presents the ideas behind the drama in the
music. The *leitmotif* says things through the orchestra that the characters don't even know and therefore can't say. For example, in the final
moments of Wagner's "The Twilight of the Gods," there are many
motifs beautifully interwoven, such as the idea of redemption through
love, even as the world of the gods is going up in flames. It's fitting for
us, toward the end of another liturgical year and of our civil year soon
thereafter, to consider the *leitmotifs* underlying our lives.

The Gospel's short parable, based on Palestinian matrimonial
customs, teaches us to be prepared at all times for the Lord's return. In
our Lord's time, the wedding day occurred long after the betrothal. On
the wedding day itself, the best man went to the bride's house and
bargained with her father over her dowry. When they had reached a
suitable contract, the best man sent for the groom to come and fetch his
bride who, along with her escorts of honor, were waiting at her house.
Because the bargaining might be a long and intricate process, no one
knew for sure when the groom would be coming, except that it would
be some time after sunset.

When the bridegroom, accompanied by his male friends, went to
the bride's house, they were greeted by the waiting bride and her
bridesmaids. Then the bride and groom, together with their friends, in
the light of oil-fueled torches, danced and sang their way to the groom's
house. The bridesmaids carried the torches to light the way. The
groom's taking the bride from her father's house to his own constituted
the ceremony of marriage. The procession took the longest route
possible, in order for the couple to receive the good wishes of as many
people as they could. Then they had a great celebration at the groom's
house, which went on for a week. In Jesus' story the groom hadn't yet
arrived at the bride's house.

Because the foolish bridesmaids brought no oil, despite their knowing that there would be no telling when the groom would arrive, they had to go to local dealers for some. (The poor dealers — but, then as now, a sale is a sale!) After the procession to the groom's house, the doors of the groom's house were locked (v. 10), a very cumbersome task. When the foolish bridesmaids returned from the oil dealer's, they cried, "Lord, Lord! Open the door for us!" (v. 11).

In the Sermon on the Mount, Jesus' first major discourse in St. Matthew's Gospel, Jesus had said, "Not everyone who says to me, 'Lord, Lord,' will enter the Kingdom. . . but only the one who does the will of my father" (Mt 7:21). Today's last of Jesus' discourses in Matthew returns to that theme. The Master's answer to the foolish is, "I do not know you" (v. 12). These five, though virgins, were lost because, contrary to the opinion of some, one needs more than chastity to enter God's Kingdom. Jesus concludes with the moral of the story: "Stay awake, for you know neither the day nor the hour" (v. 13).

Why were the foolish foolish? Because they didn't reflect on the *leitmotifs* of life, and so they didn't realize that this wedding feast, which as usual in the Scriptures represented eternal salvation, was *everything*. To be there called for the investment of one's whole being. They risked only a tentative investment, while being engaged in other interests. So they didn't come to the final accounting well prepared.

In all ages, it's only the fool who doesn't see what others see. The fool dwells in a garden of roses oblivious of the thorns. Living in mystical reverie, he or she is like the frog in a well who sees the sky as a little patch of blue no larger than the roundness of its shelter. Small-minded and foreign to vision, people can become the greatest fools because they don't see themselves as fools. They don't realize that, no matter how long or short the day, every day gets buried in the graveyard of the night.

Why were the wise wise? Because they reflected on life and were experts at making the surpluses of life subordinate to their main interest. The foolish were there for what they saw as one taste among many in the festival of life, the wise for a bedazzled foretaste of a delightful party to come, for which they prepared. While we suspect that the foolish and the wise somehow exist within each of us, we hope that the ratio of wise to foolish is better than the fifty-fifty in Jesus' story. To keep it all in perspective we pray for wisdom.

And that's what today's first reading is about. Written about a hundred years before Christ, the Book of Wisdom speaks of what its title indicates. Now, wisdom has many meanings. It means going beyond mere knowledge to the depth and breadth of the mind-boggling fullness of life. It means understanding and insight. It means the best way for one to relate to God and to other people. It means seeing every thought and word and deed in relation to the *leitmotif* of our life.

To motivate people to the arduous search for wisdom, the book personifies wisdom as an alluring woman — resplendent (v. 12) because of her divine origin, unfading, waiting in the early morning light, and caringly looking for those who are searching for her. The psychologist Karl Jung said that the creative and spiritual sides of the psyche are feminine. The possession of wisdom results in parents who take their vocation seriously, leaders who look to the needs of their people, and persons who take into consideration all the dimensions of life, including death.

In today's second reading, St. Paul in his First Letter to the Thessalonians approaches more directly the *leitmotif* of the wise foresight we should develop for the coming events of our lives which cast their shadows before. He talks about the Thessalonians' mourning excessively for their dead (v. 13) and provides a contrasting description of the resurrection of believers.

The scene of Christ's Second Coming will be at God's word of command, accompanied by the voice of an archangel and with God's trumpet. The majestic sound of the trumpet played a role in many First Testament appearances of God: for instance, at the assembly of God's people at Sinai. At Sinai, in anticipation of God's coming Moses had the people prepare themselves. When God came then, there were glorious manifestations of nature: clouds, and thunder, and lightning. Like Sinai, Paul's scene of Jesus' Second Coming in terms of Jewish literature and then-current ideas of the cosmos, approaches sheer art and lends itself to drama.

Unless the Christian Thessalonians straighten up, says Paul, they will give in to an unrestrained mourning like the pagans, who have no hope. The pagans' so-called hope is minimal. In the face of death the pagan world, then and now, becomes fearfully mute and despairing. The object of Christian hope is specific: Jesus died and rose (v. 14).

Our age, like the pagans in Thessalonia, looks upon death with horror, embalms people to make it appear that they aren't dead, uses euphemisms like "slumber rooms" in funeral homes, adorns the dead with expensive surroundings, and does all kinds of inconsequential things to assuage guilt. In these respects our age isn't much different from whole civilizations that have been built in death's dominion. The ancient Egyptians turned their land into a vast necropolis, and the Aztecs conquered Mexico not for booty but for human sacrifices to blunt the lethal appetites of their man-eating gods.

True Christians look upon the *leitmotif* of death that courses through our lives not as a dreadful end to everything, or solely as a time of judgment, but as a participation in Jesus' death and resurrection and as our last act of giving to our heavenly Father. Nothing illustrates that better than the story of the West Virginia widow who had to face that indescribably tragic day when word came of her son's death in action in World War II. Their family Bible had come down through generations and in it were recorded family marriages, births, and deaths. Now her son's name must be added. But when she went to write it in she found that on the page headed *Deaths* a heavy line had been drawn through the word. Above it, in her son's handwriting, were the words: "There is no death." And below, where his name would have been entered, he had written, "Mom, I love you."

Every classic work on spirituality urges us to think about death. From the *Imitation of Christ* through the *Introduction to the Devout Life* of St. Francis de Sales to the *Spiritual Exercises* of St. Ignatius of Loyola, all urge us to consider that we're going to die. The old saying that "no one gets out of this world alive" is in one sense true, but in another sense we're going to get out of this world to live forever with the Lord. Death isn't a trap door to nothingness. It involves the survival of the self and an encounter with God. Nor should we regard life after death as a butterfly that flutters away above the grave and is preserved somewhere; rather, it's life's completion.

Death is the *leitmotif* of our lives. The British poet John Donne wrote: "Never send to know for whom the bell tolls; it tolls for thee." But that *leitmotif* needn't fill us with dismay. An Italian tourist brochure, in connection with the volcanic Mt. Vesuvius and the towns of Herculaneum and Pompeii which it destroyed, says, "The nearness of death exalts life." In other words, it's only in daring to accept death as a companion that we may really possess our life. Let's develop the wisdom to do now what at the time of our death we would like to have done in our lives!

THIRTY-THIRD SUNDAY IN ORDINARY TIME
Pr 31:10-13, 19f., 30f.   1 Th 5:1-6   Mt 25:14-30

Actively Daring Risk Rather
Than Being Passively Acceptable
Using All Your Talents; Eager Zeal Over Lazy Complacency;
Vibrant Preparedness for God's Judgment; Your Reach Should Exceed
Your Grasp; Sticking Your Neck Out; Venture Nothing, Lose All

Sometimes we Christians, in favor of smooth security, are smugly disinclined to take the bold risks that others take in behalf of their business and personal ventures. Perhaps we watch our diet carefully, exercise more or less scrupulously, buckle up religiously, and always do the "sensible" thing. We may feel that we're not living fully every day, but we feel safe and virtuous. Today's liturgy on this next-to-last Sunday of the Church year tries to set us straight.

Jesus' story of the talents teaches us to boldly prefer taking active risk in our lives over passive complacency. It is reminiscent of the pre-Christian story of the sword of Damocles, which goes like this.

There once was a king named Dionysius who ruled in Syracuse, at that time the richest city in Sicily. He lived in a fine palace where there were many beautiful and costly things, and he was waited upon by a host of servants.

Naturally, there were many in Syracuse who envied his good fortune. One of these was Damocles, one of Dionysius's best friends. He was always saying to Dionysius, "You must be the happiest man in the world."

One day Dionysius, tired of hearing such talk, said, "Perhaps you would like to change places with me."

"Oh, I would never dream of that," said Damocles. "But if I could only have your riches and your pleasures for one day, I should never want any greater happiness."

"Very well. Trade places with me for just one day."

And so, the next day, Damocles was led to the palace, and all the servants were instructed to treat him as their master. They dressed him in royal robes, and placed on his head a golden crown. He sat at the head of a table in the banquet hall, and rich foods were set before him. There were costly wines, beautiful flowers, rare perfumes, and delightful music, and he rested himself among soft cushions.

"Ah, this is the life," he sighed to Dionysius, who sat at the other end of the long table. "I've never enjoyed myself so much."

As he raised a cup to his lips, he lifted his eyes to the ceiling. What was that dangling above him, with its point almost touching his head? Damocles stiffened. The smile faded from his lips, and his face turned ashen. His hands trembled. He wanted no more food, no more wine, no more music. He only wanted to be out of the palace, far away. For directly above his head hung a sword, held to the ceiling by only a single horsehair. Frightened that any sudden move might snap the thin thread and bring the sword down, he sat frozen in his chair.

"What's the matter, my friend?" asked Dionysius. "You seem to have lost your appetite."

"That sword! That sword!" whispered Damocles. "Don't you see it?"

"Of course I see it," said Dionysius. "I see it every day. It always hangs over my head, and there's always the chance someone or something may cut the slim thread. Perhaps one of my advisors will grow jealous of my power and try to kill me. Or someone may spread lies about me, to turn the people against me. Or maybe a neighboring Kingdom will send an army to seize my throne. Or I might make an unwise decision that will bring my downfall. If you want to be a leader, you have to accept these risks. They come with the power."

Damocles said, "I see now that I was mistaken, and that you have much to think about besides your riches and fame. Please take your place, and let me go back to my own house."

And as long as he lived, Damocles never again wanted to change places, even for a moment, with the king.

The standard of God's judgment of every person is relative to the talents given: the greater the gifts, the greater the responsibility. We're the servants in today's Gospel parable, and the absentee master is a symbol of Christ; his return is a scene of judgment. The depiction of the master of the time is accurate. He frequently had to travel and turn over the management of his affairs to his trusted servants.

As with most parables, though, the comparison can't be pressed too far. While God isn't a cosmic patsy who forgives anything, even when we have no inclination to apologize, the key to Jesus' moral practice — in every case, without exception — involves the humility to admit that you've wandered. As for hell, of nearly 4,000 verses in the Gospels, Jesus speaks of it in Mark only once, in Luke three times, in Matthew six times, in John not at all. He speaks of judgment in Mark only once, in Luke twice, in Matthew and John six times each. In his lengthiest consideration of judgment (Mt 25:31-46), which comes right after today's passage, his crucial question pivots on the issue of one's sensitivity to the suffering of the hungry, the thirsty, the imprisoned. If you contrast the relative rareness of Jesus' speaking about hell or judgment with the profusion of times in the Gospels when he both spoke and acted as one come to heal and forgive, you come away with a picture of Christian moral practice far different from what many Christians have come to expect.

The worthless servant used the most popular bank of the time: a hole in the ground. In ancient cultures that was the safest place to guard a treasure against times of uncertainty, or upheaval, or war, or marauders and thieves. Like all of us when we haven't done what we should, the worthless servant rationalized excuses. For one, he thought of his master as a demanding person (v. 24). The truth is that, while the master does require an accounting, he's not *demanding*. The worthless servant's second excuse was that he was afraid (v. 25). For that kind of irrational fear we can only say that one should do everything necessary to overcome it. The truth of the matter is what the master said: the servant was lazy (v. 26).

It's always easy to give in to rationalization, especially the one that says that "what little talent I have will never be missed." In 1645, one vote gave Oliver Cromwell control of England; in 1776, one vote gave the United States the English language instead of German; in 1845, one vote brought Texas into the Union; in 1868, one vote saved President Andrew Johnson from impeachment; in 1875, one vote changed France from a monarchy into a republic; in 1923, one vote gave Adolf Hitler leadership of the Nazi party; in 1941, just weeks before Pearl Harbor was attacked, one vote saved Selective Service.

To paraphrase a poet (Michel Quoist, *Breath of Life*): If each note of music were to say "one note does not make a symphony," there would be no symphony; if each word were to say, "one word does not make a book," there would be no book; if each brick were to say, "one brick does not make a wall," there would be no house; if each seed were to say, "one grain does not make a field of corn," there would be no harvest; if each of us were to say, "one act of love cannot save mankind," there would never be justice and peace on earth. To have an impact, you must get involved. No one is impressed with the won-lost record of the referee.

The punishment for the worthless man — who had done nothing, really — was as harsh as that for more positive sins. We're not all equal in talent, but we're all called to collaborate in the work of the Gospel according to our personal opportunity, ability, and gifts. The reason why the master, perhaps paradoxically, took away what little the worthless servant had and gave it to the most profitable servant was that it's with using God's gifts as it is with learning a language or playing golf: if we don't use it, we lose it.

But let's not exaggerate our talents' importance, either, by setting our standards unrealistically high. That's the surest way to fail. By such standards, Socrates was a failure. His ambition was to make people happy by making them reasonable and just, and he didn't do that. John Milton was a failure. In writing *Paradise Lost*, his aim was to justify the ways of God to humankind. Inevitably, he fell short and wrote only a monumental poem. Beethoven, who conceived his music to transcend fate, was a failure, because his music didn't.

Many people by external standards will be "successes." They will own nice homes, eat in the best restaurants, dress well, and, in some cases, perform socially useful work. Yet, too few people are putting themselves on the line, getting involved in something noble enough for their talents that's worth failing at. Jesus wants us to know that salvation will come to those who are prepared to risk their lives for him.

To think that way is a part of wisdom. The Book of Proverbs, from which we get today's first reading, is a collection of wise sayings, some attributed to Solomon, but actually written by many people over a period of 500 years up to a few centuries before Christ. Today's beautiful and poetic portion, which contains rules on how to choose an exemplary wife, was a small foretaste of Jesus' theme of praising those who use their talents for the sake of the Kingdom.

Today, some will see in the passage a beautiful description of the ideal wife, mother, and home-maker who is the center of family happiness; others will see the woman it describes as being in an out-dated lesser role relegated to her by a demanding, unjust, male-oriented society. Still others see in these verses (especially vv. 14-17, on her industriousness, missing from today's selection) a justification for wives and mothers working outside the home. And her rewards (vv. 18,

25f., and 28, also missing) share in what her hands have worked for. She
enjoys the success of her dealings, strength, dignity, foresight, wisdom,
and the praise and love of her husband and children.

What's certain is that this passage shows the worthy wife to be a
model of energetic faithfulness to the small tasks which God gives all
of us, male and female, every day. That's the passage's connection with
today's Gospel. Like the profitable servant we're all called to be, the
worthy wife takes what has been given her and improves upon it. She
thus improves the lives of all she touches.

On this next-to-last Sunday of the Church year, one reminder in
this passage that seems eternally true is that charm is deceptive and
beauty fleeting (v. 30). This is not to deny the attraction of charm and
beauty, in which women probably excel over men. What the text
downgrades is *empty* charm and *skin-deep* beauty. A time like ours that
stresses youth needs that reminder.

Equally timeless is the only explicitly religious element in this
whole passage: the reminder that great praise is to go to the woman who
has a reverential respect for God's sovereignty, goodness, and justice
toward humankind. This is the foundation of religion. The true charm
of the model wife is her religious spirit. Today's Responsorial Psalm,
the "Marriage Psalm" which praises the happily married man, indicates
that the same spirit is to characterize him.

The *why* of using our talents is, as we've seen, the glory of God,
the service of other people, and our own fulfillment. God the Father said
to St. Catherine of Siena (from her *Dialogue*): "I have distributed all my
gifts in such a way that no one has all of them. Thus I have given you
reason, necessity in fact, to practice mutual charity. I could well have
supplied each of you with your needs. . . but I wanted to make you
dependent upon one another so that each of you would be my minister,
dispensing gifts and graces you have received from me. So whether you
will it or not you cannot escape my charity."

In today's second reading, St. Paul addresses another question
that concerns us all: When are we going to have to answer for our
talents? The Thessalonians had been overly concerned with when Jesus
was going to come again. Against the chance that his return was
imminent, some had quit their jobs and were idly waiting.

Paul speaks of the sleep of indifference, which is deadly. He
warns the Thessalonians to keep busy in order to be prepared for "the

day of the Lord" (v. 2). That was a phrase common in the Jewish Scriptures. Among its characteristics were that it would come suddenly, involve a cosmic upheaval, and be a time of judgment. The New Testament identified it with Jesus' Second Coming, and in the New Testament all its characteristics in the Jewish Scriptures are applied to that event. Naturally, everybody wanted to know when this awesome day would come. Paul uses two striking similes to describe its suddenness: (1) It will come "like a thief at night" and (2) like the onset of labor pains for a pregnant woman. Paul doesn't seek to terrify, but to encourage. However, he gives no excuse for anyone not being prepared.

One of the most difficult conditions for us to fight against is indifference. The poem *Indifference* (G. A. Studdert-Kennedy, in George Stewart, ed. *Redemption: An Anthology of the Cross* [New York: Doran Co., 1927]) said:

> When Jesus came to Golgotha they hung him on a tree,
> They drove great nails through hands and feet, and made a
>   Calvary;
> They crowned him with a crown of thorns, red were his wounds
>   and deep,
> For those were crude and cruel days, and human flesh was cheap.
> When Jesus came to our small town they simply passed him by,
> They never hurt a hair of him, they only let him die;
> For men had grown more tender, and they would not give him
>   pain,
> They only just passed down the street, and left him in the rain.
> Still Jesus cried, "Forgive them, for they know not what they do,"
> And still it rained the winter rain that drenched him through and
>   through;
> The crowds went home and left the streets without a soul to see,
> And Jesus crouched against a wall and cried for Calvary.

Let's keep in mind that there can be no true religion without adventure. For this, we should cultivate imagination and initiative as well as moral vigilance. Recalling our gifts, let's imitate the industry, cheerfulness, and generosity of the talented people in Jesus' parable, of the Book of Proverbs' ideal wife, and the best of the Thessalonians.

FEAST OF CHRIST THE KING
Ezk 34:11f., 15-17   1 Cor 15:20-26, 28   Mt 25:31-46

Better than Camelot
Christ the King: a State Religion?; Making Christ's Kingdom
Alive in Us and in Our World; What Christ's Kingdom Is Like;
Our Shepherd-King; Our King's Standards of Judgment;
The Dominant Virtues in Christ's Kingdom; Compassion

Today's Feast of Christ our King gives us an opportunity to think about
some important issues, not least among them what a wonderful world
we could create if we really put our minds to it.

Through Ezekiel, God gives us a beautiful picture of Himself as
the shepherd — one of the earliest passages in the Bible to do so. It's
a picture that undoes, point by point, the harm done to the people by
bad rulers. It's a picture of a shepherd walking in the middle of his
sheep, going back and forth among them, guiding them, talking with
them, looking for the lost, and carrying the weak and the wounded in
his arms. It's a picture of the shepherd which in biblical times always
had overtones of kingship, as with David the shepherd-king. It's a
picture reflected in today's Responsorial Psalm: "The Lord is my
shepherd." As with the shepherd-king's love for his sheep, God's love
for us is personal and individual, and there's nothing beyond it that we
need.

Yahweh's judging between one sheep and another and between
rams and goats in Ezekiel isn't too different from Jesus' description of
the beautiful (but fearful) scene of the Last Judgment in St. Matthew's
Gospel. Among Matthew's ways of painting a kingly portrait of Jesus
is to have Jesus refer to himself as "the Son of Man" (v. 31). This
ambiguous title may mean simply a humble person, such as Jeremiah
used it, or it could refer to a triumphant figure standing between heaven
and earth, as Daniel used it (7:14). Here the title has cosmic overtones
and refers to Jesus in kingly glory at the Last Judgment.

In addition to that title, many other titles try to capture Jesus:
Suffering Servant, for example, and Lord, and Prophet, and Lamb.
Often we speak of our Lord as if Jesus were his first name and Christ
were his last name. Jesus was his first name all right, but Christ is the

Greek rendering of "Messiah," a Jewish term with an entire theological history behind it. In comparison, "king" is a relatively weak word. Despite our not knowing much today about monarchies, either, calling Christ our king gets us away from pietistic sentimentalism, and provides the idea that Jesus is more than just a nice buddy or emotional crutch. Supporting the notion of his kingship, in today's Gospel Jesus also mentions the angels attending him, all the nations assembled before his throne. It's a picture better than any Camelot, congress, or parliament.

Our king tells us that the sole criterion for his judging our worthiness for citizenship in his Kingdom is our exercise of love. Jesus illustrates his criterion with simple things that everybody can do: feeding the hungry, giving thirsty people a drink, making strangers welcome, providing covering for the ill-clothed, comforting the sick, and visiting those in jail. All of these can be interpreted literally —the whole world has more than its share of the homeless and the hungry — but often we're called to meet needs which require looking below the surface and demand creativity and initiative.

With the hungry, creativity and initiative may suggest feeding people's hunger for knowledge by volunteering at a literacy organization, feeding people's hunger for companionship by welcoming a new neighbor in for coffee, or feeding the hunger for intimacy by lending our ear to people in need of sympathy. Looking below the surface may suggest slaking people's thirst for justice by contacting legislators about issues of concern, or people's thirst for equality by not discriminating, or people's thirst for self-worth by helping battered spouses or other people on the edge. We can welcome the stranger by helping at a shelter for the troubled, by teaching children to accept people of all colors and cultures, or by volunteering at a hotline for people with problems.

To clothe the naked, we might supply a poor family with such essentials for good grooming as soap, detergent, toothpaste, or cosmetics. We might visit the sick by helping people who suffer from substance abuse, calling on shut-ins, or listening to a friend who is depressed. As for prison, we can help people who are locked up by many things besides the police: materialism, loneliness, loss of a sense of their human dignity and of hope about the meaning of their lives.

But the list of the "corporal works of mercy" shouldn't be limited to these. If we have compassionate hearts, which is the badge of the nobility in Jesus' Kingdom, there will swim into our vision thousands of ways to be of help to people who need us. To emphasize the actions' importance, Jesus goes through the scene a second time, from the viewpoint of the condemned. Their surprise (v. 44) is easy to understand: They never accepted the idea of encountering Jesus in other people. Too often people's attitude is: "If only I'd known it was you, I'd have helped." But the idea is that Jesus is in the unattractive.

No matter how repulsive some people may appear to us, Jesus identifies himself with *all* who need to be served. He doesn't say that he will *consider* these things as if done to him; he says it *is* done to him (v. 40). Mother Teresa said, "If sometimes our poor people have had to die out of starvation, it is not because God didn't care for them, but because you and I didn't give, were not instruments of love in the hands of God, to give them that bread, to give them that clothing; because we did not recognize Christ, when once more Christ came in distressing disguise."

St. Paul had the same vision when he wrote his famous chapter on the resurrection. It adds a new side to the kingship of Christ. Paul's idea is that Jesus shows his royal power in bringing us from death to life, in putting all his evil enemies under his feet, and in gathering all to God. Paul calls Jesus "the firstfruits" (v. 20) of those who have died. The Jews knew this term well. They offered God the first sheaves of their grain harvest in the Temple — an act symbolic of giving God the entire harvest. Their offering took place at the Feast of Passover, which wasn't only a commemoration of the deliverance of the Israelites from Egypt, but also a great harvest festival. It therefore took place at a time very close to the resurrection of Jesus. Paul sees in Christ's resurrection the beginning of an entire harvest of risen people — the first, from whom others flow as effects.

Paul goes on to teachings familiar to every Jew of his day. Death came through a human being, says Paul (v. 21), referring to the teaching of Genesis (3:1-19) that it was through Adam's sin that death came into the world. Like every good Jew, Paul had a great sense of the solidarity of the human race. To the ancient Jews, no one could do anything that would affect only oneself: everyone was bound up with all of life in general and with the lives of everyone else. Adam being the father of the race, the whole species was in him.

With Jesus, something new came into the world: He was sinless, and he conquered death (v. 22). Christ the King made it possible to defeat sin, vanquish death, and free humankind (vv. 24-28). Paul describes the completion of Christ's task (v. 28) in picturesque terms: the Son will return to his heavenly Father like a victor returning home from battle. The Father had sent forth His son to redeem the world, and the Father will receive back a world redeemed. With the completion of Christ's mission, there will be nothing anywhere, in heaven or on earth, outside the love of God. In that line of thinking, every Sunday is a little feast of Christ the King, and every Sunday in the Creed we profess that "his Kingdom will have no end."

While we live on this earth, we're not to dream about heaven as "pie in the sky when you die bye'n'bye," an escape from the present. All the way to heaven can be heaven if we honor our present responsibility. That responsibility is to love. Love is the meaning of life. It's the essence of what God showed us in Christ. It's our opportunity for fulfillment. What's done out of love lasts forever — the only thing that lasts forever. The chances to express it are all around us —especially in needy people, with whom Jesus identifies.

If we were to follow the advice of today's liturgy, everybody in the world would feel accepted, and thus would be more able to live in harmony with others. Because this would mean the salvation of every individual, it would be also the salvation of the whole world. For the Christian, the achievement of Christ's Kingdom in the world begins not when we give others what they have a right to, which is justice; it begins when we go beyond justice to accept others as persons by seeing Christ in them, and then giving them ourselves. And it ends in presenting to the heavenly Father, through Christ our King, in the words of today's Preface, a Kingdom of truth and life, a Kingdom of holiness and grace, a Kingdom of justice, love, and peace.